The Politics of Leadership

Superintendents and School Boards in Changing Times

a volume in

Educational Policy in the 21st Century: Opportunities, Challenges, and Solutions

Series Editor: Bruce Anthony Jones

Educational Policy in the 21st Century: Opportunities, Challenges, and Solutions

Bruce Anthony Jones, Series Editor

Policy and University Faculty Governance (2004)
Michael T. Miller and Julie Caplow

The Politics of Leadership

Superintendents and School Boards in Changing Times

Edited by

George J. Petersen
California Polytechnic State University,
San Luis Obispo

and

Lance D. Fusarelli
North Carolina State University

INFORMATION AGE
PUBLISHING

Greenwich, Connecticut • www.infoagepub.com

Library of Congress Cataloging-in-Publication Data

The politics of leadership : superintendents and school boards in
changing times / edited by George J. Petersen and Lance D. Fusarelli.
    p. cm. -- (Educational policy in the 21st century)
  Includes bibliographical references and index.
  ISBN 1-59311-168-1 (pbk.) -- ISBN 1-59311-169-X (hardcover) 1.
School superintendents--United States. 2. School boards--United States. 3.
Educational leadership--Political aspects--United States. I. Petersen,
George J. II. Fusarelli, Lance D. (Lance Darin), 1966- III. Series.
  LB2831.72.P65 2005
  371.2'011--dc22

                2005004486

Printed in the United States of America

CONTENTS

SERIES FOREWORD

Bruce Anthony Jones

The Politics of Leadership: School Boards and Superintendents in Changing Times, by Professors George J. Petersen and Lance D. Fusarelli is a significant contribution to the series on *Educational Policy in the 21st Century: Opportunities, Challenges, and Solutions.* With regard to K-12 public education, the series has dealt extensively with issues that concern the principalship and with issues that concern the intertwining political roles of the government and private sectors in shaping how schools and school districts operate. Therefore, this volume fills a critical void with its research emphasis on school boards and the superintendency.

Over 40 years ago W. B. Spaulding wrote, "Superintendents have more anxiety than any other people who I have tested outside of mental institutions" (1954, p. 1). This is an amazing assertion—for 40 years ago—given the exceedingly complex political environments that superintendents must operate in today.

This volume by Petersen and Fusarelli is a reality check. The volume places the critical roles of the superintendency and school board in a modern context through the explication of said roles in often volatile and intense policy settings. This explication can help bring a better understanding and some level of *sanity* to the dynamic roles that school leaders need to play in the twenty-first century.

REFERENCE

Spaulding, W. B. (1954). *The superintendency of public schools: An anxious profession*. Cambridge, MA: Harvard University Press.

FOREWORD

Theodore J. Kowalski

In the midst of increasingly intense criticisms of public elementary and secondary education during the 1980s, many administrators and school board members viewed the need for reform with skepticism. They concluded that demands for change, promoted primarily by prominent corporate executives and elected officials, were meant to be diversions. More precisely, they thought their intent was to make public schools the scapegoat for America's declining economic stature in an emerging global economy. This skepticism was nurtured by a prevailing institutional culture in which educators had come to believe that periods of intense dissatisfaction were inevitable but temporary distractions. Consequently, many education leaders concluded that pressures to change would subside after world economic concerns diminished. Evidently, the past few decades have proven that the doubters were incorrect. Not only have demands for reform persisted for an unusually long period, the nature of the change proposals have become progressively focused—and at least for the last 10 years, they have concentrated heavily on local school district governance. Critics have started to point fingers at both superintendents and school boards and more than a few of them have concluded that Mark Twain was correct when he opined: "In the first place, God made idiots. That was for practice. Then he made school boards."

Local control of public education is a deceptively simple concept for at least three reasons. First, the demarcation presented in the literature between board member as policymaker and superintendent as policy implementer is arguably unambiguous. In practice, however, we discover that this dividing line is frequently very thin and at times, even invisible. Second, board members are supposed to be trustees—that is, public officials acting on behalf of all district residents. In practice, they are much more likely to be delegates advancing their personal agenda or the agenda of supporting political groups. Third and most important, the process of public policymaking is more difficult and contentious than it has been in the past. The reason is apparent; as America has become a much more diverse society competing values have ensured school improvement proposal will be opposed, at least by some segment of the community.

During the last half of the twentieth century, changes in the world magnified tensions between two equally important but arguably competing values—liberty and equality. The former has been expressed by creating and then preserving local control of public schools, including taxpayer power to determine programming scope, resource deployment levels, and the fiscal parameters. School improvement ideas such as parental choice, charter schools, and site-based councils are nested in this disposition. The latter value has been expressed by creating and then preserving reasonably equal statewide educational opportunities. School improvement ideas such as increased state funding, forced busing, and equalization of state funding formula are nested in this disposition. Clearly, the opposing values of liberty and equality promote radically different iterations of school governance and these perspectives have shaped most contemporary reform initiatives. As examples, liberty advocates argue that local district officials should be given greater autonomy and control and they promote strategies such as state deregulation and district decentralization. Equality advocates argue that federal and state government should take a more activist role and they promote centralized controls and increased funding. These nearly opposite perspectives undeniably encourage distinctively different roles for both superintendents and local school boards.

In our democracy, politicians have been reticent to eliminate the tensions between liberty and equality fearing that doing so would alienate a large percentage of the population. Instead, they have preferred compromises intended to produce temporary relief. This proclivity applied to public education has resulted in what scholar Hans Weiler described as directed autonomy applied to public education. On the surface, local district officials appear to have been given greater freedom to chart their own course with respect to improving schools. But more intense scrutiny reveals that state deregulation typically is less liberating than intended, especially when the strategy includes broad state goals, mandatory student testing, and legal accountability provisions. In essence, the current policy of pushing reform to the district level demonstrates how political figures seek to mollify both conservatives and liberals. Even more recently, the federal government has become more active in setting public education policy as evidenced by the passage of the No Child Left Behind Act.

Future decisions about education governance will have far reaching consequences extending even to the school administration profession itself. Whether public education becomes more decentralized and centralized will have an obvious influence on the expected roles of superintendents and other school administrators in coming decades. As an example, changing school boards to policy boards—an alteration that requires board members to focus almost entirely on visioning, planning, and curriculum—would enhance the professional stature of superintendents because their leadership and management responsibilities would be broadened. Conversely, increasing federal and state authority at the expense of local school board authority would diminish the stature of superintendents because their role would entail managing predetermined and pervasive policy.

The future of local district governance can be decided in two ways; exclusively by political elites or collectively by political elites and education professionals. More than 10 years ago, prominent policy analysts, such as Michael Kirst, Jacquelyn Dansberger, and Michael Usdan, began asking if we dare depart from standard political maneuvering by actually redefining the roles of schools boards and superintendents. In so doing, they encouraged members of the education profession to become reformers. The uncertainty that still surrounds the future of local school districts is why this empowering book is so important. George Petersen and Lance Fusarelli, the editors, have selected a collection of research studies and scholarly perspectives that broaden our understanding of the complexity of policy development and implementation at the local district level. This knowledge gives readers a deeper understanding of the realities of practice, permits them to make more informed choices, and prepares them to take an active role in improving the governance of local districts.

The editors and authors make available an array of historical, contemporary, and future points of view. As examples, the first chapter provides an historical context of board and superintendent relationships; the last chapter looks to the future by addressing administrator preparation and the state's role in this function; the intervening chapters present research on the book's foci; the investigations range from case studies to quantitative investigations testing widely accepted theory. Collectively, the editors and authors have succeeded in painting a mosaic of critical insights contributing to the ongoing discourse on governance reform.

The primary contribution of this book, however, is not its advocacy of a specific position but rather, its objective analysis of cogent topics. The content prompts us to consider governance in relation to quality education and to ponder alternative policy strategies that have yet to be fully evaluated. As a young doctoral student more than a few years ago, William Van Til, an eminent scholar and a mentor, reminded me almost daily that members of the education profession had a moral responsibility to address the most difficult questions about education and democracy. These enduring queries, he argued, extended to determining how this critical social service should be organized and controlled and to determining the appropriate roles for administrators and teachers. Those in our profession who fail to heed his advice by remaining indifferent to these philosophical dilemmas should consider Plato's long-standing warning: "One of the penalties for refusing to participate in politics is that you end up being governed by your inferiors."

CHAPTER 1

SUPERINTENDENT-BOARD RELATIONS

An Historical Overview of the Dynamics of Change and Sources of Conflict and Collaboration

Lars G. Björk

The history of American education describes an integral relationship between schools and local communities (Cremin, 1988). They were viewed as extensions of local communities and were organically related and bound together by shared circumstances, agricultural work, notions of family, and religion (Beck & Foster, 1999; Tyack, 1974). During the middle of the nineteenth century, the notion that schools were bound to local communities provided a foundation for Horace Mann's idealistic vision of a common school system that not only served neighborhoods but also helped unify a highly decentralized nation (Tyack & Hansot, 1974). The notion that the primary purpose of schools was to serve the nation by preparing numerate and literate citizens and workers by institutionalizing prevailing cultural norms, values, beliefs, and attitudes persisted throughout the close of the century. The social, economic, and political life of the

The Politics of Leadership: Superintendents and School Boards in Changing Times, 1–22
Copyright © 2005 by Information Age Publishing
All rights of reproduction in any form reserved.

nation changed dramatically as the nation expanded in geographic size, population, and complexity during this era.

Throughout the first two decades of the twentieth century, the nature of schooling changed to reflect industrial and technological developments, urbanization, population characteristics, corporate values of efficiency and productivity, and abiding faith in bureaucratically structured and scientifically managed organizations (Beck & Foster, 1999). As was the case during previous eras, schools sought to prepare youth for work in corporate and industrial settings and adopted many of the organizational and managerial practices of business. Tyack (1974) observed that school boards and superintendents embraced the notion of centralized control and created large, comprehensive school systems. In addition, they adopted new bureaucratic organizational structures that divided schools into grades (Goodlad & Anderson, 1963) and managed school affairs and directed activities of principals, teachers, and pupils through hierarchical chains of command. In doing so, they instituted roles and practices that had an indelible effect on schooling throughout the remainder of the twentieth century (Tyack, 1974). As a consequence, the role of boards of education and superintendents changed dramatically. Boards adopted decision making models used in modern business, superintendents employed corporate notions of management to administer district affairs, and principals abandoned notions of being principal teachers to serving as executive managers. In retrospect, school boards and administrators made every effort to align schools with "economic and social conditions of an urban-industrial society" (Cubberly, 1916, p.126).

This brief discussion of the emergence of American public schools illustrates that schools are inexorably bound to local communities and that changes in social, economic, political, and industrial/technological contexts influence the nature of organizational structures, administrator roles, and superintendent-board relations. Understanding the dynamic relationships between the external environment, schools, and the nature of governance and superintendent-board relations can provide a framework for examining present circumstances as well as a discussion of promising future directions. The organization of this chapter provides a succinct discussion of theoretical perspectives on the relationship between the external environment and organizational change; a review of the structure of public school governance; an examination of changing education contexts; consideration of research findings on the relationship between community power structure, board political configurations, and superintendent roles; and a discussion of future prospects for superintendent-board relations.

THEORETICAL PERSPECTIVES

Theoretical perspectives on organizations and their environments provide a framework for understanding the fundamental structure of schooling and dynamics of superintendent-school board relations. For example, Talcott Parsons (1956) and others posit that organizations are social inventions and are both fluid and dynamic, move in time and space, act and react, and are shaped by a combination of historical and external environmental factors that both threaten their survival and provide the impetus for change (Fullan, 1993; Meyer & Rowan, 1978). This notion suggests that when significant changes in an organization's social, economic, political, and technological environment occur, it seeks equilibrium by modifying internal structures and adjusting relations with other organizations in the task environment (Meyer, 1978; Senge, 1990). The nature of these adaptive responses may be patterned according to both historical precedent (Meyer, 1978) and sources of the organizational legitimation (Pfeffer, 1978).

A decade later, Parsons (1967) underscored the importance of organizations maintaining connection with the community. In his general theory of formal organizations, he posits that rather than existing in isolation, organizations are interdependent with the larger social system from which they derive legitimacy, meaning, and support. The ecology of organizations is characterized as a symbiotic relationship in which organizations and society derive mutual benefits. With regard to public education, this relationship is rather straightforward: Society supports schools in exchange for their creating numerate and literate citizens. The inability of schools to meet these expectations can jeopardize continuing public support and threaten their survival.

During the last half of the twentieth century, notions derived from systems thinking influenced the work of political and social scientists trying to understand the relationship between organizations and environments, institutional behavior, and organizational learning. David Easton (1965) described the political system as a subsystem of the larger social order. He referred to his conceptualization of these interactions between the political system and the larger environment as political systems analysis. Subsequently, political and social scientists rationalized that schools are part of the political subsystem because board members are elected and make authoritative decisions regarding the allocation of resources (Campbell, Flemming, Newell, & Bennion, 1987). Their actions are legitimated by the larger community (Thompson, 1967) and persist in society as a means through which schools and society can adapt to changes (Easton, 1965). Wirt and Kirst (1982, 2001) applied Easton's political analysis approach to understanding the relationship between education organizations and society. They persuasively argued that because school boards mediate inputs (demands and supports) from the external environment and convert them into appropriate outputs (action, program, or policy) schools are part of the political subsystem. Campbell et al. (1987) extended the work of Easton (1965) and Wirt and Kirst (1982, 2001) in developing an open-systems view of school administration. This perspective provided a more definitive framework on how systems thinking can be used in order to increase the effectiveness and efficiency of schools as organizations.

For example, during the last several decades, the American public has persistently demanded that schools align their work with changing demographic, social, economic, political, and technological realities of society. Systems thinking provides a framework for understanding the relational nature between schools and society and the changing dynamics of board and superintendent roles (Hoy & Miskel, 2001). Recently, Björk and Keedy (2001) examined interactions among school boards and superintendents and found that external events influence internal board dynamics and consequently board members and superintendents mutually define their respective roles. In this regard, complex community, board, and superintendent influence patterns contribute to superintendent role definition and redefinition. Theoretical perspectives and research findings provide insight into enduring practices as well as sources of change that may influence superintendent-board relations.

The District Role in Education

State governments established local school districts to administer its system of public education. This organizational approach reflected congruence with citizen expectations to preserve long-standing traditions of local control and support of education as well as direct democracy. School districts function as political subdivisions of the state or quasi-public corporations and, as such, are subject to the will of state legislatures, and are obligated to conduct their affairs in accordance with state constitutional provisions and laws (Kowalski, 1999). State authority for public education is included in state constitutions, specified in state statutes and regulations that allow local boards of education to act on its behalf related to school district operations. Although the public education system is dispersed, state legislatures have considerable authority in directing the affairs of local school districts, including retaining the prerogative to assume operational control when districts are malfeasant or negligent, to change district jurisdictional boundaries or eliminate it entirely, and to alter the powers of boards of education (Cooper, Fusarelli & Randall, 2004; Kowalski, 1999). States delegate powers to local school boards to act on their behalf in the provision of education. Although state and federal constitutional provisions, statutes, regulations, and policies proscribe board decision making authority, they have considerable discretion in making education decisions with regard to raising revenue through property taxes, managing school property, employing professional and support staff and, influencing instructional programs (Kowalski & Reitzug, 1993). In other words, the autonomy of school districts is conditional and limited to powers granted by the state legislature that are specifically related to its role in providing education (Knezevich, 1984; Kowalski, 1999).

Although school districts vary in terms of student enrollments and geographic size, Ramirez (1992) and Björk & Gurley (2005) contend that district size is related more to historical antecedents and political preferences than concerns for organizational efficiency. In this regard, district size will reflect political preferences of local communities as well as patterns of governance, superintendent board relations, and administration. On the one hand, large urban districts have larger boards that reflect a broader range of diversity and interests that heighten the level of conflict between superintendents and boards of education. In addition large districts are organizationally complex and have central office support staff that often preclude superintendents from having direct involvement in managing district operations. In these circumstances, superintendents function much like chief executive officers (CEOs) of large corporations. On the other hand, superintendents in small, often rural districts must attend to the nuances of community cultures and power structures as well as function with the lack administrative support staff. As a consequence, they have a more direct hand in district operations than their urban counterparts. Those serving in mid-size districts often must contend with a wide range of unique social, political and administrative circumstances that define their relations with local boards of education and how they do work.

Glass, Björk, and Brunner (2000) estimate the number of superintendents at 13,700: a number that closely reflects the number of functional public school districts in the United States. They range in size from large urban districts like New York City with over one million students enrolled, to rural districts, with fewer than 300 students attending. Approximately 21% of school districts in the nation enroll more than 2,500 students; however, they are responsible for educating 80% of children in public education. On the other hand, 79% of districts enroll fewer than 2,499 students; however, they educate only 20% of all students (Lunenberg & Ornstein, 1991).

Although school districts commonly include grades P-12, some states have other types of configurations including elementary districts (K-8), high school districts (9-12), those that span elementary through community college (K-14), as well as other districts for special education and correctional agencies (Kowalski & Reitzug, 1993). School districts are distributed geographically and typically align with county boundaries or city jurisdictions. Some have crosscutting jurisdictions for the delivery of special services and oddly, others do not have any students (Glass et al., 2000). In addition, school districts can be classified as being either dependent or independent. These two designations describe authority granted by the state legislature for a local district to levy property taxes needed to support district operations. For example, independent districts administer their own budgets and are allowed to set their own tax rates; however, their actions are restricted by state statutes and are subject to review by state agencies. These districts have greater discretion with regard to taxation and budgetary decision-making. Dependent districts, however, have less discretion. They have neither the discretion to levy taxes nor to administer their budgets as they are under the auspices of either city or county governing bodies. These data underscore the importance of acknowledging the influence of district size in defining patterns of governance, superintendent-board relations, and administration as well as the difficulty in offering a simplistic descriptions of how districts are or should be governed, lead, and managed. Understanding district contexts is central to fathoming the nature of superintendent-board relations.

The Role and Characteristics of Local Boards of Education

Local school boards are delegated powers by the state to act on its behalf to ensure that schools are operated properly and all children learn. Although constitutional provisions, state and federal statutes, regulations and policies limit board decision making, boards have considerable discretion in making education decisions with regard to raising revenue through property taxes, managing school property, employing professional and support staff and, influencing instructional programs. Responsibilities common to most local boards of education include engaging in two-way communication with citizens, parents, teachers, and special interest groups to help understand their needs and expectations; providing a platform for open discourse on important issues; and informing the community on district affairs. This provides a basis for formulating policies, rules, and regulations to enhance organizational effectiveness and support student learning. Other responsibilities include monitoring the effectiveness of academic curricula and instructional programs, approving budgets and maintaining fiscal responsibility, levying taxes and approving capital projects, negotiating contracts with labor unions, establishing school attendance boundaries, and ensuring that constitutional due process provisions are followed when grievances are

adjudicated. In most instances boards of education rely on superinten-
dents to handle day-to-day administrative responsibilities (Kowalski &
Reitzug, 1993, Lunenburg & Ornstein, 1991; Norton, Webb, Dlugash, &
Sybouts, 1996).

The vast majority of school board members are elected, which is in
concert with prevailing democratic notions that this ensures that they will
be responsive to public demands and accountable to the community
(Kowalski & Reitzug, 1993; Lunenburg & Ornstein, 1991). The number of
members serving on local school boards varies by state, however, the average number falls within a range of 7 to 9 members. Demographic characteristics of school boards reflect the political dynamics of local
communities. For example, most boards are composed of members who
are older than the general population (79% over 40 years of age), are predominantly Caucasian (93%), male (60%), and are college educated
(68%). They also tend to be professionals (50%), many own their own
businesses (12%), and have incomes above $70,000 per year (46%)
(Lunenburg & Ornstein, 1991). Problems faced by local boards of education over the past several decades have remained relatively unchanged
and include inadequate financial resources, conforming to state and federal mandates, developing and aligning curriculum, and responding to
disciplinary issues and drug abuse. Although citizen responses to public
opinion polls may indicate a different order with regard to perceived
severity of problems faced, they are in agreement as to what problems are
most severe (Lunenburg & Ornstein, 1991). Glass et al. (2000) found that
superintendents identified five significant problems: the lack of adequate
financing, difficulty in assessing learner outcomes, state accountability,
demands for new teaching strategies and changing curriculum priorities.
Their analysis of previous AASA ten-year reports on the American superintendency suggest that these problems are enduring and may stimulate
political interest group activity that contributes to tensions among citizens, board members, and superintendents.

The Role and Characteristics of District Superintendents

The superintendent of schools serves as the chief executive officer of
the local board of education and is charged with the responsibility for car-
rying out their policies and administering district affairs. As CEOs, their
administrative role includes reviewing and recommending board policy
options, advising them on district operations, providing information on
the status of school community relations and student academic progress,
as well as leading district strategic planning initiatives. In addition,

boards expect superintendents to monitor the academic program; keep them informed about personnel matters; maintain collaborative relations with local, state, and federal education agencies; and are primarily responsible for keeping the public informed about district affairs through linkages with news media (Kowalski, 1999). In this regard, superintendents of schools enact several roles including educator, business executive, democratic leaders, applied social scientist (Björk, 2000; Brunner, Grogan, & Björk, 2002; Cuban, 1976; Griffiths, 1966), and communicator (Kowalski, 2001).

Understanding the characteristics of superintendents may help chart new courses in relations with boards of education. During recent years, scholars studying superintendents' characteristics report findings that are generally consistent (Glass et al., 2000; Hodgkinson & Montenegro, 1999; Johnson, 1996; Kowalski, 1999). For more than a half a century (1950-2000), the median age of superintendents has remained at about 50 years of age. This statistic is not surprising given the time involved in "moving through the chairs," a process that characterizes superintendents' typical career patterns. The most common track for becoming a superintendent (48.5%) was from teacher, to assistant principal or principal, to central office administrator, to superintendent. The majority of superintendents became a CEO in their early to mid 40's, held several three-year contracts within the same district and stayed an average of 8.5 years. On average they served in 2-3 districts over a career spanning approximately 15-18 years. Most (68%) superintendents indicated they were hired from outside their present district, confirming observations of the transient nature of the position; however, 87.5% spent their professional careers in only one state.

Community Power Structures, Board Politics and Superintendent Roles

During the past several decades (1983-2003), the press for reform has influenced changes in how superintendents enact their roles. A loss of confidence in institutions and leaders, increased levels of interest group activism, and public demands for involvement in local policy making processes require a different set of skills than during previous eras. In addition, analysts report that a growing cultural divide among citizens, divergent ideological positions on major issues, and a shift in policy making to the state level and the devolution of decision-making authority to schools have increased superintendent-board conflict. These circumstances have increased the complexity of superintendents' work and highlight a need to improve superintendent-board working relationships (Björk & Lindle, 2001).

Understanding the tie between communities and schools as well as how political power structures influence superintendent-board roles and relationships can provide a framework for analyzing sources of conflict. The nature of school district politics and the relationship between superintendents and local school board members has captured the interest of scholars since the nineteenth century (Björk & Lindle, 2001; Burlingame, 1988; Iannaccone, 1991; Tyack & Hansot, 1982). During the first several decades of the twentieth century, superintendent-board conflict was believed to result from political corruption and consequently, reformers called for separating board member selection from the electoral process by either creating non-partisan elections or appointing board members (Björk & Lindle, 2001; Iannaccone & Lutz, 1995; Tyack & Hansot, 1982). By the1950s, scholars began to view often heated debates among school board members and contentious local elections as an essential dimension of representative democracies and concurred that they were a legitimate political arena worthy of study (Burlingame, 1988). Chubb and Moe (1990) observe that because effective authority for education resides at the local level, decision-making processes will attract political groups that have a vested interest in policy decisions. Although some scholars argue for developing a better understanding of the dynamics of community politics (Björk & Lindle, 2001), few studies have focused on the dynamics among community power structures, political configurations of boards of education, and superintendent roles (Björk & Lindle, 2001). A line of inquiry, began by McCarty and Ramsey (1971) was recently extended by Glass et al. (2000) and Björk & Lindle (2001), provides some insight into these political relationships.

McCarty and Ramsey (1971) examined relations among superintendents and local board members and sought to understand their political behavior and roles through an analysis of community political structures. They contend that community political power structures influence the selection and actions of members of local boards of education. McCarty and Ramsey (1971) also conjectured that superintendents would be politically astute enough to ascertain political power configurations of their respective boards and adjust their leadership roles to fit community and board power configurations. Their research findings generally confirmed these relationships. McCarty and Ramsey (1971) developed four theses to describe power relationships including: (a) the nature of political power varies from one community to another; (b) those who have political power in communities influence community-wide boards and professionals implementing board policies; (c) power structures are observed directly through interaction among community power figures, community-wide boards, and professionals; and (d) community power structures are composed of interrelationships that exhibit different forms and patterns, and understanding them enables individuals to predict dispositions on issues and adjust their behavior to enhance their performance.

McCarty and Ramsey's (1971) typology of community-board-superintendent relations that aligned community and board power structures with the superintendents' role was used by Glass et al. (2000) in their recent nation-wide study of the superintendency. Their work examined superintendent perceptions of board of education power configurations and how they characterized the way they worked with board members. Their findings generally confirmed relationships established by McCarty and Ramsey (1971) and identified that over nearly a 30-year period (1971-2000), superintendents exhibited two dominant roles in working with their boards of education—professional advisor and decision maker. Superintendents' role preferences that have persisted over the past 30 years indicate how they view their work. As professional advisors, they are inclined to work collaboratively with boards yet have the political acuity to adapt to changes in board political power configurations. Findings reported by Glass et al. (2000) indicate that 48% of CEOs characterize the way they work with boards of education as being a professional advisor and nearly half (49.5%) of superintendents indicated that they viewed their role as decision-makers, primarily concerned with making the district organization work effectively.

The work of McCarty and Ramsey (1971) and other scholars underscore the importance of superintendents having the acuity to understand political power configurations of communities and board members to enhance their effectiveness in reform environments. This is particularly important as the demographic characteristics of communities change, public scrutiny of schooling increases, and multiple and diverse interest groups demand greater participation in decision making and governance processes (Carter & Cunningham, 1997). Although public sentiment and professional norms tend to reinforce the notion that partisan and interest group politics should not intrude on education decision making arenas, scholars concur that open debate around the purposes of public education and partisan political activity in support of preferred education policies is both common practice and a hallmark of democratic traditions established during the colonial period (Björk & Lindle, 2001; Rowan & Miskel, 1999). In this regard, an inherent characteristic of American schooling is the role of local school boards in providing forums for expressing ideological positions, airing differences, and building consensus about education in local communities (Björk, Bell, & Gurley, 2002; Kirst & Wirt, 1982). Thus, understanding the politics of community and school board relations and superintendent roles, as well as being able to negotiate the local political terrain will largely determine the success or failure of educational reform in the United States during the coming decades (Björk, 2000; Björk & Lindle, 2001; Carter & Cunningham, 1997; Kowalski, 1999).

SUPERINTENDENT-BOARD POLICY MAKING: NORMATIVE MODELS AND PRACTICE

Although normative models are useful in defining superintendent and board roles and arenas of action, they tend to be overly simplistic and, as such, may often be misleading. Models of superintendent-board relations suggest that boards enact district policies and superintendents carry them out as part of their administrative duties. How their respective roles are actually enacted, however, may be different. For example, although boards of education tend to view superintendents as responsible for managing district affairs, they are inclined to micro-manage district affairs. This intrudes upon superintendent prerogatives, heightens tension, adds to superintendent-board instability, and contributes to superintendent turnover. Glass et al. (2000) examined the effect of board conflict and found that only 15% of superintendents in the nation, and 24% in small districts with fewer than 300 students, leave their positions because of conflict with their boards. Although this may present a serious problem to some districts, the majority of superintendents and boards appear to have amicable relations despite tendencies on both to intrude upon the others' formal prerogatives particularly in the area of formulating district policies. Although conventional wisdom says that school boards formulate policy, superintendents, by virtue of their expert knowledge and accessibility to data and staff, tend to play a significant role. Glass et al. (2000) found that boards initiated policies less than 8% of the time and accepted proposals offered by superintendents 89% of the time. They also found that nearly 50% of superintendents enacted their role as professional advisors (47.7%) or maintained relations with all board factions (1.6%), suggesting a tendency towards collaborative work relationships.

The inclination to work as partners in the policy making process appears to be increasing. For example, in 1992, only 28.5% of superintendents described policy making as a shared responsibility; however, in 2000, nearly 37% indicated that was the case (Glass et al., 2000). It is evident that discrepancies between normative models and actual practices in districts governance and administration suggest that board members and superintendents tend to work together as teams. Even though their roles may overlap, they have the capacity to accommodate differences that arise from infringement on the formal roles of each. These findings may suggest promising directions for redefining superintendent-board roles and relationships.

CHANGING EDUCATION CONTEXTS: IMPLICATIONS FOR FUTURE SUPERINTENDENT-BOARD RELATIONS

Theoretical perspectives discussed previously suggest that changing external circumstances (e.g., community and student demographics) will influence governance and administrative patterns and relations. During the past several decades, demographic changes (Reyes, Wagstaff, & Fusarelli, 1999); heightened interest groups activity; expanding policy making role of the courts (Björk & Lindle, 2001); unstable economic circumstances; and competing values have altered the landscape of American public education. As a consequence, educators have been compelled to develop a better understanding of the dynamic relationship between society and schools (Björk & Keedy, 2001a). In addition, it has become necessary for school boards and leaders to develop "very different ways of thinking about the purposes of their work, and the skills and knowledge that go with these purposes" (Elmore, 2000, p. 35). An examination of numerous macro-level forces suggests that changes in social contexts are collectively placing increasing demands on schools as institutions and heightening demands for changing how they are governed, led, and contribute to the nations economic well being.

Changing Demographics and Public Expectations for Education

Changing demographic patterns and social characteristics of the nation as well as the composition of students who attend public schools in part influence changing public expectations for public education. Release of education reform reports through the reform era (1983-2004) provided a forum for a protracted public debate among educators, politicians, economists, business leaders, and ideologues about aligning schooling with the needs of a more diverse student population and demands of a global, information-based service economy. Although education reform reports were highly critical of American public schools, they also affirmed the belief that education is linked to individual success and that a sound education system is essential to the national well-being and public faith in schools (Brogan, 1962; Cuban, 1990; Murphy, 1995).

Changing Population Demographics

Analysts presented convincing demographic evidence that projected growth in the nation's minority population will have significant implications for society, and articulated the need to ensure that all children learn (Kingdon, 1995). For example, projections indicate that the African American population in the United States will increase to 44 million by the year 2020 (Hodgkinson, 1991a, p.5). In addition, the Hispanic segment of the population is increasing rapidly and became the largest minority group in the nation in 2002. Projections that this cohort will grow to 47 million by the year 2020 are being increased. In addition, a new and expanded system of racial record keeping developed by the United States Census Bureau in 2000 enables individuals to define themselves by selecting as many as six racial categories. Analysts estimate that between 3% and 6.6% of the population (8.4-18.5 million people) may identify themselves as being multiracial. Demographic projections indicate that the nation's population will grow to 265 million by the year 2020. At that juncture, more than 91 million Americans, or one third of the nation, will be non-white (Hodgkinson, 1985, p.5).

Students of color are the fastest growing segment of the American public school population. The United States Census in 2000 reported that out of the nation's 49 million elementary students 38 million were white, 8 million were African American, 7.3 million were Hispanic, and 2.1 were Asian or Pacific Islander. Based on Hodgkinson's (1991) projections, the percentage of students of color in public schools will steadily increase during the coming decades moving from 36% in 2000, and to 48% by 2020. This segment of the student population often requires significant levels of academic support (Hodgkinson, 1991; Sergiovanni et al., 1987) to ensure academic success. Most reformers recognize that as the proportion of students of color as well as those with low SES backgrounds attending public schools increases in the twenty-first century, they will have a significant impact on school learning, teaching, leadership, and governance. For example, the United States Congress recently enacted the No Child Left Behind Act (2002) that underscores the importance of redesigning teaching to enhance student learning particularly for at risk children. Although the purpose of the No Child Left Behind Act (NCLB) enjoyed an uncommon level of bipartisan support in Congress, critics assert that it is the most comprehensive yet punitive and inadequately funded education mandate handed to states in the history of American history (Hoyle et al., 2004).

Demographic projections indicating that a larger proportion of the nation's youth would have to be more highly educated to meet workforce demands during the next century were identified by education commissions and task forces during the 1980s and raised important concerns about how well schools served all children. Demographic data showed that minority groups would provide the preponderance of workers in the 21st century. Realizing that schools were strategically positioned to develop the nation's human capital during the coming decades motivated conservative business leaders to join progressives in actively supporting education reform (Björk, 1995). The contentious debate surrounding issues of access and excellence that troubled policy makers during earlier decades were no longer viewed as being mutually exclusive. As morality became pragmatic, liberal and conservative adversaries became tentative allies in promoting the education of all children as a means of supporting the nation's quest for economic self-preservation (Henderson, 1977).

This emerging perspective contributed to altering public expectations for schools and led to questioning the deep structures of educational practice. In the past, schools served as sorting machines and children who successfully navigated bureaucratic school contexts were expected to fit into regimented industrial settings (Spring, 1986). They were prepared to meet these work demands by being taught the importance of obeying superiors, following rules, and complying with regulations, and engaging in rote learning in static classroom environments. Continuation of practices that fit nineteenth century conditions were viewed as being tantamount to preparing the next generation of American workers for planned obsolescence. Business leaders, educators, and policy makers recognized that in the future, work would require a different set of behaviors that aligned with a postindustrial economy. All children would have to be educated at higher levels by optimizing learning; cultivating the ability to question the status quo; developing critical thinking skills; using technology to access, manipulate and analyze information, and working independently as well as collaboratively in solving real-world problems. They also acknowledged schools not only would be held responsible for preparing a large segment of the nation's youth, who have been poorly served by schools, but also help meliorate a wide array social problems that inhibit their academic success.

During the early 1990s, Wong (1992) observed: "increasingly, external politics and economic forces are found to shape school finance, leadership, succession, the student population, racial desegregation and issues related to education of the disadvantaged" (p. 3). In large measure, the dynamic relationship between the environment and public schools call for greater attention to social society and organizational justice in schools as well as aligning the characteristics of those who govern and lead public schools with citizens and students they are intended to serve.

Education Reform and Emerging Views on Learning, Leadership, and Governance

During the past several decades, widespread concern for the quality of public education launched what arguably is the most intense, comprehensive, and sustained effort to improve education in American history (Björk, 2001). National commission and task force reports, accompanied by unrelenting calls for school reform by a broad spectrum of reformers both within and outside of traditional educational circles, are challenging conventional assumptions about teaching and learning and changing the manner in which schools are structured, managed, and governed. As a consequence, roles of superintendents, their relationship with school boards, and how they are prepared have emerged as prominent themes in the discourse on reform in the nation.

Since release of *The Nation at Risk* report by the National Commission for Excellence in Education (1983), three successive waves of educational reform contributed to shifting policy initiatives from accountability, to teacher professionalism, to learning (Björk, 2001, 1996). Since the mid-1980s, reformers focused on the role of principals in ensuring the success of school improvement. Subsequently, in the late 1980's, heightened interest in large-scale, systemic reform shifted the focus to the superintendency. Legislators, practitioners, and professors raised questions as to how devolution of decision making to the building level and shift of policy making to the state level would change landscape of superintendents' work and governance (Björk, 2000; Crowson, 1988; Cuban, 1988; Johnson, 1996).

One of the most important developments in the field of educational administration during the past several decades, the organization of the field's knowledge base, provides insight into how changing contexts influence district leadership, community interaction, and school board relationships. In the past, Halpin (1957) and Boyan (1988) structured the knowledge base around organizational, managerial, and environmental issues. Murphy and Louis (1999), in an effort to re-center the field, incorporated these elements within a broad discussion of leadership for school improvement and student learning. Thus discussions of the knowledge base shifted away from the acquisition of formal knowledge or "knowing about" administration to knowledge use or "knowing for" management and school improvement (i.e. craft knowledge) emphasized during the first wave of education reform (1983-1986). Although this change reflects the field's evolution from a theory-orientation to a knowledge-practice configuration, Björk, Lindle, and Van Meter (1999) contend that it is insufficient to understand changes in the context of schooling or respond to calls for a different type of leader and leadership practices. New expectations for school and district leaders emerged during the second wave of educational reform (1986-1989). Emphasis shifted away from effective management to student learning, teacher professionalism, decentralization, distributed leadership, and shared governance and underscored the importance of superintendents' educational and democratic leadership roles (Björk, 1993; Björk & Gurley, 2005). Thus, "knowing how" to improve teaching and learning, engaging teachers, and parents, as well as generating broad-based community support became increasingly important.

To adequately address issues facing schools, however, discourse on the relationship between the social, economic, and political contexts in which schools are embedded must accentuate notions of "knowing how" to change schools (Björk, Lindle, & Van Meter, 1999). Thus, leadership focused on improving teaching and learning, engaging teachers, and parents, as well as generating broad-based community support became increasingly important. Themes of inclusive participation were carried into and expanded during the third wave of reform (1989-2001) and underscored the value ofconstructivist's notion of "knowing why" reforms are needed (Björk, 1996). As the push for systemic reforms brought superintendents into more frequent contact with a wide range of community citizens, agencies, and interest groups they were expected to articulate how caring for and educating all children were central to sustaining an inclusive democratic society and a vigorous national economy. Thus, "knowing why" educational reform is needed, helped to redefine how superintendents view schooling, leadership, and community interaction (Björk & Gurley, 2003).

At the close of the twentieth century, the confluence of a number of external environmental factors is altering the landscape of American education and changing the nature of the superintendency. Factors, including expanding social diversity in ethnicity and race, persistent demands for reform, and changing expectations for education that underscore the importance that all children learn have increased the intensity of relations between schools and communities and placed superintendents at the nexus of local politics. Although superintendents are required to have acuity for working with multiple and diverse community groups, circumstances also compel them to act as moral and transformational leaders. It is moral in the sense that superintendents' work will be increasingly guided by "knowing why" reforms are essential to ensuring social justice (Starratt, 1996). As moral leaders, superintendents are expected to articulate the purpose of schooling, analyze how well or how poorly students are served, meliorate problems that inhibit change, seek common ground for productive discourse, and create meaning in the work of teachers and students. It is transformational in terms of building community capacity to participate in education policy and decision-making venues as well as organizational capacity with regard to engaging those in the system to alter conventional patterns of work to enhance learning and teaching. In these circumstances, they will be confronted with the need to reconsider conventional notions of power (Brunner, 1995) and control and accept the notion of agency in sustaining long-term change. Rather than using power to make others subservient as is typical in modern industrial settings, they will use it to ensure voices of all citizens are valued; support the creation of communities of caring; and broaden involvement of teachers, parents, and citizens in decision-making and governance.

Reconceptualizing Superintendent-Board Relations

During the past several decades (1970-2003), changing social contexts and reform initiatives have altered patterns of district governance and board of education-superintendent relations. Since the early 1970s, state legislatures assumed increasing responsibility for public education—a trend that gained momentum during the education reform movement (1983-2003). During this period, primary responsibility for educational policy making shifted from districts to state levels of government and with the adoption of school-based management and distributed leadership, decision-making devolved to the school level. These circumstances altered conventional governance arrangements leading some analysts to speculate on the pending crisis; however, others view them as opportunities to redefine the superintendent-board roles.

IMPLICATIONS FOR PROFESSIONAL PREPARATION

Understanding the nature and future direction of decision-making and governance patterns will influence how the next generation of superintendents are identified, prepared, selected and evaluated. Several themes woven through the warp and weft of educational reform reports during the past two decades (1983-2004) have a direct bearing on the nature and direction of superintendent preparation. The first theme, improving learning, require that district leaders have a working knowledge of learning, teaching, curriculum construction and alignment (Björk, 1993; Cambron-McCabe, 1993; Murphy, 1993). The second theme, distributed leadership, involves superintendents working to broaden and deepen levels of participation in decision-making and governance. The third theme, reconfiguring professional preparation, stresses aligning training with the new realities of practice and emphasizes preparing them to be excellent administrators; knowledgeable about curriculum, learning and teaching; working as a member of a district governance team; having a political acuity for working with multiple and diverse groups in the community, and building the capacity of people in organizations to change.

The theme of reconfiguring professional preparation has two distinct yet complimentary dimensions including: (1) acquiring professional knowledge that grounds their work as educators and CEO's and, (2) attaining experience in leading high performing districts. At this juncture, the academic and practice arms of the profession have a common interest in identifying and preparing excellent district leaders. Thus, universities and districts should be equally responsible for identifying the next generation of superintendents as well as reconfiguring how they are prepared including: integrating knowledge about instructional leadership, educational statesmanship (politics and board relations), communication, management, and social sciences into the curriculum (Björk & Kowalski, 2005) and orienting it more explicitly toward problems of practice; adopting work embedded learning strategies, and using standards-based performance assessments (Björk, 2001; Murphy, 1990). In sum, they must possess knowledge about and for administration, knowledge of how to improve schooling, and why reforms are essential to sustaining a democratic society (Björk, Lindle, & Van Meter, 1999). The changing landscape of district governance and decision-making suggests the importance of aspiring and veteran superintendents as well as board members cooperating with each other in laying a new foundation for policy and decision-making.

CONCLUSION

The notion that organizations are social inventions (Parsons, 1956) implies that they can be reconfigured when faced with significant changes in the environment. Continuing patterns of governance, heightened levels of political interest group activity, the press for school reform, and changing environmental contexts are increasing the probability for superintendent-board conflict as well opportunities for redefining the nature of superintendent-board relations. During the past two decades, a simultaneous shift of policy making from local boards of education to states and the devolution of decision-making from superintendents to schools present a unique set of circumstances that invite a search for new forms of governance and administration. For example, research findings suggest that collaborative working relationships, rather than being a recent phenomenon, may be an enduring characteristic of how boards and superintendents work. Thus, building upon these long-standing relationships may help chart promising new directions in governance and administration. In addition, changing demographics suggest that governance patterns will be more inclusive and the nature of decisions will underscore the importance of achieving social and organizational justice. These changes also will reframe how the next generation of superintendents will be identified, recruited, prepared, hired and evaluated.

REFERENCES

Beck, L., & Foster, W. (1999) Administration and community: Considering challenges, exploring possibilities. In J. Murphy & K. Seashore Louis (Eds.), *Handbook of research on educational administration* (pp. 337-358). San Francisco: Jossey-Bass.

Björk, L. (1993). Effective schools-effective superintendents: The emerging instructional leadership role. *Journal of School Leadership, 3(3)*, 246-259.

Björk, L. (1995). Substance and symbolism in the education commission reports. In R. Ginsberg & D. Plank (Eds.), *Commission reports and reforms: Fashioning educational policy in the 1980's and beyond* (pp. 133-149). New York: Praeger.

Björk, L. (1996). The revisionists' critique of the education reform reports. *Journal of School Leadership, 7(1)*, 290-315.

Björk, L. (2000). Personal characteristics. In T. Glass, L. Björk, & C. C. Brunner (Eds.), *The study of the American superintendency 2000: A look at the superintendent in the new millennium* (pp. 15-32). Arlington, VA: American Association of School Administrators.

Björk, L. (2001). Preparing the next generation of superintendents: Integrating formal and experiential knowledge. In C. C. Brunner, & L. Björk (Eds.), *The new superintendency: Advances in research and theories of school management and educational* (pp. 19-54). Greenwich, CT: JAI Press.

Björk, L., Bell, R. & Gurley, D. (2002). Politics and the socialization of superintendents. In G. Perreault (Ed.), *The changing world of educational administration*, (pp. 294-31). Lanham, MD: Scarecrow Press.

Björk, L., & Gurley, K. (in press). Superintendent as educational statesman. In L. Björk & T. Kowalski (Eds.), *The contemporary superintendent: Preparation, practice and development*. Thousand Oakes, CA: Corwin Press.

Björk, L. & Keedy, J. (2001). Politics and the superintendency in the United States: Restructuring in-service education. *Journal of In-Service Education* 27(2), 277-305.

Björk, L. G., & Kowalski, T. J. (Eds.). (2005) *The contemporary superintendent: Preparation, practice and development*. Thousand Oaks, CA: Corwin.

Björk, L., & Lindle, J. C. (2001). Superintendents and interest groups. *Educational Policy, 15(1)*, 76-91.

Björk, L., Lindle, J. C., & Van Meter, E. (1999). A summing up. *Educational Administration Quarterly, 35(4)*, 657-663.

Boyan, N. (Ed.). (1988). *Handbook of research on educational administration: A project of the American Educational Research Association*. New York: Longman.

Brogan. D. (1962). *The American character*. New York: Vintage Books.

Brunner, C. C. (1995). By power defined: Women and the superintendency. *Educational Considerations, 22(20)*, 21-26.

Burlingame, M. (1988). The politics of education and educational policy: The local level. In N. Boyan (Ed.), *The handbook of research on educational administration* (pp. 439-451). New York: Longman.

Cambron-McCabe, N. (1993). Leadership for democratic authority. In J. Murphy (Ed.), *Preparing tomorrow's leaders: Alternative designs* (pp. 157-176). University Park, PA: University Council for Educational Administration.

Campbell, R., Flemming, T., Newell, L., & Bennion, J. (1987). *A history of thought and practice in educational administration.* New York: Teachers College Press.

Carter, G. & Cunningham, W. (1997). *The American school superintendent: Leading in the age of pressure.* San Francisco: Jossey-Bass.

Cooper, B., Fusarelli, L., & Randall, E. (2004). *Better policies, better school: Theories and applications.* Boston: Allyn & Bacon.

Cremin, L. (1988). *American education: The metropolitan experience.* New York: Harcourt, Brace, and World.

Crowson, R. L. (1988). Editors introduction. *Peabody Journal of Education, 65(4),* 1-8.

Cuban, L. (1976). *Urban school chiefs under fire.* Chicago: University Chicago Press

Cuban, L. (1988). *The managerial imperative and the practice of leadership in schools.* Albany: State University of New York Press.

Cuban, L. (1990, December). Four stories about national goals for American education. *Phi Delta Kappan, 72(4),* 264-271.

Cubberly, E. (1916). *Public school administration.* New York: Houghton-Mifflin.

Easton, D. (1965). *A systems analysis of political life.* New York: Wiley.

Elmore, R. (2000). *Building a new structure for school leadership.* Washington, DC: The Albert Shankar Institute.

Fullan, M. (1993). *Change forces: Probing the depths of educational reform.* Sussex, England: Falmer Press.

Glass, T., Björk, L., & Brunner, C. C. (2000). *The study of the American superintendency 2000: A look at the superintendent in the new millennium.* Arlington, VA: American Association of School Administrators.

Griffiths, D. E. (1966). *The school superintendent.* New York: Center for Applied Research.

Goodlad, J., & Anderson, R. (1963). *The nongraded elementary school.* New York: Harcourt, Brace, and World.

Halpin, A. W. (1957). A paradigm for research on administrator behavior. In R. F. Campbell & R. Gregg (Eds.), *Administrative behavior in education.* New York: Harper.

Henderson, H. (1977). A new economics. In D. Vermilye (Ed.), *Relating work and education* (pp. 227-235). San Francisco: Jossey-Bass.

Hodgkinson, H. (1985) *All one system: Demographics of education, kindergarten through graduate school.* Washington, DC: Institute for Educational Leadership.

Hodgkinson, H. (1991) Reform versus reality. *Phi Delta Kappan, 73(1),* 8-16.

Hoy, W., & Miskel, C. (2001). *Educational administration: Theory, research and practice* (6th ed.). New York: McGraw-Hill.

Hoyle, J., Björk, L., Collier, V., & Glass, T. (2004). *The superintendent as CEO: Standards-based performance.* Thousand Oaks, CA: Corwin Press.

Hodgkinson, H., & Montenegro, X. (1999). *The U.S. school superintendent: The invisible CEO.* Washington, DC: Institute for Educational Leadership.

Iannaccone, L. (1991). Micropolitics of education: What and why. *Education and Urban Society, 23,* 465-471.

Iannacone, L. & Lutz, F. W. (1995). The crucible of democracy: The local arena. In J. D. Scribner & D. H. Layton (Eds.), *The study of educational politics, the 1994 commemorative yearbook of the Politics of Education Association (1969-1994)* (pp. 39-52). Philadelphia: Falmer Press.

Johnson, S. M. (1996). *Leading to change: The challenge of the new superintendency.* San Francisco: Jossey-Bass.

Kingdon, J. (1995). *Agendas, alternatives, and public policies* (2nd ed.). New York: HarperCollins.

Knezevich, S. (1984). *Administration of public education: A sourcebook for the leadership and management of educational institutions* (4th ed.). New York: Harper & Row.

Kowalski, T. (1999). *The school superintenden: Theory practice, and cases.* Upper Saddle River, NJ: Merrill-Prentice Hall.

Kowalski, T. J. (2001). The future of local school governance: Implications for board members and superintendents. In C. C. Brunner & L. G. Björk (Eds.), *The new superintendency: Advances in research and theories in school management and educational policy* (Vol. 6, pp. 183-204). Oxford, England: JAI.

Kowalski, T., & Reitzug, R. (1993). *Contemporary school administration: An introduction.* New York: Longman.

Lunenburg, F., & Ornstein, A. (1991). *Educational administration: Concepts and practices.* Belmont, CA: Wadsworth.

McCarty, D. J., & Ramsey, C. E. (1971). *The school managers: Power and conflict in American public education.* Westport, CT: Greenwood.

Meyer, J. (Ed.). (1978). *Environments and organizations.* San Francisco: Jossey-Bass.

Meyer, J. W., & Rowan, B. (1978). The structure of educational organizations. In M. W. Meyer (Ed.), *Environments and organizations* (pp. 78-109). San Francisco: Jossey-Bass.

Murphy, J. (Ed.). (1990). The reform of school administration: Pressures and calls for change. In *The reform of American public education in the 1980's: Perspectives and cases.* Berkeley, CA: McCuthan.

Murphy, J. (1995). Changing role of the teacher. In M. O'Hair & S. Odell (Eds.), *Educating teachers for leadership and change* (pp. 311-323). Thousand Oaks, CA: Corwin Press.

Murphy, J., & Louis, K. S. (Eds.). (1999). *Handbook of research on educational administration: A project of the American Educational Research Association.* San Francisco: Jossey-Bass.

Norton, S., Webb, L., Dlugosh, L., & Sybouts, W. (1996). *The school superintendency: New responsibilities, new leadership.* Needham Heights, MA: Allyn & Bacon.

Parsons, T. (1956). Suggestions for a sociological approach to the theory of organizations. *Administrative Science Quarterly, 1,* 63-85.

Parson, T. (1967). *Sociological theory and modern society.* New York: Free Press.

Pfeffer, J. (1978). The micropolitics of organizations. In M. W. Meyer (Ed.), *Environments and organizations* (pp. 29-50). San Francisco: Jossey-Bass.

Ramirez, A. (1992). *Size, cost, and quantity of schools and school districts: A question of context.* (ERIC Document Reproduction Service No. ED 361162).

Reich, R. (1983). *The next American frontier.* New York: Times Books.

Reyes, E., Wagstaff, L., & Fusarelli, L. (1999). Delta forces: The changing fabric of American society and education. In J. Murphy & K. Seashore Louis (Eds.), *Handbook of research on educational administyratioon* (2nd ed., pp. 183-201). San Francisco: Jossey-Bass.

Rowan, B., & Miskel, C. (1999). Institutional theory and the study of educational organizations. In J. Murphy & K. Louis (Eds.), *Handbook of research on educational administration* (2nd ed., pp. 359-383). San Francisco: Jossey Bass.

Sergiovanni, T., Burlingame, M., Coombs, F., & Thurston, P. (1987) *Educational governance and administration.* Englewood Cliffs, NJ: Prentice-Hall.

Senge, P. (1990). *The fifth dicipline.* New York: Doubleday.

Spring, J. (1986). *The American school 1642-1985.* New York: Longman.

Starratt, R. (1996). *Transfroming educational administration: Meaning, community, and excellence.* New York: McGraw-Hill.

Thompson, J. (1967). *Organizations in action.* New York: McGraw-Hill.

Tyack, D. (1974). *The one best system: A history of American public education.* Cambridge, MA: Harvard University Press.

Tyack, D. B., & Hansot, E. (1982). *Managers of virtue: Public school leadership in America.* New York: Basic Books.

United States v. Butler, 297 U.S. 1, 56S. Ct. 312 (1936).

Wirt, F., & Kirst, M. (2001). *The political dynamics of American Education.* Berkeley, CA: McCutchan.

Wirt, F., & Wirst, M. (1982). *Schools in conflict* (3rd ed.). Berkely, CA: McCutchan.

Wong, K. (1992). The politics of urban education as a field of study: An interpretive analysis. In J. Cibulka, R. Reed, & K. Wong (Eds.), *The politics of urban education in the United States* (pp. 3-26). London: Falmer.

CHAPTER 2

THE BOARD PRESIDENT AND SUPERINTENDENT

An Examination of Influence Through the Eyes of the Decision Makers

George J. Petersen and Barbara Morrow Williams

A significant body of literature has pointed to the relationships among the district superintendent and the board of education and the influences of those relationships on the quality of the educational programs and academic success of children. A major contributor in facilitating and modulating the relationship of the superintendent and board of education is the board chair or president. Using components found in social capital theory, this study examined the perceptions of school board presidents and superintendents regarding the influence of their relationship on district leadership and the decision-making responsibilities of boards of education.

The findings suggest that attributions of superintendent leadership were enhanced through the networks and connections that they facilitated with the board president through the transmission of human, cultural and economic capital. Finally, constituents and stakeholders construct *influen-*

The Politics of Leadership: Superintendents and School Boards in Changing Times, 23–49
Copyright © 2005 by Information Age Publishing

tial others as leaders on the basis of valued forms of human, cultural, social and economic capital. The caveat here, however, is that the superintendent must have the ability to gain prior knowledge of what capital is valued by others, that is, his or her constituents in order to have influence and to be perceived as a leader.

THE CURRENT POLITICAL MÊLÉE

Historically in the United States, much of the authority over educational policy has been delegated to local school districts by state government. However, reform and restructuring efforts as well as a weakening domestic economy have placed enormous political and financial pressure on schools to do more with less, yet continue to demonstrate effective leadership at the district level (Usdan, McCloud, Podmostko, & Cuban, 2001). Research literature focused on district leadership has repeatedly stated that the relationship between the superintendent and board of education has a significant impact on the quality of a district's educational program (Allison, Allison, & McHenry, 1995; Fusarelli & Petersen, 2002; Hoyle, English, & Steffy, 1998; Kowalski, 1999; McCurdy, 1992; Petersen & Short, 2001). In fact, Blumberg and Blumberg (1985) suggest that the most critical association in running a school system is the interplay between the superintendent and board of education. A major player in facilitating and modulating the relationship of the superintendent and board of education is the board chair or president (Allison et al., 1995; Lunenburg & Ornstein, 1996). Although important, very few empirical investigations have examined the relationship in any depth (Allison et al., 1995; Campbell & Greene, 1994; Lunenburg & Ornstein, 1996; Petersen & Short, 2001, 2002). Because of this gap in the literature, we have undertaken an examination of the relationship of the district superintendent and board president and the influence of their relationship on school board decision-making.

Superintendent-School Board Relations

Boards of education and superintendents often find themselves targets of criticism in both the professional literature and popular press. Recent reforms and heightened expectations of accountability have created a permanent state of turbulence and pressure (Kowalski, 2003; Usdan et al., 2001). Studies that have previously concentrated on issues of school governance and reform have emphasized the importance of the school board in the educational process of the district (Bullard & Taylor, 1993; Danzberger, Kirst & Usdan, 1992; Wirt & Kirst, 1989). Although school boards have decision-making power, they are usually unpaid, part-time, and untrained and, except for the information presented to them by the superintendent or perhaps what they pick up informally, they know little of the underlying issues for the scores of complex decisions requiring their approval at each board meeting (Cuban, 1976). Because of this, school boards will rely on the professional judgment of the superintendent, especially in the area of technical-core educational issues (Kowalski, 2003; Petersen, 2002).

To the casual observer, the role that the superintendent and board of education play in the leadership and governance of the district appear well-defined, yet a myriad of investigations examining the subtleties and dynamics of this relationship and the impact it has on the leadership of the school organization indicate otherwise (Campbell & Greene, 1994; Carpenter, 1987; Crowson, 1987; Glass, 1992; Kowalski, 1999; McCurdy, 1992; Norton, Webb, Dlugosh, & Sybouts, 1996; Tallerico, 1989). As district leaders attempt to manage ever more complex changes and pressures, extant literature has continually pointed to the fact that their success centers on the relationship they have established with their board president (Allison et al., 1995; Campbell & Greene, 1994; Lunenburg & Ornstein, 1996; Petersen & Short, 2001, 2002) as well as the board of education (Berg, 1996; Carter & Cunningham, 1997; Danzberger, 1993; Feuerstein & Opfer, 1998; Hoyle et al., 1998; Kowalski, 1999; McCurdy, 1992; Norton et al., 1996; Tallerico, 1989). Numerous scholars have asserted that a poor relationship between the superintendent and the board of education poses a threat to the district's ability to meet its goals. For example, a precarious relationship deters school improvement (Danzberger, 1992); affects the quality of educational programs (Boyd, 1976; Nygren, 1992); increases conflict over district instructional goals and objectives (Morgan & Petersen, 2002; Petersen, 1999, 2002); impairs superintendent-board communication around technical-core issues (Kowalski, 2003; Petersen & Short, 2002); weakens district stability and morale (Renchler, 1992); negatively influences the superintendent's credibility and trustworthiness with board members (Petersen & Short, 2001); impedes critical reform efforts, such as district restructuring (Konnert & Augenstein, 1995) and collaborative visioning and long-range planning (Kowalski, 1999); and it eventually results in an increase in the "revolving door syndrome" of district superintendents (Carter & Cunningham, 1997; Renchler, 1992).

Clearly the dynamic of the relationship among the board president, superintendent, and the larger board is pivotal in addressing reform and restructuring efforts. Further, a key component in the superintendent's success is intricately tied to his or her ability to influence critical policy decisions made by the board of education (Blumberg, 1985; Crowson, 1987; Zeigler, Jennings, & Peak, 1974). Although some recent research points to the fact that superintendents have considerably more control and influence in the establishment of the board agenda than previously thought (Petersen & Short, 2001), formal authority for policy articulation and decision-making still resides with the board of education. As a result, superintendents must, in most instances, attempt to influence votes of each individual board member (Blumberg, 1985).

Superintendent Influence

As superintendents find themselves at the center of a complex web of interpersonal relationships, their ability to define and receive support for often complex policy issues will result in other's perceptions of their expertise, truthfulness and referent power. Scholars on the one hand have emphasized the importance of the superintendents' expertise and the ability to communicate with their board presidents (Campbell & Greene, 1994; Council, 1994; Feistritzer, 1992; Lunenburg & Ornstein, 1996; Petersen & Short, 2001, 2002) and boards of education (Glass, Björk, & Brunner, 2000; Hoyle et al., 1998) in leading the school district. On the other hand, scholars also note that it is difficult to establish precisely the impact on decision-making within school districts (Zeigler et al., 1974). Research investigating superintendents has attributed a variety of factors for the success or failure of the superintendent and board relationship. Many conclude that interpersonal skills such as communication, empathy, trust, persuasiveness, and clarity of role are essential in the development and maintenance of a cooperative relationship between the superintendent and board of education (Berg, 1996; Bratlein & Walters, 1999; Carter & Cunningham, 1997; Glass, 1992; Kowalski, 1999; McCurdy, 1992; Tallerico, 1989).

THEORETICAL FRAMEWORK

Public school superintendents, board presidents, and school boards operate in a socio-cultural context that in many instances defines the issues and establishes priorities on the decisions and actions that must be taken (Pitner & Ogawa, 1981). Although both the board president and superintendent retain formal authority and, as a result, are a source of influence in the leadership of the district (Deem, Brehone, & Heath, 1995; Feuerstein & Opfer, 1998; Goldhammer, 1964; Holdaway & Genge, 1995; Lunenburg & Ornstein, 1996; Tallerico, 1989), in the contemporary area of school reform, influence of the superintendent is critical in moving the district through the gauntlet of initiatives (Hoyle et al., 1998; Kowalski , 2003).

In an exploratory investigation of the board president-superintendent relationship, Petersen and Short (2001) used social influence theory and social style as frameworks to assess the superintendent's ability to sustain the relationship with the board president and to operate the district within the social context of the board of education and decision making responsibilities. This study revealed that the ability of one person to influence another is contingent upon the one who would seek to influence (that is, the communicator) possessing social attractiveness and credibility. Social attractiveness is based upon the perceived similarities of experiences, background, and the desire of the one who would be influenced to emulate or to identify with the influential person (Cooper & Croyle, 1984; Goodyear & Robyak, 1981; Martin, 1978; Strong, 1968). Credibility, the second contingent of social influence, itself has two components, trustworthiness and expertness (Martin, 1978; Strong, 1968; Strong & Schmidt, 1970), both based upon the perceptions of those who would be influenced by the communicator. Trustworthiness is the perceived motivation of a communicator to use his or her knowledge and skill for the good of the audience (Strong, 1968), while expertness is the perception that the communicator possesses specialized knowledge or skills to solve a problem (Martin, 1978; Strong, 1968; Strong & Schmidt, 1970)

Petersen and Short (2001), found a "strong association of the attributes found in social influence and social style with the superintendent's ability to define, recommend, and receive board support on a majority of policy issues facing the district" (p. 561). Social influence theory and social style suggest that credibility, social attractiveness, assertiveness, and emotiveness are effective compelling elements of influence.

As a recommendation for future research, they suggested that prospective investigations use other conceptual frameworks to examine this relationship as well as more interactive data gathering methods, rather than relying solely on behavior measures. For this follow-up investigation, we decided to use the conceptual framework of social capital. Social capital is related to issues of trust, reciprocity, exchange, and connectedness of networks and groups (Pretty & Ward, 2001). Previous work in this area has demonstrated these personal and organizational characteristics are germane when examining the school board president and superintendent relationship and issues of influence and decision-making.

For this study, we used the integrated social capital model of Spillane et al. (2003) in an attempt to further examine issues of influence of the superintendent-board president relationship on district level decision-making (Petersen & Short, 2001). Social capital is an appropriate lens for this investigation because it focuses on board presidents' and superintendents' perceptions of how their relationship develops reciprocal levels of trust and collaboration through the accumulation of the various types of capital (e.g., social, human, cultural and economic). Spillane et al.'s (2003) work in this area clearly indicates that if the capital enacted by others is valued, then followers attribute leadership to the actors. Their integrated model provides an appropriate lens for viewing the leadership of superintendents, and the forms of capital they enact that may or may not be valued by others in a given situation. It also prompted us to examine specific areas related to the development of capital:

1. The superintendent's ability to establish a collaborative relationship with the board president and members of the school board.

2. Demonstrated characteristics and actions of superintendent that foster confidence and trustworthiness with the president and school board.

3. Demonstrated characteristics and actions of superintendent that foster mistrust.

4. The importance of the superintendent and the board president relationship in the leadership of the district.

5. The influence of the superintendent at board meetings and on board decision-making.

We believe focusing participants' responses to these areas and analyzing their responses through the integrated model of social capital of Spillane et al. (2003) will permit a clearer perspective and understanding of the role of public school superintendents in enacting forms of capital and influence.

Social Capital

Social capital can be defined as established social networks of trust and relationships that are exercised between individuals in a group, communities, or organizations (Putnam, 1995; Spillane, Hallett, & Diamond, 2003). These social networks, composed of social norms, sanctions, trust, and collaboration, are arenas in which individuals work together to form shared resources for the community and its members. The fundamental elements of social capital are rooted in the social relations and basic social networks of individuals leading to social trust. "[S]ocial capital is productive, making possible the achievement of certain ends that in its absence would not be possible" (Coleman, 1988, p. 81). Unlike other forms of human capital, social capital inheres in the structure of relations between individuals and among individuals. Putnam (1995) refers to them as "a dense network of reciprocal social relations" (p.19). Petersen and Short (2001) found a relationship of social trust between superintendents and board presidents in the context of the board agenda, particularly how items were added to the agenda. In fact, the context of the board agenda strongly suggests a conceptual overlay between social trust and social capital; both rely upon an established relationship or network for successful culmination.

At this point, however, to begin the discussion, we will explore capital as an over arching term that encompasses cultural capital, human capital, economic capital, as well as social capital. In his examination of the idea of social space, Bourdieu (1991) identified the kinds of capital as powers that define the chances of profit in fields or subfields, each of which has its own types of capital (p. 230). He observed further that an individual's position in the social space was determined by the power distributed to him or to her in that field. These powers or forms of capitalare what Bourdieu termed 'symbolic' or prestige, reputation, fame, etc.—and are distributed to individuals in a multi-dimensional field according to the *volume* and the *composition* of the capital they possessed (p. 231).

Understanding the overarching term 'social capital' is particularly important because it is central to understanding the uses of the other forms of capital mentioned here in the context of schools and district leadership. Coleman (1990) expanded his conception of social capital to include economic constructs. He cited the economist, Granovetter (1985), and his writings on the new institutional economics in which the economist analyzed social and organizational relations. Coleman observed specifically Granovetter's (1985) exposition of the importance of networks of personal and social relations and their significance in "generating trust, establishing expectations, and in creating and enforcing norms," and how they were embedded in economic transactions (Coleman, p. 302). In constructing the idea of social capital, Coleman (1990) articulated the concept that relationships between individuals or among groups of individuals could have value or worth in situations that did not involve money.

In their study of the construction of leadership among 84 teachers at eight Chicago elementary schools, Spillane et al. (2003) adopted the construct of social capital and used it to create a theoretical framework, "an integrated model" that focused how followers construct *others* as leaders on the basis of various forms of capital. Influenced by Bourdieu (1991, 1986, 1984, 1979), Coleman (1988), and others (Lamont & Lareau, 1988; DiMaggio 1982; Schultz 1961, as cited in Spillane et al., 2003), they described four constructs of capital: human capital, cultural capital, social capital and economic capital. The integrated model described by Spillane et al., (2003), was not dominated by the leader or pure construction by the followers; instead, the researchers believed that people enacted forms of capital as they went about tasks of leadership. If the capital enacted by others was valued, then followers attributed leadership to them (Spillane et al., 2003, p. 3).

Human Capital

Generally, capital is a resource that accumulates wealth or value and has worth to others (Agnes et al., 2001). Human capital is substantive, the accumulation of a person's knowledge, skills, and expertise, and is acquired through the development of skills and capabilities that enable people to perform in new ways (Becker,1964; Coleman, 1988; Schultz, 1961, as cited in Spillane et al., p.3). Human capital is evident in the *volume* of capital (Bourdieu 1991) inherent in the interaction between the superintendent and others, for example, the board president (Spillane et al., 2003).

Cultural Capital

Spillane et al. describe *cultural capital* as internalized dispositions acquired through the life course (p.7). Cultural capital plays out as acquired ways of being and doing, interactive styles that are of value to the participants in particular contexts (p. 3). These acquired ways of being and doing are institutionalized in durable social statuses that are socially recognized or legally guaranteed (Bourdieu, 1991, p. 231) to those who possess them, as in the example of superintendents and board presidents.

Economic Capital

Economic capital includes money and material resources (Spillane et al., 2003). We examined *economic* capital separately here in the context of the superintendency because it is one of the various roles that superintendents have been expected to fulfill over the years as *expert manager* (Brunner, Grogan & Björk, 2002). In what the authors refer to as the third discursive stage of the superintendency (out of seven), superintendents were expected to follow the business model of management and be effective, efficient managers of the budget in a strongly hierarchical management system. This concept has resurfaced in today's economic climate that includes state reduction of spending on education, children with higher needs, communities with fewer economic resources, and indeed, Petersen and Short's (2001) research suggested those attributes of the superintendent linger.

METHODS

Sample and Procedures

Creswell (1994) defined a qualitative study as "an inquiry process of understanding a social or human problem, based on building a complex, holistic picture, formed with words, reporting detailed views of informants, and conducted in a natural setting" (p. 24). The nature of the problem surrounding the influence and decision-making processes at the district level points to the need for a qualitative study in this area for two reasons: (a) the complexity of the problem, and (b) the need for deeper understanding of the issues surrounding the problem (Marshall & Rossman, 1989).

The data presented in this paper are the result of a follow-up investigation of a previous study focused on analyzing the relationship between the superintendent and the board president through the theoretical frameworks of social influence and social style theory (Petersen & Short, 2001).

Participants

Individuals selected for this study were chosen from school districts that had participated in the previous Petersen and Short (2001) study. Using purposeful sampling (Bogdan & Biklen, 1998; Strauss & Corbin, 1998) thirteen key informants were identified and contacted. Participants included seven school board presidents, three district superintendents, two executive directors at the state school board association, and one executive director at the state administrators' association. The executive directors were chosen for this investigation because of their work with boards of education and superintendents throughout the state and are in a unique position to provide a more cosmopolitan perspective of the board president-superintendent relationship and its influence on decision-making in school districts.

Each participant was interviewed using face-to-face, in-depth, semi-structured interviews regarding their perceptions of the influence of the district superintendent and the board president and whether or not this relationship had an affect on board decision-making. This investigation was grounded around three overarching research questions:

1. How influential is the district superintendent in the decision-making process of the board of education?
2. Are there characteristics that support the superintendent in leading the school district? What would those characteristics be?
3. What is the board president's perception of the influence the superintendent has in generating the board agenda?

These research questions were explored by asking participants to respond to inquiries about the school organization, roles and functions of both the superintendent and school board president, and how that relationship influenced decision-making at the board level. Follow-up questions probed for deeper meaning and clarification of the interviewee's experience (Lofland & Lofland, 1984).

Data Analysis

All interviews were conducted in person by the first author. Interviews were audio taped and transcribed. Data collection and analysis occurred simultaneously and continued throughout the study (Glaser & Strauss, 1967). Ongoing analysis influenced the focus and direction of succeeding interviews. To form some kind of reciprocity with study participants, transcribed interviews were returned to each individual for their clarification, review, and feedback (Marshall & Rossman, 1989; Peshkin, 1993; Seidman, 1991).

The process of open and axial coding (Strauss, 1987; Strauss & Corbin, 1998) guided the analytical procedures resulting in inductively derived explanatory themes. Coding processes included identifying concepts embedded within the data, organizing discrete concepts into categories, defining the properties and dimensions of categories, and linking them according to their properties and dimensions into broad, explanatory themes.

The interview data were first compiled by question, with each series of responses identified. The themes that emerged from each question were noted. Documentation was examined for triangulation of identified themes. Then, the themes were traced throughout the entire body of data. Finally, the data and themes were viewed against the backdrop of the research questions.

Credibility

Merriam (1988) suggested three ways to insure dependability in a study: (a) fully explain researcher's assumptions and theory behind the study (b) triangulate data collection, and (c) establish an audit trail. Credibility was insured in this study by having each of the authors individually analyze the interview transcripts for regularities, patterns, and topics and then code into categories for further analysis (Bogdan & Biklen, 1998; Taylor & Bogdan, 1998). Triangulation of findings was achieved by the use of data sources provided by participants as well as by independent data analysis by both authors (Bogdan & Biklen, 1998; Patton, 1990). Concluding individual analysis, the authors met and discussed individual findings and arrived at the themes presented here. Transcripts, themes, and findings were also returned to each participant for their clarification, review, and feedback (Marshall & Rossman, 1989; Peshkin, 1993; Seidman, 1991).

FINDINGS

When asked the question, *"what makes the superintendent successful in his/her relationship with you [board president] and the board of education?"*, respondents repeatedly characterized the superintendent as using "influence not intimidation" with the board and members of the community; and he or she "educates the board," is a "good communicator" and has "respected experience," and is "serious, dedicated, goal oriented," "makes the school look good" as opposed to worrying about how [he or she] looks in the community, and is "child-centered." Clearly, their responses point to the intersection of the characteristics defined first by the integrated model of Spillane et al. (2003), as well as the research of Petersen and Short (2001). One board president observed,

> I think the critical issues are that they have to have a political nature to them. In the Greek sense that they are able to respond to people and understand what is being said to them and be able to listen as well as discuss topics. You got to remember, of course, that seven board members are not professional educators, that isn't always the case, so we don't always bring something to the superintendent with the proper jargon. It is up for him to do the interpretation. You got to be an open person and we have been lucky. (Board president #3).

Another board president was very specific about what makes the superintendent successful with the board and the community:

> I think being child centered, having a strong emphasis on curriculum is important, and knowing the numbers is important. I think those are three things that lead to a successful superintendent. Then you've got to go with the personal skills with both staff (which is a large variety of individuals) and dealing with parents as the public as well. Then, of course, being successful with the community, I think being a good communicator and being consistently support [sic] the decisions and the positions of the district. And they've got to be a good money person there too, which is knowing the numbers. (Board president #4)

The importance of being up front and open with the board was an essential superintendent characteristic, noted by another board president when asked what makes a superintendent successful:

> Being open with the board, not trying to hide anything with them, making the board as informed as they possibly can be, not holding any information

back. The superintendent, I feel, has his opinion just as much as the board president, or anybody on the board, but he has to be that way to give you all of the information. Let you make the decision because if he doesn't, you found out he held something back from you, then you're going to resent him a lot more than if he made the wrong decision. I feel our school superintendent is very open with us. He doesn't hold a thing back; we told him, and our principals, too, "do not hold a thing back. You let us know everything, and we'll all make this decision together'. I think that's what makes the superintendent successful. I feel the board then can work with the superintendent, and have 100% trust with [sic] him. (Board president #2)

In all of the interviews, board presidents attached value to those characteristics demonstrated by the superintendent identified as human capital by Spillane et al. (2003) including skills, knowledge, and expertise in the conduct of the job of superintendent; as a result, they constructed the superintendents as leaders.

Similarly, the social style factors measured by Petersen and Short (2001) formed overlapping paradigms to human capital characteristics and were standards applied to the superintendent, as well as valued by the observing board presidents who articulated preferences for specific superintendent behaviors. Those behaviors characterized by assertiveness and demonstrations of control, influence, and task orientation, and emotiveness with sensitivity to the feelings of others, trust, sociability, composure, and social attraction were behaviors that were critical to the success of the superintendent in the *eyes of the board presidents*. The attribution of leadership to the superintendents turned upon their ability to persuade others to value the form of capital the superintendents had constructed or enacted in that situation. That is, the superintendents had to use their position of social influence, with its components of social attractiveness and credibility, to get others to value what he or she represented to the organization.

The superintendents and executive directors of the administrative organizations we interviewed concurred with these observations and seemed to appreciate the dynamics between the board and the superintendent as represented by the statement of this superintendent:

Communication. The better you inform your board, the better you keep them informed, the better you listen to them and their concerns, the better you will be. Now, you can't be all things to all people, and you can't be all things to the board, but if you are listening to them and you understand their concerns and they are listening to you, then you are communicating what is taking place and I feel you can be successful. You may not always like to hear what you are hearing but we are not going to kill the messengers; we are going to understand what we are hearing. (Superintendent #3)

All of the superintendents in this investigation articulated the notion that the district leaders are individuals who are able to incorporate actions and characteristics that build and sustain openness and trust with their constituents. Likewise, they understood what permitted them to be influential and what made them socially attractive; in particular, their emotiveness, the ability to listen empathetically, demonstrate interpersonal solidarity and trust, was a key attribute that supported their tenure as superintendents.

Board presidents also singled out credibility and trustworthiness as required characteristics of superintendents, and again, there was substantial overlap of those characteristics of human capital found in the superintendent that attributed leadership to them. For example, board presidents frequently described desirable characteristics of superintendents as including "open," "trustworthy," "mature," "very fair," with information for the board and with people when asked the question, "*what would the superintendent have to do to be considered not trustworthy or not credible with the board of education?*"

> I haven't had a long experience with superintendents but if their word wasn't good that would be number one. You are who you say you are and if your word isn't any good or if you are talking about one or the other outside, I'm always of the idea with the seven guys we got, men or women, we are always trying to work together even though we have different parts, and if he made the mistake of picking up one group against the other, I wouldn't think much of that. He's got to be clever enough, smart enough not to do that. (Board president #1)

Several board presidents echoed those sentiments regarding the error of withholding information, and while the withholding of information might have been a sin of omission in the *eyes of these board presidents*, the sin of *commission* was equally repugnant to participants. Another board president was more succinct when asked how superintendent breached trustworthiness and credibility: "Someone that is more concerned about keeping their job than doing the right thing." When asked how would he know if that were true, the president admitted that it might be difficult, especially if the superintendent was skilled at making others believe [he] was doing the job. That president also had experienced real life situations with a previous superintendent: "He wanted to do things that made him look good rather than what was good for the school, and over the last 6 or 8 years, we have seen a lot of the results of those decisions." In this board president's perception, the superintendent's focus on his own image and his own needs was carried out through decisions that had long range consequences for the district and demonstrated a lack of trustworthiness, an essential component of credibility. As a result, that superintendent's social influence was greatly diminished in *the board president's eyes*. Further, the superintendent's human capital, his store of knowledge, skills and expertise, was greatly diminished in the content of his interaction (Spillane et al., 2003) with the board president. In this case, the superintendent's perceived self-serving behavior demonstrated a lack of interest in using his knowledge and skill for the benefit of the district in that situation, and as a result, the board president did not attribute leadership to the superintendent.

The observations and perceptions of these board presidents are bolstered by earlier research examining organizational leadership. Pitner and Ogawa (1981) followed 20 superintendents from diverse school districts across Ohio to examine the leadership roles enacted by superintendents. They observed that superintendents sat at the intersection of the organization's information network, and thus, in the role of mediator, superintendents had the opportunity to influence the process in which shared meanings for the institution are constructed. In that role of constructing shared meanings for the organization, the superintendents could construct or enact a form of human capital that was based upon ability to gather knowledge, skills, and expertise that was, in turn, a result of their vantage point occupied at the intersection of the organization's network.

Thus, the combined components of social attractiveness and credibility create the environment for the development of the superintendent's human capital in the social context of the school district. When followers value the human capital of leaders, human capital becomes a basis for the construction of leadership (Spillane et al., 2003). Pitner and Ogawa (1981) found superintendents in their study, like those in Petersen and Short's (2001) investigation, must be able to clearly communicate and transmit information in a persuasive manner to maintain their credibility. Similarly, Petersen and Short (2001) found their board presidents emphasized the need for superintendents to be persuasive and strong communicators. In order to maintain their social influence through their human capital (e.g., knowledge, expertise, and skills), however, superintendents must understand what their audience values and clearly and consistently communicate that understanding to their audience; otherwise, the human capital has no value in that situation.

In the context of the integrated model, we suggest that social influence and human capital form two halves of a continuous cycle in the leadership of the district (see Figure 2.1).

If superintendents develop stocks of human capital and use them to mediate communication within their organization, and do a good job of it (so that it is valued by others) followers will attribute leadership to them and that leadership will translate to social influence, including social attractiveness, and credibility. Social influence then contributes to the opportunity to develop more stocks of human capital.

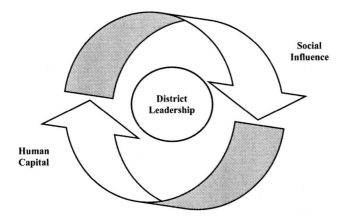

Figure 2.1.   The continuous cycle of social influence and
human capital in district leadership.

Cultural Capital

Petersen and Short (2001) describe social style as perceptions of behavioral patterns observed by others. The crucial overlapping element of cultural capital and social style is *style,* or what Swidler (1986) called a *cultural
tool kit,* a range of behaviors that dictate how people interact with each
other, or habitual ways of being and doing that are acquired throughout
life and used in social interaction (Spillane et al., 2003). Superintendents
in small districts may be particularly visible and vulnerable to adverse
perceptions of the impact of their style. One board president was candid
in her observations about what she saw happening in her district as a consequence of the superintendent's style.

> Well, I think that morale is one of the best keys for how things are going in
> the district. And morale was dropping. We were hearing a lot of complaints
> that when you stopped to listen to them were pretty petty complaints, but
> then you ask, "Why are you raising these?", and it just kept pointing back to
> the administration. Not communicating well, not communicating accu-
> rately, changing minds [sic] perhaps. It appeared among all of our staff that
> they were losing confidence in the leadership that we had. (Board President
> #6)

The superintendent's style prompted not only a loss of confidence but
when his reputation spread throughout the small community, the board
president perceived that the bond issue failed as well: "And at the same
time in the community that reports were coming back that, 'oh, this was

seen as the superintendent's project, it isn't the school's project'. There had been an eroding of credibility."

Petersen and Short (2001) distinguished social style as a form of communication behaviors, with perceived levels of assertiveness and emotiveness. Assertiveness was defined as the observable and measurable effort to control others, and emotiveness was described as the degree to which a person is perceived as expressing feelings when relating to others. Their research found that highly assertive superintendents were perceived to be more attractive, that is they were perceived as confident, ambitious, powerful, competent, and versatile. Highly emotive individuals received more positive evaluations and were more likely to be perceived as trustworthy, versatile, and socially attractive with interpersonal solidarity.

Likewise cultural capital manifests itself in the stylistic form of the interaction between the leader and the followers but only to the extent that followers value that style (Spillane et al., 2003, p. 3). When asked what carried more weight the superintendent's level of expertise or their knowledge about a particular issue, a board president observed,

> Both, I think. I think you still have to have that personality. I think you still have to sell yourself to the board and the community. The personality can make things a lot easier on the board. If your superintendent is out in the community, and being friendly, and being cheerful, and being helpful to people when they ask you questions, and being open with the community, just as open as he is with the board. I feel it makes the board a lot easier job. (Board President #2)

Another board president gave an example of the importance cultural capital has in public relations. Their previous superintendent carried a substantial public relations burden that that had been enacted through his personal style. In this case, the district was undergoing a bond election. This superintendent was perceived as lacking the cultural capital or social style valued by the members of the community, which eventually became a liability in the school district's attempt to pass a much needed bond initiative. It wasn't until after a new superintendent was hired that the bond election was successful.

Again, the earlier work of Pitner and Ogawa (1981) illuminates why cultural capital and social style are so important to the success of a leader. They found that superintendents were constrained by social and organizational structures but possessed organizational influence, again because of their position as mediator. The researchers noted that in one of their studies, the superintendents reported spending over 80 percent of their time directly interacting with people. The superintendents were central figures in articulating their community stakeholders' preferences for the schools and ensuring that there was no conflict of values between the methods of operation of the schools, school programs and curricula, and the community; they needed to facilitate the communication of information among board members, subordinates, and community members. Such intense human interaction places substantial weight on the superintendent to demonstrate a style that is valued by others and can become a basis for attributing leadership. In order to accomplish this, the successful superintendent must be able to juggle the contents of a cultural tool kit, that is, the symbolic vehicles of meaning such as beliefs, ritual practices, art forms, and ceremonies, as well as informal cultural practices such as language, gossip, stories, and rituals of daily life (Swidler, 1986). Spillane et al. (2003) noted the teachers in their study paid particular attention to the administrators' ways of being and doing in their social interaction with others, ascribed value to them, and attributed leadership to the administrators who had a supportive style. The research of Petersen and Short (2001), Pitner and Ogawa (1981), and Spillane et al. (2003) suggests that for superintendents to gain value for the cultural capital they possess, they must display a style and be socially attractive in ways that are valued by others in the situation.

As a leader, trustworthiness, versatility, confidence, power, and competency, for example, are all characteristics likely to be admired by followers, and followers are likely to attribute leadership to those demonstrating such traits. We suggest that cultural capital, social style, and social attractiveness are on the same continuum with social influence, by now a by-product of human capital, serving as an additional element on the continuum. Based upon Spillane et al. (2003) and their findings, without a style that is valued by constituents, a superintendent cannot gain the stocks of cultural capital needed to gain the trust and confidence of constituents because he or she is not socially attractive to constituents.

Board Agenda

The concept that emerged repeatedly as a theme in multiple ways was embodied in the word *agenda*. How the agenda was assembled and presented and who had input on the agenda topics reflected how the board presidents viewed a number of social relations affecting the dynamic of the superintendent and the board, as well as the dynamic of the superintendent and the community. Certainly, the superintendent's influence for decision-making for the district was often reflected in how the agenda was put together. Petersen and Short (2001) found the interpersonal skills such as communication, honesty, and sharing information as greatly facilitating the superintendent's ability to influence agenda construction.

When asked, "do you work with the superintendent in setting the agenda?" the board president stated

> He [the superintendent] is basically the one who is going to set the agenda except for where we bring things that we want to add. Most of the agenda is his. But as I said, he is in tune to board members saying in response to a citizen comment or whatever, we'd like to see more information about this. (Board President # 13)

Another board president noted, "the superintendent is the one who indeed drafts many of these recommendations [for agenda items for board decision], but it is certainly with the direct input from the board coming at board meetings" (Board President #12).

But a related question that asked where the *nitty gritty* discussions and decision-making regarding the board agenda occurred, one board president's view of social trust as an important aspect in agenda setting:

> if for example the superintendent brings a business and management item to the board, then I think those decisions are being made in the central office and they are being brought to the board for ratification and board says fine, or whatever. The board is saying, "if you want our support, fine, bring them to us and we'll approve them." (Board President #10)

The agenda in some ways represented the social networks in the community. Social relations are based in social networks composed of community norms, sanctions, trust, and collaboration that work together to form resources for the community. Members of the community have reciprocal obligations where favors are exchanged among members in an atmosphere of social trust. When communities are built on social trust, everyone knows what resources are available, where to find them and, perhaps more importantly, who has been consuming the resources; thus, it is possible to keep track of resources and reciprocity. Dense social networks encourage honesty; reputations are at stake and they are usually worth more than momentary treachery (Putnam, 1995).

Economic Capital

Economic capital refers to money, material resources, and attributing legitimacy to those who control those resources (Spillane et al., 2003). This concept continues to be a central focus because of today's economic climate that includes reduction of spending on education, coupled with a growing population of communities with limited economic resources. Indeed, previous research (Glass et al., 2000; Kowalski, 2003; Petersen &

Short, 2001) suggested those attributes of the superintendent linger. Several of the board presidents in this study emphasized the need for superintendents to be good fiscal managers, and phrases like "knowing the numbers" were typical of comments describing expectations of superintendents.

> When we sit down for a finance meeting with the superintendent, if he's no good on budget, then we're lost because obviously I work, everybody on the board works different jobs, and we can't be up there messing with the budget. He's got to have an expertise in finance. (Board President #2)

Even though the board voted on the budget, the superintendent was expected to provide the *expert* background intelligence on the budget to the board for that vote, as well as then manage the budget that resulted from that vote.

Spillane et al. (2003) note in their research, however, that the way the administration spreads it economic capital may also influence how others construct leadership. Leaders in that study were often perceived as those who controlled resources that facilitated human capital. In the same way, superintendents who use their human, cultural, and social capital to manage resources in a way that encourages others to attribute leadership to them can be successful in spite of reduced economic resources. Forms of human, cultural, and social capital are crucial companions of economic capital, especially in financially strapped environments. The superintendents' abilities to marshal the social influence inherent in both human capital and cultural capital can help them lead others through financial crises.

SUMMARY

The development and facilitation of social capital lowers the cost of collaborating, while facilitating cooperation among organizational members. The dense networks provide people with the confidence to invest in collective activities, knowing that others will participate as well. Individuals are less likely to engage in unregulated individual actions that may negatively impact the organization; Pretty and Ward (2001) have identified four central aspects related to this: (a) relations of trust; (b) reciprocity and exchange; (c) common rules, norms, and sanctions; (d) connectedness among networks and groups.

Superintendents again are in a transformational setting with the pressures of drastically reduced state budget allocations, changing demographics, a shifting local tax base, the accountability pressures of the No

Child Left Behind Act of 2001, as well as impact of the economic down turn on the children and families in the communities in their districts. Children and their communities are coming to schools with issues and challenges that the schools are expected to remedy, or at least develop strategies to deal with them. All of these pressures require a level of human skills that is almost *in*human, but the superintendents' understanding of the role played by social influence, social style, and forms of capital and their ability to incorporate those strategies into their *cultural tool kits* will determine which leaders skillfully steer the district to prosperity and which fail, and who are successful, and who find other employment.

Social capital enacts attributions of leadership first by providing the networks and connections that can actually facilitate the transmission of human capital (Spillane et al., 2003, p. 8). For example, one board president facilitated the superintendent's human capital in his district.

> We want a superintendent we can support publicly. That we can support him by taking him around which we have done and introducing him to different groups and pockets of people and then he can meet people in supporting him before he needs to meet the people. When it is a crisis and they are at your door with the hot tar and it is too late then. You want to know them on a personal basis before then. (Board President #3)

Board presidents in this investigation understood the importance of developing stocks of social capital, as well as the importance of the superintendents' need in developing their own stocks of social capital perhaps even independent of that of the board. Not only does access to social capital benefit superintendents in the context of the district as someone the board can publicly support, but it also benefits them individually for survival as a professional.

In the study by Spillane et al. (2003), the school principals were able to draw upon the social networks or connections from their previous schools to benefit the classroom practices of the teachers at their current school. Similarly, the superintendents in this study were able to draw upon the social networks that they have developed at least partly as a function of the relationships they have established with help from, but independent of, the board and the board president. As a result, those networks would facilitate the transmission of human capital, that is, skills, knowledge, and expertise, to benefit the district as well as the superintendents.

Second, social capital constructs leadership by creating the group norms that foster trust. Spillane et al. (2003) observed that social capital is relational in nature, and relationship trust is a form of social capital embedded in interpersonal relationships. Putnam (1995) identifies *thick trust* and *thinner trust*: thick trust is "embedded in personal relations that are strong, frequent, and nested in wider networks" (p. 136). Thin trust is more generalized but is still embedded in some background of shared social networks and expectations of reciprocity. Thinner trust is more useful because it extends the radius of trust beyond the roster of people whom we can know personally (Putnam, 1995). The board president was succinct in his assessment of the level of trust with the superintendent: "we believe that he knows what he is talking about and we trust him. That if he tells us that, it will be true." Superintendent #3 concurred with the assessment of the board president: "I think the relationship there is the trust. If he trusts you, he is going to back out and let you run the district. He is going to trust that you had that leadership when the entire board hired you." In both instances, the radius of trust between the superintendent and the board president extended beyond the two of them and out to the board, and presumably to the community at large.

The superintendents in Pitner and Ogawa's (1981) study were able to generate social capital that gained the trust of their constituents by communicating with the various elements in their district to determine the opinions and preferences of their constituents. In this way, the superintendents contributed to the development and maintenance of group norms. The constituents of the superintendents, in turn, benefited from the social trust placed in the superintendents in the development of the group norms that acknowledged and secured their opinions and preferences. In Petersen and Short (2001), the board meetings provided an opportunity for the community and the board to exchange stocks of social capital. When asked if the board meetings were a symbolic gesture, one of the superintendents [#3] said, "No ... the board doesn't always agree with every decision I make but this is an opportunity to share with them what is good and bad that is going on; it is not just a symbolic gesture." A board president concurred:

> Well, on a number of issues on different occasions, you'll spend a lot of time discussing what, how, what gets you to that point, where should we go from here, what options do we have, what direction you should go with. I can see some superintendents could be very manipulative and directive and they take you only in the direction you want to go, but the person that I want working for me is somebody that shows us all the options and lets us decide which direction we should go. I want to know what their opinion is because they are the ones that have to implement it. They still need our input to determine what the community wants. (Board President #4)

The superintendent here, like those in the earlier studies by Pitner and Ogawa (1981), was entrusted with the management of group norms, and in this instance, communicating important information to the board so that they could make decisions, and then implement those decisions.

Cultural capital and its dominant element of style can be a major component of social capital (Spillane et al., 2003), as may be social attractiveness (Petersen & Short, 2001). Each construct focuses on style and perceived similarities of experiences and background that contribute to the ability of diverse constituents and leaders to form relationships of trust and networks that form valuable social capital. The board president queried about the superintendent's credibility talked about that superintendent's social location in the community, commenting, "we are good friends outside of there. Maybe that makes it harder for me to answer that question. It is just that I know him. I know the kind of person that he is. We go to church together. He teaches Sunday school. I just know that he is a good, decent person." When the social power of the community is invested in superintendents, or as long as the social power of the community is entrusted to, and invested in superintendents, leadership is attributed to them and they control the reciprocity, the favors, the norms, and sanctions of the school community in that situation.

While Spillane et al. (2003) have identified social capital as a distinct form of capital that includes networks, trust, collaboration, and a sense of obligation, the application of social capital as a lens to view the superintendency suggests that it can be a more inclusive, comprehensive construct. For superintendents to have social capital, have it valued by others, and have others attribute leadership power to them as a result, then superintendents must possess the other forms of capital as well. When they possess those forms of capital, human, cultural, and social, and they are integrated into their style, then they are more likely to have social influence, credibility, and are more likely to be perceived as trustworthy. Trustworthiness is a key characteristic identified by board presidents as crucial in their relationships with the superintendents and in the ability of the superintendents to govern their districts.

CONCLUSION

If superintendents are to prevail in the leadership of their districts, then they must demonstrate specific forms of capital that are valued by others, specifically the board president and other members of the school board. The superintendents must undergo a process of valuation (Spillane et al., 2003). They must understand how various forms of capital work together to facilitate the creation of other capital. For example, the cultural capital of the superintendents, their style of behavior or doing things, may assist in developing social capital, networks of trust and collaboration that facilitate the business of the district. Constituents and stakeholders construct influential others as leaders on the basis of valued forms of human, cultural, social and economic capital. The caveat here, however, is that superintendents must have the ability to gain prior knowledge of what capital is valued by the others, that is, their constituents or stake holders. In other words, superintendents must have some insight into what is respected by constituents and stakeholders in the numerous and varied leadership and decision-making situations they face as leaders as well as insight into their own styles.

REFERENCES

Agnes, M., et al. (Eds.). (2001). *Webster's new world collegiate dictionary* (4th ed.). Cleveland, OH: IDG Books Worldwide.

Allison, D. J., Allison, P. A., & McHenry, H. A. (1995). Chiefs and chairs: Working relationships between effective CEOs and board of education chairpersons. In K. Leithwood (Ed.), *Effective school district leadership: Transforming politics into education* (pp. 33-50). Albany: State University of New York Press.

Becker, G. S. (1962). Investment in human capital: A theoretical analysis. *Journal of Political Economy, 70,* 9-49.

Berg, J. H. (1996). Context and perception: Implications for leadership. *Journal of School Leadership, 6,* 75-98.

Blumberg, A. (1985). A superintendent must read the board's invisible job description. *American School Board Journal, 172*(9), 44-45.

Blumberg, A., & Blumberg, P. (1985). *The school superintendent living with conflict.* New York: Teachers College Press.

Bogdan, R. C., & Biklen, S. K. (1998). *Qualitative research for education: An introduction to theory and methods.* Boston: Allyn & Bacon.

Bourdieu, P. (1991). *Language and symbolic power* (G. Raymond & M. Adamson, Trans.). Cambridge, MA: Harvard University Press.

Boyd, W. L. (1976). The public, the professionals, and educational policy: Who governs? *Teachers College Record, 77*(4), 539-578.

Bratlein, M. J., & Walters, D. L. (1999). The superintendency: Preparing for multi-dimensional roles in complex and changing environments. In F. K. Kochan, B. L. Jackson, & D. L. Duke (Eds.), *A thousand voices for the firing line* (pp. 87-102). Columbia, MO: The University Council for Educational Administration.

Brunner, C. C., Grogan, M., & Björk, L. (2002). Shifts in the discourse defining the superintendency: Historical and current foundations of the position. In J. Murphy (Ed.), *The educational leadership challenge: Redefining leadership for the 21st century* (pp. 211-238). Chicago: National Society for the Study of Education.

Bullard, P., & Taylor, B. O. (1993). *Making school reform happen.* Needham Heights, MA: Simon and Schuster.

Campbell, D. W., & Greene, D. (1994). Defining the leadership role of school boards in the 21st century. *Phi Delta Kappan, 75*(5), 391-395.

Carpenter, D. C. (1987, February). *Minnesota superintendents' perceptions of their role and influence in school board agenda setting.* Paper presented at the Annual Meeting of the American Association of School Administrators, New Orleans, LA. (ERIC Document Reproduction Service No. ED342049)

Carter, G. R., & Cunningham, W. G. (1997). *The American superintendent: Leading in an age of pressure.* San Francisco: Jossey-Bass.

Coleman, J. (1990). *Foundations of social theory.* Cambridge, MA: Harvard University Press.

Coleman, J. (1988). Social capital and the creation of human capital. *American Journal of Sociology, 94,* 95-120.

Council, B. (1994). Steer a steady course. *The American School Board Journal, 181*(1), 25-27.

Cooper, J., & Croyle, R. T. (1984). Attitudes and attitude change. *Annual Review of Psychology, 35,* 395-426.

Creswell, J. W. (1994). *Research design: Qualitative and quantitative approaches.* Thousand Oaks, CA: Sage.

Crowson, R. (1987). The local school district superintendency: A puzzling administrative role. *Educational Administration Quarterly, 23*(3), 49-69.

Cuban, L. (1976). *Urban school chiefs under fire.* Chicago: University of Chicago Press.

Danzberger, J. P. (1993). Governing the nation's schools: The case for restructuring local school boards. *Phi Delta Kappan, 75*(5), 367-373.

Danzberger, J. P., Kirst, M. W., & Usdan, M. D. (1992). *Governing public schools: New times new requirements.* Washington, DC: The Institute for Educational Leadership.

Deem, R., Brehone, K., & Heath, S. (1995). *Active citizenship and the governing of schools.* Buckingham, UK: Open University Press.

Feistritzer, C. E. (1992). A profile of school board presidents. In P. F. First & H. J. Walberg (Eds.), *School boards: Changing local control* (pp. 125-147). Berkeley, CA: McCutchan.

Feuerstein, A., & Opfer, V. D. (1998, July). School board chairmen and school superintendents: An analysis of perceptions concerning special interest groups and educational governance. *Journal of School Leadership, 8,* 373-398.

Fusarelli, L., & Petersen, G. J. (2002). Changing times, changing relationships: An exploration of current trends influencing the relationship between superintendents and boards of education. In G. Perreault & F. C. Lunenburg (Eds.), *NCPEA 2002 yearbook: The changing world of school administration* (pp. 282-293). Lanham, MD: Scarecrow Press.

Glass, T. E. (1992). *The 1992 study of the American school superintendency: America's education leaders in a time of reform.* Arlington, VA: American Association of School Administrators.

Glass, T. E., Björk, L., & Brunner, C. C. (2000). *The 2000 study of the American school superintendency: A look at the superintendent of education in the new millennium.* Arlington, VA: American Association of School Administrators.

Glaser, B. G., & Strauss, A. L. (1967). *The discovery of grounded theory: Strategies for qualitative research*. New York: Aldine.

Granovetter, M. (1985). Economic action, social structure, and embeddedness. *American Journal of Sociology, 83*, 1420-1443.

Goldhammer, K. (1964). *The school board*. New York: The Center for Applied Research in Education.

Goodyear, R., & Robyak, J. (1981). Counseling as an interpersonal influence process. A perspective for counseling practice. *Personnel and Guidance Journal, 60*, 654-657.

Holdaway, E. A., & Genge, A. (1995). How effective superintendents understand their work. In K. Leithwood (Ed.), *Effective school district leadership: Transforming politics into education* (pp. 13-32). Albany: State University of New York Press.

Hoyle, J. R., English, F. W., & Steffy, B. E. (1998). *Skills for successful 21st century school leaders: Standards for peak performance*. Arlington, VA: American Association of School Administrators.

Konnert, W. M., & Augenstein, J. J. (1995). *The school superintendency: Leading education into the 21st century*. Lancaster, PA: Technomic.

Kowalski, T. J. (2003, April). *Superintendent as communicator: The fifth role conceptualization*. Paper presented at the annual convention of the American Educational Research Association, Chicago, IL.

Kowalski, T. J. (1999). *The school superintendent: Theory, practice and cases*. Upper Saddle River, NJ: Prentice-Hall.

Lofland, J., & Lofland, L. H. (1984). *Analyzing social settings* (2nd ed.). Belmont, CA: Wadsworth.

Lunenburg, F. C., & Ornstein, A. C. (1996). *Educational administration: Concepts and practices* (2nd ed.). Belmont, CA: Wadsworth.

Marshall, C., & Rossman, G. B. (1995). *Designing qualitative research* (2nd ed.). Thousand Oaks, CA: Sage.

Martin, R. P. (1978). Expert and referent power: A framework for understanding and maximizing consultation effectiveness. *Journal of School Psychology, 16*, 49-55.

McCurdy, J. M. (1992). *Building better board-administrator relations*. Arlington, VA: American Association of School Administrators.

Merriam, S. (1988). *Case study research in education: A qualitative approach*. San Francisco: Jossey-Bass.

Morgan, C., & Petersen, G. J. (2002). The superintendent's role in leading academically effective school districts. In B. S. Cooper & L. D. Fusarelli (Eds.), *The promise and perils of the modern superintendency* (pp. 175-196). Lanham, MD: Scarecrow Press.

No Child Left Behind Act of 2001, Pub. L. No. 107-110 (2002).

Norton, M. S., Webb, L. D., Dlugosh, L. L., & Sybouts, W. (1996). *The school superintendency: New responsibilities new leadership*. Boston: Allyn and Bacon.

Nygren, B. (1992). Two-party tune up. *American School Board Journal, 178*(7), 35.

Patton, M. Q. (1990). Qualitative evaluation and research methods (2nd ed.). Newbury Park, CA: Sage.

Peshkin, A. (1993). The goodness of qualitative research. *Educational Researcher,* 22(2), 23-29.

Petersen, G. J. (2002). Singing the same tune: Principal's and school board member's perceptions of the superintendent's role in curricular and instructional leadership. *Journal of Educational Administration 40(2),* 158-171.

Petersen, G. J. (1999). Demonstrated actions of instructional leaders: An examination of five California superintendents. *Educational Policy Analysis Archives,* 7(18). Retrieved June 24, 2004, from http://epaa.asu.edu/epaa/v7n18.html

Petersen, G. J., & Short, P. M. (2002). An examination of the school board president's perception of the district superintendent's interpersonal communication competence and board decision-making. *Journal of School Leadership,* 12(4), 411-436.

Petersen, G. J., & Short, P. M. (2001, October). The school board president's perception of the district superintendent: Applying the lens of social influence and social style. *Educational Administration Quarterly 37(4),* 533-570.

Pretty, J., & Ward, H. (2001). Social capital and the environment. *World Development, 29(2),* 209-227.

Pitner, N. J., & Ogawa, R. T. (1981). Organizational leadership: The case of the school superintendent. *Educational Administration Quarterly, 17(2),* 45-65.

Putnam, R. D. (1995). *Bowling alone: The collapse and revival of American community.* New York: Simon & Schuster.

Renchler, R. (1992, Winter). Urban superintendent turnover: The need for stability. *Urban Superintendents' Sounding Board, 1(1),* 2-13.

Seidman, I. E. (1991). *Interviewing as qualitative research.* New York: Teachers College Press.

Spillane, J. P., Hallett, T., & Diamond, J. B. (2003). Forms of capital and the construction of leadership: Instructional leadership in urban elementary schools. *Sociology of Education, 76,* 1-17.

Strauss, A. (1987). *Qualitative analysis for social scientists.* New York: Cambridge University Press.

Strauss, A., & Corbin, J. (1998). *Basics of qualitative research: Techniques and procedures for developing grounded theory* (2nd ed.). Thousand Oaks: Sage.

Strong, S. R. (1968). Counseling: An interpersonal influence process. *Journal of Counseling Psychology, 15(3),* 215-224.

Strong, S. R., & Schmidt, L. D. (1970). Expertness and influence in counseling. *Journal of Counseling Psychology, 17,* 81-87.

Swidler, A. (1986). Culture in action: Symbols and strategies. *American Sociological Review, 51,* 273-286.

Tallerico, M. (July, 1989). The dynamics of superintendent-school board relationships: A continuing challenge. *Urban Education, 24(2),* 215-232.

Taylor, S. J., & Bogdan, R. C. (1998). *Introduction to qualitative research methods: A guidebook and resource.* New York: John Wiley & Sons.

Usdan, M., McCloud, B., Podmostko, M., & Cuban, L. (2001). *Leadership for learning: Restructuring school district leadership.* Washington DC: Institute for Educational Leadership.

Wirt, F. M., & Kirst, M. W. (1989). *Schools in conflict.* Berkeley, CA: McCutchan.

Zeigler, L. H., Jennings, M. H., & Peak, G. W. (1974). *Governing American schools: Political interaction in local school districts.* North Scituate, MA: Duxbury Press.

CHAPTER 3

TOWARD A MORE COMPLEX UNDERSTANDING OF POWER TO BETTER GRASP THE CHALLENGES OF THE CONTEMPORARY SUPERINTENDENCY

Sheldon Watson and Margaret Grogan

This chapter suggests that the notion of power in educational research has been conceptually limited and laced with normative biases. In the case of the superintendent and school board relationship, this has resulted in a truncated understanding of the power relations that influence school district operations. In addition, a narrow view of power diminishes the capacity of leadership preparation programs to develop leaders who can navigate the contested terrain of district politics, particularly if the goal of such leaders is school reform. A reappraisal of the concept as it relates to educational research is necessary. Specifically, we suggest that a feminist poststructuralist (Brunner, 2002a; Grogan, 2000a) perspective on power offers a useful lens for examining the contemporary superintendency. This being said, our aim is not to supplant existing the-

The Politics of Leadership: Superintendents and School Boards in Changing Times, 51–72

oretical convention, but rather to argue for an expanded multi-paradig-matic perspective (Capper, 1993).

Examining the foundations of our contemporary conceptions of power is a daunting task. Power is a concept central to the human experience. The term is used widely in everyday discourse, yet rarely defined with much specificity. As with many fundamental concepts, we assume to know the meaning of the term—but do we? Here, we set out to briefly review some of the more influential conceptualizations of power. We view this as an indispensable first step to developing a more robust application of the concept of power to the superintendent and school board relationship. In the course of this inquiry, we have noted a number of valuable reviews of power (Clegg, 1989; Flyvbjerg, 1991, 2001; Haugaard, 1997; Hindess, 1996). We do not seek to duplicate the work of these authors. Our aim is to offer a synthesis of some of the significant work on this topic with a focus on that which might be of particular interest to educational researchers. We frame the review with a brief discussion of literature on the superintendency that leads us to believe that research using some of the more complex notions of power offered here might be useful in future studies of the superintendency. This seems particularly pertinent in the current climate of mandated educational reform and diminishing local control.

Power relations enveloping these educational leadership positions are under-researched. It is possible that school board chairs, community leaders, and superintendents understand power very differently. It is also likely that each school district's structures of decision-making and policy formulation provide a particular environment within which power is defined and exercised. To use power as a resource to effect reform, a superintendent must understand fully what is going on in his or her district. Moreover, superintendents who understand well the power dynamics in their communities have a better chance of remaining in the position long enough to accomplish their goals. Because the superintendency is a prominent, executive-level social position, it follows that there is great interest in the promise or threat of power.

Throughout history, our conceptions of power have been intimately tied to the idea of control. This tradition has impacted the structural conditions that frame the decision-making process in many organizational contexts. People have power *over* another when they have control over that person's behavior. There are two common ways to conceive of power. Power has been viewed as an object, an abstract tool, or a quality, something one can acquire and possess. Acquisition of power, and the ability to exercise it, corresponds to one's position in an organizational hierarchy. The higher the status, the more likely one has some degree of power over those below. The common theme of this view of power is a focus on the *capacity* to act in such a way as to influence others. A second conception of power has dominated the literature alongside the capacity model. Its emphasis is upon *legitimacy*, or a *right*, to act. The legitimacy model and capacity models encompass the dominant pre-Foucauldian strands of inquiry into power (Clegg, 1989; Hindess, 1996).

With the introduction of Foucault's (1970, 1973, 1977) work into the power discussion, new strands of conceptualization took prominence. These include: the praxis of power and knowledge—power/knowledge, emphasis on the role of subjectivity in interpretation, and the contextualization of truth. The anti-normative focus of Foucault's work offers alternatives that are often attractive to traditionally marginalized voices of inquiry. For instance, feminist scholars have not hesitated to assimilate poststructuralist ideas into their own paradigms. In doing so, they now offer additional ways to look at both power and leadership.

POWER AND THE SUPERINTENDENCY

Studies of the superintendency have illuminated both the personal power (and its absence) associated with the position, and the power relations between superintendent, policy actors, and community stakeholders. The latter includes but is not limited to: boards of education, county or city governing boards, interest groups, parents, teachers, and a variety of unions. Consensus seems to point to a loss of faith in the aggregate power of the superintendent, at least over time.

Brunner, Grogan, and Björk's (2002) historical analysis of the superintendency revealed a "powerful position embedded in politics" (p. 222). However, with the development of lay leadership in the community to include such avenues as school advisory boards, school improvement councils, and self-study committees for accreditation, some of the control of education that once resided in the superintendency has been eroded (Rallis, Shibles, & Swanson, 2002). Further, as more and more state and federal education mandates curtail local control, both superintendents and boards of education are witnessing a shift in their spheres of influence. Cronin and Usdan (2003) even argue that in urban settings, if not elsewhere, the move to more representative and diverse boards weakens their traditional power. Earlier trusteeship boards had more direct political and economic ties with the local elites. This is a troubling notion, for the superintendent has long been understood as playing a vital role in community power brokering, while drawing on extended influence through the board of education, (Cuban, 1976; Keedy & Björk, 2002; Lutz & Iannaccone, 1978; Petersen & Short, 2001).

Scholars of the superintendency have identified this power as facilitative power or *power-with* rather than *power-over* (Brunner, 2000a; Leithwood, 1995). Calling it the power to transform politics into education, Leithwood (1995) sees it as central to the success or failure of the contemporary superintendent. The superintendent must somehow "proactively transform the values, aspirations and interests of the increasingly diverse constituents served by today's schools into a set of sophisticated educational services that address those values, aspirations, and interests" (Leithwood, 1995, p. 5).

As researchers and practitioners study the superintendency today in order to understand what executive leadership skills, dispositions, and knowledge will best serve students and families, it becomes clear that a more highly developed comprehension of power is required. We read more today than ever before about the turbulent conditions of the superintendency, the increasing incidents of student violence, the high turnover of urban district superintendents, single-agenda board members, and dysfunctional boards. Some have described a crisis in the superintendency (Cooper et al., 2000; Rist, 1991). And while others have debunked the myth of a severe shortage of qualified applicants for the position (e.g., Special Issue of *Journal of School Leadership*, 2003, *The Superintendent Shortage: Myth or Reality*, edited by Björk & Keedy); there is still a growing sense of unease about the future effectiveness of the position. Björk and Keedy (2003) blame dysfunctional boards for the failure of many districts to retain superintendents. In the same issue, Kowalski (2003) argues that self-interested school board members and their associations, and superintendents and their associations may be framing the issue as a crisis to serve their own economic and political needs. Scholars studying women and minorities in the superintendency have long been suspicious of the claims of reduced numbers of quality applicants for executive educational leadership positions (Brunner, 2003; Grogan, 1999; Tallerico, 2000). The way the discourse on "quality applicants" has been formulated, largely from a white, male, traditional perspective, keeps alive the tension between the non-white, female aspirant and the white, male superintendent norm. Each of these dimensions of the superintendency is enmeshed in a power struggle between competing interests and interpretations.

Perhaps the most scrutinized role of the early twenty-first century superintendent is the relationship between the superintendent and student academic achievement. There has been some interest in establishing a fruitful nexus between the superintendent and instruction (Bredeson, 1996; Hallinger & Murphy, 1986; Petersen, 2002). And, while few studies identify a direct influence, there is more acceptance of the notion that the superintendent must use his or her power (however that is defined) to ensure at least raised test scores throughout the district. Indeed, under the current George W. Bush administration, the impact of the No Child Left Behind Act (2001) leaves no doubt that superintendents will be more fully involved, generally, in curriculum and instructional issues than ever before. Moreover, since each sub-group of minority students and other marginalized students must show sustained adequate yearly progress for districts to stay out of trouble, superintendents must become much more knowledgeable of diversity issues that influence student learning.

Consequently, there is heightened attention being paid to district approaches to equity and equality issues of access to human and material resources. Educational leaders are expected to eliminate achievement gaps amongst their populations by turning to school communities for support and guidance (Furman, 2002; Ryan, 2003). Studies have found that even with the best will, superintendents cannot wield enough personal power to achieve these goals single-handedly (Grogan & Sherman, 2003; Lipman, 1998). The intersections of such social structures as race, class, poverty, gender, disability, religion, and sexuality demand a highly complex understanding of power and power relations in communities.

In dealing with these sensitive, political issues, it is particularly important for superintendents to create and maintain a productive working relationship with their local school boards. Danzberger and Usdan (1992) argue that school boards contribute a vital power to the policy debates surrounding educational reform. "[School boards] possess the power to hire and fire the superintendent and other key personnel, have the ultimate budget responsibility, and set policy parameters in a wide spectrum of school matters. School boards set the tone for the district, and their support is essential if efforts to 'restructure' schools and schooling ... are to be implemented successfully" (p. 95). Studies have highlighted the necessity for a tight relationship between the board president and the superintendent (Feuerstein & Opfer, 1998; Petersen & Short, 2001). The power to set the agenda for board meetings, in the hands of both superintendent and board president cannot be underestimated in terms of influencing district direction and priorities. Indeed, even in this period of increased state and federal oversight, the current governance structure of schools retains a powerful local board in the majority of districts. Professing allegiance to their constituencies, and sometimes at the mercy of activist interest groups, boards can provide vehicles for genuine democratic deliberation or they can stifle healthy discussion and debate (Rallis, Shibles, & Swanson, 2002). It goes without saying; superintendents need a sophisticated understanding of power and community power structures to operate effectively in this environment.

As a place to start, we offer an opportunity to look more closely at power. In the following sections, we (a) survey briefly a number of traditional ways to conceptualize power; (b) provide a discussion of power in the context of education; (c) consider the contribution of Foucauldian notions of power, and the discourse of poststructuralism, including feminist poststructuralism; and (d) comment on the utility of some of these newer conceptions of power to understanding the superintendency and school boards.

CONCEIVING POWER

The antiquarian origins of the discussion of power in the West could easily take us back to Plato and *The Republic*, even to the Homeric Hymns and the age of Epics. In the Renaissance and the Enlightenment, Machiavelli and Hobbes are founding figures of the modern debate. Machiavelli is credited as a precursor to the contemporary focus on context-specific subjectivities by many European theorists (Clegg, 1989; Flyvbjerg, 2001). Hobbes has enjoyed a long period in the spotlight of democratic social theory. These historical traditions and connections have been explored by others (e.g., Clegg, 1989) with particular lucidity.

In the nineteenth century, Marx and Weber set the stage for contemporary theorizing on social power relations. Marx (1967) focused on control of the means of production as the source of power in society. Within his economic paradigm of social relations, power was constituted through the control of labor, resources, and capital. In a capitalist system, with its inherent focus on competition leading to stratification, power always takes the form of domination through the determinism of the structures of social relations. In Marx's world individual human agency is subsidiary to structural determinism.

Weber (1968) defined power in terms of the likelihood that actors can see their own goals materialized despite the opposition of others. Power was tied to intent, desire, and motivation. Weber further indicated that domination occurs when an actor is observed to obey specific directives from another actor. In these cases, subordinates are operating under the influence of their own belief in the legitimacy of their subordinate status. Domination becomes a consensual relationship. Three types of legitimacy were identified: traditional, charismatic, and legal. Like Marx (1967), Weber emphasized the structural environment. The concept of legitimacy is linked to the structural context of the relationship in question.

Structural context was a focal point in the debates over community power in the United States in the 1950s through 1970s (Clegg, 1989; Dahl, 1961; Hindess, 1996; Haugaard, 1997). Sociologists known as *community power theorists* (Hunter, 1953; Mills, 1959) began developing the idea that democracy in the United States is mediated by the dominance of elite groups holding the real power in society. This perspective on power has been very influential with critical theorists seeking to discern power relations within class conflict intrinsic to social structures. The debate has framed much of American theorizing on power to this day.

Dahl (1961) contributed to this debate by pointing out that the community power enclave had simply revealed that an unequal balance of resources is present in American society. There was no unequal balance of power. Access to the resources of power does not immediately translate into realization of power. There are confounding factors endemic to the structures of democracy that limit the utilization of resources. Competition results in a distribution of power that negates the hegemony of any one elite subunit. Dahl insists that observable conflict is an intrinsic and natural aspect of the exercise of power. Dahl identified power with its exercise. The use of power is our orienting reference. Power is defined as one agent, A, causing an effect in another agent , B, that would not occur without A's influence having been present.

Reaction to Dahl's work included claims that power could not reasonably be limited to observed conflict (Bachrach & Baratz, 1962). Power is also identified in the frequently clandestine mobilization of bias within systems and organizations. A fundamental example of this is the case of issue identification and agenda setting, or nondecision-making as Bachrach and Baratz (1963) refer to it. In this scenario, power is exercised by limiting the potential scope of debate. Alternatives are eliminated and discussion is suppressed through indirect means. Conflict is present, but more subtle.

Lukes (1974) proposed a conceptual synthesis of Dahl (1961) and Bachrach and Baratz (1962, 1963), and suggested a third dimension. The synthesis is known as the Three-Dimensional Power model (Lukes, 1974). Dahl's identification of power as observed conflict is given status as the first dimension of power. Bachrach and Baratz (1963) contribute the second dimension of power with their emphasis on the covert exercise of power through nondecision-making. Lukes (1974) adds the third dimension of power and a model for the interaction of the three. Bias and conflict are not only framed by individual acts of coercion and influence, but also social structure and culturally patterned group behavior. Power does not materialize in a vacuum; rather it is constituted within a social and cultural context. Furthermore, the dominated are frequently complicit in the subordination due to a false sense of freedom and/or power. They do not see that their genuine desires and interests are marginalized.

Not all theorists accepted that power and politics went hand in hand. Parsons (1963) argued that Mills (1959) had incorrectly identified a unified power elite dominating American society. However, where Dahl (1961) had used democracy as a normative template for assessing power relations and criticizing Mills, Parsons employed capitalism. He suggested that the United States was a non-political country, owing to its unbridled pursuit of economic values to the neglect of ideological pursuits. Parsons (1963) further stated that a well-defined elite is a natural development within the business world. The diffusion of power to smaller units is unlikely. Selective access to power is thus justified via the internal logic of capitalism.

Parsons (1963) is a capacity theorist, like Mills (1959); he simply chooses to emphasize the mobilization of professional expertise and entrepreneurial spirit as the resources of power. Mills (1959), on the other hand, had emphasized accumulated wealth for the most part. One of the more intriguing elements of the Parsons-Mills debate is that Parsons comes very close to directly stating that power is a context-specific phenomenon. Through his own analysis of Mills' work he convincingly, though quite inadvertently, communicates the postmodernist idea that the recognition of power is contingent on the referential knowledge of the observer.

Barnes (1988) attempted to advance the work of Parsons (1963) and other capacity theorists by developing an interactive set of social processes, which generate and grant power to specific individuals and institutions. For Barnes, power is a cognitively constituted capacity for action gained via social interaction. Power is constituted *with* others. Collective action, rather than domination, is the manifestation or exercise of power. Social objects, positions, and relations are constituted through interactive rings of self-referential social knowledge. Power is produced in an actor when that actor believes he or she has power and when others behave and act as if the actor has power.

Barnes (1988) suggests that the referent is not simply the position or behavior of the actor, but rather the praxis of the social knowledge of the actor and that of others. In respect to the holder of power, power is an externally constituted phenomenon. Barnes' work is consistent with generalized social contract theory, yet it liberates the individual from the constraints of purely collective action. Barnes is able to escape many of the normative implications associated with the Three-Dimensional Power model.

Haugaard (1997) reviews many of the conceptual strands discussed above. He emphasizes the relationship between power, knowledge, and structure. Knowledge and structure are linked to, and constituted through, social power relations. Agency is a balance between individual autonomy and structural determinism. Haugaard rejects the universalizing theories of the past, favoring a pluralist approach. Differing conceptualizations of power are more or less applicable in different contingencies or contexts. Power is put in a shifting conceptual box, resulting in a somewhat ambiguous and postmodernist approach.

POWER AND EDUCATION

The literature of educational leadership, administration, and policy studies are laced with discussions of power. Power has been viewed primarily as a capacity to influence and control—legitimated by hierarchical relationships. In the area of curriculum and pedagogy (not addressed in this chapter), power is seen as a structural force of stratification that must be exposed and transformed in favor of more egalitarian alternatives. Contributions from critical theory (Popkewitz & Fendler, 1999) have been instrumental in bringing this perspective to pedagogical theory.

Business management literature has been historically linked to the conceptual toolkit of educational research, particularly in the area of leadership and administration. This is consistent with the discursive association of business management theory with education that took place in the first half of the twentieth century (Brunner, Grogan, & Björk, 2002). There is a strong normative theme throughout business management theory—representative of its source. These ideas have had a significant influence on educational researchers and practitioners.

In this tradition, power is viewed in terms of the capacity of an agent to influence one or more individuals (Mintzberg, 1983). This capacity for influence is typically connected to the authority, or legitimacy, corresponding to the position of the agent within an organizational hierarchy. The capacity and legitimacy models of power are in play. Power and authority are viewed as an interpersonal control system (Scott, 1998). This control, or influence, is constituted within the structural interaction of a superior and subordinate(s). Yukl (2002) identified three potential outcomes of influence attempts: commitment, compliance, and resistance. In addition, he posited three different types of influence processes: instrumental compliance, internalization, and personal identification. French and Raven's (1959) power taxonomy has also been widely applied in business management theory. They distinguish between five types of power: reward, coercive, legitimate, expert, and referent power. These types of power have been expanded and distributed under the domains of position power and personal power (Bass, 1960; Etzioni, 1961; Yukl & Falbe, 1991).

Acquiring and losing power are of key interest to organizational theorists. The role of power within a process of reciprocity and exchange has been examined by a number of theorists (Jacobs, 1970; March & Simon, 1958; Pfeffer, 1992). Burt (1992) offers the idea that power may also be a function of one's social capital. Networks and contacts can be a means of gaining or expanding power (Granovetter, 1973). Strategic contingencies theory (Hickson et al., 1971) suggests that the relative power of agents, specifically in subunits within organizations is a function of one's expertise. The more indispensable one is to the system, the more power one will have, and the more secure one's status will be.

From a leadership perspective, research has historically focused on the relative distribution of power within organizations (Smith & Tannenbaum, 1963) and the specific traits and tactics associated with influence behavior (Blau, 1955; Pfeffer, 1992). Mintzberg (1996) identified moments of *uncertainty* as the loci of power. Ambiguity may offer individuals, particularly those in well-situated positions, the opportunity to influence the actions of others. The interaction between leader power, particular influence behaviors, and outcomes is indeterminate in the literature (Yukl, 2002).

Theories of power have also had a significant influence in the area of policy studies. Variations on the Three-Dimensional Power Model have had a strong hold over research in this domain of educational research. For educational policy gurus, much like their counterparts in political science, the utility of theory is limited by its potential applicability on the ground and in the trenches. This is testimony to the long-standing appeal of work such as Dahl's (1961) that was grounded in case-study research.

Coplin and O'Leary (1981) offer a formula for assessing power relationships in the policy domain. Their PRINCE system is a complementary heuristic to the Three-Dimensional Power Model (Lukes, 1974). Binary permutations of power such as symmetrical versus asymmetrical power relationships (Bryson & Crosby, 1992), and distributive versus facilitative power (Mann, 1996) have added further dimensions to the mix. Mann's work, in particular, has given voice to a distinction growing within the literature between a *power-over* and a *power-with* perspective (Brunner, 2002). In Mann's (1996) terminology, distributive power is analogous with *power-over*, while facilitative power suggests *power-with*. The injection of a feminist narrative into the discussion of power has advanced a facilitative emphasis (Brunner, 1999, 2000; Grogan, 1996). We will return to this point below when we turn our focus to feminist and poststructural paradigms.

Educational research on leadership and policy has made use of these concepts of power to understand individuals' wielding of power and the idea of community power structures. What is not so common yet, is work that defines power less explicitly and more fluidly. For instance, few studies of leadership have considered power as residing outside of individuals. Poststructuralist and feminist approaches to power offer alternative insights into the complex terrain framing the relationship of superintendents and school boards. In particular, Flyvbjerg's (1991) study of a community's democratic processes provides an interesting model for other workers seeking greater understanding of local politics. Though it is located in Denmark, the poststructuralist lens used could certainly be focused on our lay leadership community structures in the United States.

FOUCAULT AND THE DISCOURSE OF POSTSTRUCTURALISM

Michel Foucault has had a dramatic impact on theories of power. His most influential works are his *archaeologies*. Foucault referred to them in this manner to emphasize that he was uncovering that which was hidden under successive strata of cultural detritus. His goal was to excavate the superficial and the apparent in order to discern the underlying foundations of the structural relations of society. His work is grounded in the historical context of particular periods of time. For instance, Foucault (1977) takes us to the time surrounding the French Revolution to reveal the advent of modern forms of subjectification. Intrinsic to this discussion is a study of power.

Foucault does not seek to offer a clean and precise definition of power, nor does he necessarily offer us a conceptual framework easily implemented. Power is the interplay of force relations constituted and organized along specific contextual dimensions (Foucault, 1977). What he offers is awareness that power is one of many cultural artifacts—constituted within the complex web of cultural interactions that we all exist within. In his complex and erudite *archaeologies*, we are shown that the underlying circumstances of power can be revealed. Through painstaking analysis we can discern the constitution of power. What exactly "it" is remains obscure. This frustrates us because we strive to categorize and label. How can we hope to grasp that which we do not understand, that which we cannot even clearly define? Definition, however, is normalizing. Normalizing is narrow and restrictive. A more inclusive approach to inquiry must embrace the ambiguity of murky and transient definitions. Definitions are ultimately just another heuristic that we allow to pass for truth.

Foucault's (1977) view of power, that multiplicity of interactions, is intimately tied to knowledge. What emerges is a dyadic concept. Neither power nor knowledge can exist one without the other. There is a symbiosis. In Foucault's (1977) words, "power produces knowledge ... power and knowledge directly imply one another ... there is no power relation without the correlative constitution of a field of knowledge, nor any knowledge that does not presuppose and constitute at the same time power relations" (p. 27). Knowledge is context-specific. Truth is what passes for knowledge in different discursive environments. Discourse is particularly important here because it is discourse that provides power with legitimacy. Power then interacts with discourse to set parameters for what shall be considered knowledge.

Foucault (1977) identifies a number of conceptual dimensions, or strands, of discipline that are the foundations of our contemporary conceptions of power. These dimensions are planes of interaction along which our social structures subjectify the individual. Control of, or influence on, the individual is the end result of these interactions, hence our difficulty in conceiving of power as anything other than control within the context of situated interaction (Hall, 1997). Foucault claims that these structures are context-specific cultural artifacts. They do not represent a totalizing social truth. Our knowledge of power originates within the confines of the structural interactions we find ourselves. Foucault argues that the subjectification of the individual within modern disciplinary structures informs our understanding of power. Conventional theories of power reflect this normative bias. They reflect our understanding of power within the context of our subjective structural environment (i.e. the Three-Dimensional Power model: Lukes, 1974). The conceptual foundation of the theory accurately captures outcomes, the power relations manifested at or near the surface of social structures. The underlying power-knowledge interactions that produce these outcomes remain largely unidentified. Poststructuralist theory seeks to peel off the layers of structure to reveal these underlying relationships. Foucault performed this task primarily using documentary analysis. Contemporary poststructuralist researchers are using a broader array of methods of data collection and analysis.

FLYVBJERG: OPERATIONALIZING FOUCAULT

Flyvbjerg's (1991) qualitative study of an award-winning urban revitalization project in Denmark offers a contemporary example of a rigorous poststructuralist analysis. Flyvbjerg examined a case from beginning to end over a 15 year span of time—conducting observations, interviews, and interpreting documents. His conceptual lenses are rationality and power, which he links in a fashion similar to Foucault's (1977) treatment of power and knowledge. Flyvbjerg's focus on rationality places the emphasis of inquiry on action. Rationality refers to a process of thinking characterized by the use of reason (Flyvbjerg, 1991; 2001). Like Foucault, Flyvbjerg resists a precise definition of power. He prefers to speak of its effects, of what it does.

Unlike Foucault's (1970, 1973, 1977) grand historical epics, Flyvbjerg (1991) offers us a focused case-study for the exploration of power/knowledge relationships. He illuminates the interplay of structure and the creation of knowledge. The structural position of actors determines their access to, and control of, knowledge (what passes for truth). Replacing genuine rationality with rationalization is the key strategy of power. Rationalization is the manipulation of reason:

> Power may very well see knowledge as an obstacle to the change power wants. This ... is the most important single characteristic of the rationality of power, that is, of the strategies and tactics of power in relation to rationality. Power, quite simply, produces that knowledge and that rationality which is conducive to the reality it wants. Conversely, power suppresses that knowledge and rationality for which it has no use. (Flyvbjerg, 1991, p. 36)

Flyvbjerg systematically documents the complex web of institutions, agencies, committees, organizations, and individuals that impacted the urban planning initiative each step of the way. As it passes through this network of social relations, the urban planning project is transformed from a rationally inspired urban revitalization effort into an example of environmental abuse and social polarization (Flyvbjerg, 1991). A dramatic narrative of the interplay of power and rationality is created. This work is a useful model for the operationalization of Foucault's (1977) concept of power.

The study is historical, particular, and examines the process of the creation of what is accepted as knowledge. Recall Foucault's (1977) observation that what is true is that which is accepted as true. Flyvbjerg's study (1991) examines the effect of this process on the relations of power between various actors, specifically on what they do and do not do. Structure, process, and agency are all touched upon both in time and in space. Flyvbjerg collects, documents, analyzes, and interprets his data using techniques readily available to researchers of school districts and the superintendency.

The time span of his study is, however, notably inconsistent with current practice within educational research. The richness of his longitudinal findings suggests we may want to move in the direction of more extended studies. The extended case method (Burawoy, 1998) offers a depth and breadth of inquiry that less-protracted research may lose. The elaborate and unpredictable web of interests and social actors is comparable to the context many superintendents face. Superintendents have always faced a complex and challenging task (Tyack, 1976), yet are currently facing an operating environment of exaggerated turbulence (Crowson, 2003; Lugg, Bulkley, Firestone, & Garner, 2002). Enhancing our understanding of the behavior of superintendents within this dynamic and complex context requires the use of conceptual tools and methods that are up to the challenge of grasping the multiple expressions of power manifest in such settings.

Applying Flyvbjerg's (1991) methods to the relationship of superintendents, school boards, and their communities may illuminate aspects of this relationship less understood using other models of power. School boards in large urban districts (Hess, 2002) frequently resemble city councils, such as the one in Flyvbjerg's study. Small rural districts can also have this politicized quality (Grogan, 2000b); although at times it may be less visible. Flyvbjerg's search for the negotiated order (Hall & Spencer-Hall, 1982) of the relationships within the Aalborg project can be applied to case studies of superintendents and school boards.

FEMINIST POSTSTRUCTURALISM

Discourse is an essential component of Foucault's (1970, 1973, 1977) vision of social relations. Discourse is also a topic of much discussion in educational research. Numerous calls have been made to include a greater plurality of voices in our social discourse on education (Corson, 1995; Delpit, 1995; Freire, 1970; McLaren & Giroux, 1997). Education has long been a field populated by a large number of women; yet like the rest of society, the discourse of a dominant white male elite has held sway (Blackmore, 2002; Grogan, 1996; Marshall, 1997). Updating and expanding the discourse of research on the superintendency to reflect the narratives of women has been the subject of recent scholarly work (Brunner, 1999, 2000a, 2000b, 2003; Grogan, 1996, 2000b). This inclusion of marginalized perspectives is expressive of a poststructuralist paradigm.

Feminist workers have attempted to grant an element of agency, an activist edge, to poststructuralism by emphasizing the potential for the exercise of individual human will (Butler, 1997). Poststructuralism can easily become very nihilistic. If everything is subjective and there is no truth other than what passes for truth, which will be different for everyone, then we are potentially left with meaningless relativism. Feminist workers have offered a glimmer of hope to this pessimistic interpretation by suggesting that individual agency is possible within the discursively constituted contexts we find ourselves embedded within (Davies, 2000; Weedon, 1997). We may live in a box of our own collective construction, but within that box each individual has the capacity to enact change. The box will always be there, but we can alter its dimensions and how it is perceived, both by ourselves and by others.

The past decade has witnessed a proliferation of writing by authors attempting to merge a feminist paradigm with poststructuralism (Blackmore, 2002; Brunner, 2002; Butler, 1997; Capper, 1993; Grogan, 1996, 2000; Holland & Blair, 1995; Lather, 1992; Marshall, 1997; St. Pierre & Pillow, 2000; Sawicki, 1991; Weedon, 1997). A particularly evocative articulation of this effort comes from Davies (2000). She states that in working with poststructuralist theory one must be cognizant of one's own discursive subjectification and explore the limits of that subjectivity. This is a reasonable assertion in light of poststructuralism's abandonment of any pretense of normative objectivity. Davies delves into this issue in some depth. She suggests that a researcher's own experience with subjectivity is a key element of poststructuralist methodology. Such a personal perspective provides avenues to new lines of conceptualization. For traditionally marginalized groups, this offers an opportunity to contribute their narratives to our discourse of power. This methodological approach is placed in opposition to one which incorporates a prescriptive formula of analysis.

According to a feminist poststructural approach, power is something other than mere oppression and coercion; it is embedded in relations between people and knowledge systems (Davies, 2000). It is constituted in two ways: power is embodied in that which is taken as knowledge; and power is manifested in the language used to express that which is taken as knowledge. The discourses we engage in, our concepts of knowledge and the praxis of the two constitute power. Structural relations within society grant unequal access to practicing and framing discourses. This both constitutes and amplifies subject relations leading to marginalization of some groups (Gaventa, 1980). Those who wield power are often unconscious of both their position in dominating discourse and the effects of that discourse on the status of others. Perceptions related to gender relations, in particular, are so integrated into the discursive practices of children that the translation of them into an oppositional structural hierarchy is virtually inevitable (Davies, 2000).

CONCLUSION

A critical focus of the application of feminist poststructural methodology to educational leadership has been to reveal the narratives of women superintendents, district office administrators, and principals in the field (Brunner, 2000b; Grogan, 1996, 2000b; Reynolds, 2002; Skrla, 2003; Smulyan, 2000; Weiler & Middleton, 1999). From a power perspective, these efforts have two primary effects. First, the marginalized voices of women are heard, thus revealing the discursive gender biases intrinsic to our models of educational leadership. Second, our collective knowledge of what constitutes leadership is fundamentally altered, thus transforming power relations within the domain of educational leadership. Power relations evolve due to shifts in discourse and an accompanying transformation of knowledge. The incorporation of new subjectivities leads to a modified conception of leadership.

The dimensions of discipline articulated by Foucault (1977) establish the discourse which has traditionally remained in the hands of dominant social groups (Marshall, 1997). These dimensions revolve around the subjectification of the individual along spatial, physiological, temporal, hierarchical, and evaluative planes of interaction (Foucault, 1977). Feminist poststructural theory suggests that examination of social interactions along these dimensional axes will reveal more complex power relations than conventional methods have done. Additionally, we shall be able to analyze traditional conceptions of power with greater depth and complexity. Essential underlying relationships between educational leaders and their stakeholders, intimately tied to the constitution of power/knowledge, may be revealed. Flyvbjerg's (1991) work contributes a model for a multi-dimensional investigation of such relationships, which facilitates a greater awareness of structure, process, and agency—particularly helpful in studying the context of the superintendency.

The context of the superintendency is a shifting one. To return to points made at the beginning of this chapter, we argue that now, more than ever, superintendents and school boards in any given district face considerable challenges. Not the least of which is to nurture the promise of democracy-in-action. To understand the potential of lay leadership as Rallis et al (2002) describe it requires a deeper, more robust comprehension of power—power harnessed for the good of children and families. Ethical decision-making, ideally a collaborative endeavor shared between superintendents and school boards is at the heart of public educators' commitment to students. Without a multi-dimensional knowledge of power and how it operates, district leaders remain limited in their activities. "To be most effective, [superintendents] convert legitimate board-determined policy decisions into operational decisions grounded in professional knowledge and judgment" (Rallis et al., 2002, p. 255). The quality of those decisions depends on the actors' full comprehension of all the local, state and federal power mechanisms.

Power is one of a group of concepts that is highly problematic to define. Leadership and culture are two others that come to mind. Power may best be conceived of as a family resemblance concept. There are a constellation of concepts revolving around the ideas of agency, control, domination, and influence that we call power. A finite definition of power is not within our grasp. Feminist poststructuralism and other poststructural accounts of power offer alternative ways of conceptualizing a relatively taken-for-granted construct. The older notions of superintendents as powerful individuals and of boards as powerful entities can be re-considered with these analytical frames. Even the idea that power lies in the community structures is too static to be really useful. With a more localized, contextually dependent understanding of power, and the way it circulates, researchers and practitioners will care less about who has it, than about how it works.

Educational leadership research will benefit from an expansion of our conception of power that will reflect a multi-paradigmatic approach. Such an analytical approach offers fresh insight into leadership relations and promises a deeper understanding of the superintendency. It is our hope that the identification and exploration of postmodern constructs of power will prove useful in our quest to prepare and develop the women and men who have the courage to embrace the challenges of the 21st century superintendency.

REFERENCES

Arvey, R. D., & Ivancevich, J. M. (1980). Punishment in organizations: A review, propositions, and research suggestions. *Academy of Management Review, 5,* 123-132.

Bachrach, P., & Baratz, M. S. (1962). The two faces of power. *American Political Science Review, 56*(4), 947-952.

Bachrach, P., & Baratz, M. S. (1963). Decisions and nondecisions. *American Political Science Review, 57*(3), 632-642.

Barnes, B. (1988). *The nature of power.* Cambridge, England: Polity Press.

Bass, B. M. (1960). *Leadership, psychology, and organizational behavior.* New York: Harper.

Björk, L., & Keedy, J. (Eds.). (2003). The superintendent shortage: Myth or reality. [Special issue]. *Journal of School Leadership, 13*(3).

Blackmore, J. (2002). Troubling women: The upsides and downsides of leadership and the new managerialism. In C. Reynolds (Ed.), *Women and school leadership: International perspectives* (pp. 49-67). Albany: State University of New York Press.

Blau, P. M. (1955). *The dynamics of bureaucracy.* Chicago: University of Chicago Press.

Bredeson, P. (1996). Superintendents' roles in curriculum development and instructional leadership: Instructional visionaries, collaborators, supporters, and delegators. *Journal of School Leadership, 6*(3), 243-264.

Brunner, C. C. (1999). Power, gender and superintendent selection. In C. C. Brunner (Ed.), *Sacred dreams: Women and the superintendency.* Albany: State University of New York Press.

Brunner, C. C. (2000a). *Principles of power: Women superintendents and the riddle of the heart.* Albany: State University of New York Press.

Brunner, C. C. (2000b). Unsettled moments in settled discourse: Women superintendents' experiences of inequality. *Educational Administration Quarterly, 36*(1), 76-116.

Brunner, C. C. (2002a). A proposition for the reconception of the superintendency: Reconsidering traditional and nontraditional discourse. *Educational Administration Quarterly, 38*(3), 402-431.

Brunner, C. C. (2002b). Professing educational leadership: Conceptions of power. *Journal of School Leadership, 12*(7), 693-720.

Brunner, C. C. (2003). Invisible, limited, and emerging discourse: Research practices that restrict and/or increase access for women and persons of color to the superintendency. *Journal of School Leadership, 13*(4), 428-450.

Brunner, C. C., Grogan, M., & Björk, L. (2002). Shifts in the discourse defining the superintendency: Historical and current foundations of the position. In J. Murphy (Ed.), *The educational leadership challenge: Redefining leadership for the 21st century* (pp. 211-238). Chicago: National Society for the Study of Education.

Bryson, J. M., & Crosby, B. C. (1992). *Leadership for the common good: Tackling public problems in a shared-power world.* San Francisco: Jossey-Bass.

Burawoy, M. (1998). The extended case method. *Sociological Theory, 16*(1), 4-33.

Burbules, N. C. (1986). A theory of power in education. *Educational Theory, 36,* 95-114.

Burt, R. S. (1992). *Structural holes.* Cambridge, MA: Harvard University Press.

Butler, J. (1997). *The psychic life of power: Theories in subjection.* Palo Alto, CA: Stanford University Press.

Capper, C. A. (1993). Educational administration in a pluralistic society: A multiparadigm approach. In C. Capper (Ed.), *Educational administration in a pluralistic society* (pp. 7-35). Albany: State University of New York Press.

Clegg, S. (1989). *Frameworks of power.* Oxford, England: Oxford University Press.

Cohen, A., & Bradford, D. (1989). Influence without authority: The use of alliances, reciprocity, and exchange to accomplish work. *Organizational Dynamics, 17,* 5-17.

Cooper, B., Fusarelli, L., & Carella, V. (2000). *Career crisis in the superintendency?* Arlington, VA: American Association of School Administrators.

Coplin, W. D., & O'Leary, M. K. (1981). *Basic policy studies skills.* New York: Policy Studies Associates.

Corson, D. (Ed.). (1995). Discursive power in educational organizations: An introduction. In *Discourse and power in educational organizations* (pp. 3-16). Cresskill, NJ: Hampton Press.

Cronin, J., & Usdan, M. (2003). Rethinking the urban school superintendency: Nontraditional leaders and new models of leadership. In W. Boyd & D. Miretsky (Eds.), *American educational governance on trial: Change and challenges* (pp. 177-195). Chicago: National Society for the Study of Education.

Crowson, R. L. (2003). The turbulent policy environment in education: Implications for school administration and accountability. *Peabody Journal of Education, 78*(4), 29-43.

Cuban, L. (1976). *Urban school chiefs under fire.* Chicago: University of Chicago Press.

Dahl, R. A. (1961). *Who governs? Democracy and power in an American city.* New Haven, CT: Yale University Press.

Dansberger, J. P., & Usdan, M. D. (1992). Strengthening a grass roots American institution: The school board. In P. F. First & H. J. Walberg (Eds.), *School boards: Changing local control* (pp. 91-124). Berkeley, CA: McCutchan.

Davies, B. (2000). *A body of writing 1990-1999.* Walnut Creek, CA: Altamira Press.

Davis, K. (1968). Attitudes toward the legitimacy of management efforts to influence employees. *Academy of Management Journal, 11*, 153-162.

Delpit, L. (1995). *Other people's children: Cultural conflict in the classroom*. New York: The New Press.

Etzioni, A. (1961). *A comparative analysis of complex organizations*. New York: Free Press.

Feuerstein, A., & Opfer, V. D. (1998). School board chairmen and school superintendents: An analysis of perceptions concerning special interest groups and educational governance. *Journal of School Leadership, 8*, 373-398.

Flyvbjerg, B. (1991). *Rationality and power: Democracy in practice*. Chicago: The University of Chicago Press.

Flyvbjerg, B. (2001). *Making social science matter: Why social inquiry fails and how it can succeed again*. Cambridge, England: Cambridge University Press.

Foucault, M. (1970). *The order of things: An archaeology of the human sciences*. New York: Vintage.

Foucault, M. (1973). *The birth of the clinic: An archaeology of medical perception*. New York: Vintage.

Foucault, M. (1977). *Discipline and punish: The birth of the prison*. New York: Vintage.

Freire, P. (1970). *Pedagogy of the oppressed*. New York: Continuum.

French, J., & Raven, B. H. (1959). The bases of social power. In D. Cartwright (Ed.), *Studies of social power* (pp.150-167). Ann Arbor, MI: Institute for Social Research.

Furman, G. (Ed.). (2002). *School as community*. Albany: State University of New York Press.

Gaventa, J. (1980). *Power and powerlessness*. Urbana: University of Illinois.

Giddens, A. (1971). *Capitalism and modern social theory*. Cambridge, England: Cambridge University.

Granovetter, M. (1973). The strength of weak ties. *American Journal of Sociology, 78*, 1360-1380.

Grogan, M. (1996). *Voices of women aspiring to the superintendency*. Albany: State University of New York Press.

Grogan, M. (1999). Equity/equality issues of gender, race and class. *Educational Administration Quarterly, 35* (4), 518-536.

Grogan, M. (2000a). Laying the groundwork for a reconception of the superintendency from feminist postmodern perspectives. *Educational Administration Quarterly, 36*(1), 117-142.

Grogan, M. (2000b, March). The short tenure of a woman superintendent: A clash of gender and politics. *Journal of School Leadership, 10*, 104-130.

Grogan, M., & Sherman, W. (2003). Superintendents in Virginia dealing with issues surrounding the black-white test-score gap. In D. Duke, M. Grogan, P. Tucker, & W. Heinecke (Eds.), *Educational leadership in an age of accountability* (pp. 155-180). Albany: State University of New York Press.

Hall, P. M., & Spencer-Hall, D. A. (1982). The social conditions of the negotiated order. *Urban Life, 11*(3), 328-349.

Hall, P. M. (1997). Meta-power, social organization, and the shaping of social action. *Symbolic Interaction, 20*(4), 397-418.

Hallinger, P., & Murphy, J. (1986). The superintendent's role in promoting instructional leadership. *Administrator's Notebook, 27*(9), 1-4.

Haugaard, M. (1997). *The constitution of power: A theoretical analysis of power, knowledge and structure.* New York: St. Martin's Press.

Hess, F. M. (2002). *School boards at the dawn of the 21st century: Conditions and challenges of district governance.* Alexandria, VA: National School Boards Association.

Hickson, D. J., Hinings, C. R., Lee, C. A., Schneck, R. S., & Pennings, J. M. (1973). A strategic contingencies theory of intraorganizational power. *Administrative Science Quarterly, 16,* 216-229.

Hindess, B. (1996). *Discourses of power.* London: Blackwell.

Holland, J., & Blair, M. (Eds.). (1995). *Debates and issues in feminist research and pedagogy.* Philadelphia: Multilingual Matters.

Hunter, F. (1953). *Community power structure: A study of decision makers.* Chapel Hill, NC: University of North Carolina Press.

Jacobs, T. O. (1970). *Leadership and exchange in formal organizations.* Alexandria, VA: Human Resources Research Organization.

Kaplan, R. E. (1984, Spring). Trade routes: The manager's network of relationships. *Organizational Dynamics, 12,* 37-52.

Katz, D., & Kahn, R. L. (1978). *The social psychology of organizations* (2nd ed.). New York: John Wiley.

Kelman, H. C. (1958). Compliance, identification, and internalization: Three processes of attitude change. *Journal of Conflict Resolution, 2,* 51-56.

Kowalski, T. (2003). Superintendent shortage: The wrong problem and wrong solution. *Journal of School Leadership, 13*(3), 288-303.

Lather, P. (1992). Critical frames in educational research: Feminist and post-structural perspectives. *Theory into Practice, 31*(2), 87-99.

Leithwood, K. (Ed.). (1995). *Effective school district leadership.* Albany: State University of New York Press.

Lipman, P. (1998). *Race, class and power in school restructuring.* Albany: State University of New York Press.

Lugg, C. A., Bulkley, K., Firestone, W. A., & Garner, C. W. (2002). The contextual terrain facing educational leaders. In J. Murphy (Ed.), *The educational leadership challenge: Redefining leadership for the 21st century* (pp. 20-41). Chicago: National Society for the Study of Education.

Lukes, S. (1974). *Power: A radical view.* London: MacMillan.

Lutz, F., & Iannaccone, L. (1978). *Public participation in local schools: The dissatisfaction theory of American democracy.* Lexington, MA: Lexington Books.

Mann, M. (1996). *The sources of social power: Vol. 2. The rise of classes, and nation-states, 1760-1914.* New York: Cambridge University Press.

March, J. G., & Simon, H. A. (1958). *Organizations.* New York: John Wiley.

Marshall, C. (1997). Dismantling and reconstructing policy analysis. In C. Marshall (Ed.), *Feminist critical policy analysis* (pp. 1-40). London: Falmer Press.

Marx, K. (1967). *Capital: A critique of political economy.* New York: International.

McLaren, P., & Giroux, H. (1997). Writing from the margins: Geographies of identity, pedagogy, and power. In P. McLaren (Ed.), *Revolutionary multiculturalism: Pedagogies of dissent for the new millennium.* New York: Westview Press.

Mills, C. W. (1959). *The power elite.* New York: Oxford University Press.

Mintzberg, H. (1983). *Power in and around organizations.* Englewood Cliffs, NJ: Prentice Hall.

Mintzberg, H. (1996). The professional bureaucracy. *Harvard Business Review, 74*(4), 61-66.

No Child Left Behind Act of 2001, Pub. L. 107-110 (2001).

Parsons, T. (1963). *Structure and process in modern societies.* New York: Free Press.

Petersen, G. J., & Short, P. M. (2001). The school board president's perception of the district superintendent: Applying the lenses of social influence and social style. *Educational Administration Quarterly, 37*(4), 533-570.

Petersen, G. J. (2002). Singing the same tune: Principals' and school board members' perceptions of the superintendent's role as instructional leader. *Journal of Educational Administration, 40*(2), 158-171.

Pfeffer, J. (1992). *Managing with power: Politics and influence in organizations.* Boston: Harvard Business School Press.

Popkewitz, T. S., & Fendler, L. (Eds.). (1999). *Critical theories in education: Changing terrains of knowledge and politics.* New York: Routledge.

Rallis, S., Shibles, M., & Swanson, A. (2002). Repositioning lay leadership: Policy-making and democratic deliberation. In J. Murphy (Ed.), *The educational leadership challenge: Redefining leadership for the 21st century* (pp. 239-260). Chicago: National Society for the Study of Education.

Reynolds, C. (2002). *Women and school leadership: International perspectives.* Albany: State University of New York Press.

Rist, M. (1991, December). Race, politics and policies rip into the urban superintendency. *Executive Educator, 12*(12), 12-14.

Robinson, V. M. J. (1995). The identification and evaluation of power in discourse. In D. Corson (Ed.), *Discourse and power in educational organizations.* Cresskill, NJ: Hampton Press.

Ryan, J. (2003). *Leading diverse schools.* Boston: Kluwer.

Sawicki, J. (1991). *Disciplining Foucault: Feminism, power, and the body.* New York: Routledge.

Scott, R. W. (1998). *Organizations: Rational, natural, and open systems.* New York: Prentice Hall.

Skrla, L. (2003). Mourning silence: Women superintendents' (and a researcher) rethink speaking up and speaking out. In L. Skrla & M. Young (Eds.), *Reconsidering feminist research in educational leadership.* Albany: State University of New York Press.

Skrla, L., Scott, J., & Benestante, J. (2001). Dangerous intersection: A meta-ethnographic study of gender, power, and politics in the public school superintendency. In C. Brunner & L. Björk (Eds.), *The new superintendency.* New York: JAI Press

Smith, C. G., & Tannenbaum, A. S. (1963). Organizational control structure: A comparative analysis. *Human Relations, 16,* 299-316.

Smulyan, L. (2000). *Balancing acts: Women principals at work.* Albany: State University of New York Press.

St. Pierre, E. A., & Pillow, W. S. (Eds.). (2000). *Feminist poststructural theory and methods in education.* New York: Routledge.

Tallerico, M. (2000). *Accessing the superintendency: The unwritten rules.* Thousand Oaks, CA: Corwin Press.

Tyack, D. B. (1976). Pilgrim's progress. Toward a social history of the school superintendency, 1860-1960. *History of Education Quarterly, 16*(3), 257-300.

Wartenberg, T. E. (1992). *Rethinking power.* Albany: State University of New York Press.

Weber, M. (1968). *Economy and society: An outline of interpretive sociology.* New York: Bedminster Press.

Weedon, C. (1997). *Feminist practice and poststructuralist theory* (2nd ed.). New York: Basil Blackwell.

Weiler, K., & Middleton, S. (Eds.). (1999). *Telling women's lives: Narrative inquiries in the history of women's education.* London: Open University Press.

Wrong, D. H. (1979). *Power.* New York: Harper & Row.

Yukl, G. (2002). *Leadership in organizations.* New York: Prentice Hall.

Yukl, G., & Falbe, C. M. (1991). The importance of different sources of power in downward and lateral relations. *Journal of Applied Psychology, 76,* 416-423.

CHAPTER 4

PERSONALIZATION OF INTEREST GROUPS AND THE RESULTING POLICY NONSENSE

The Cobb County School Board's Evolution Debate

V. Darleen Opfer

The role of interest groups in the functioning of our democracy is unclear. While some researchers argue that interest groups serve a number of important functions,[1] others contend that their participation has negative consequences.[2] Compounding this uncertainty is the recent rise in the use of grassroots influence tactics by these groups.[3] In today's political environment, interest groups are less likely to approach policy makers as groups and increasingly more likely to attempt influence through individual contact.

While most political scientists have concentrated their investigation of interest groups at the state and national level (Bjork & Lindle, 2001), evidence suggests that local school boards are not immune to their influence.

The Politics of Leadership: Superintendents and School Boards in Changing Times, 73–93
Copyright © 2005 by Information Age Publishing
All rights of reproduction in any form reserved.

A study by the American Association of School Administrators indicated that more than 90% of school superintendents in large urban districts reported that interest groups exerted pressure on school board policies and operations. Further, more than half of the superintendents (57%) acknowledged that interest groups were active in their communities (Glass, Bjork, & Brunner, 2000). Other studies have also suggested that school boards are susceptible to interest group influence (Arocha, 1993; Danzberger, 1994; Feuerstein & Opfer, 1998; McCarthy, 1996). This chapter attempts to clarify the role(s) of interest groups in school board policymaking, and more generally, in the functioning of our democracy.

The chapter examines the relationship between school boards and interest groups by investigating the events surrounding the adoption of science textbooks and the subsequent science curriculum policy adoption process by the Cobb County (Georgia) School Board over a period of approximately six months. The case study method was chosen to better understand interest group influence on school boards (Stake, 1995). This instrumental case study was constructed by relying on multiple sources of information as suggested by Yin (1989). These sources include: observations of school board meetings, interviews with interest group members and school board members, media coverage of the adoption and subsequent science policies, and documents produced by the school board and the interest groups.

Contrary to scholars who attribute a positive role to interest groups in a democracy, the case illustrates that the interest groups involved in Cobb County impeded both the textbook adoption and subsequent policymaking related to science curricula. The Cobb County case illustrates that interest group actors may operate out of a sense of personalism and that such personalism can result in the absence of policy or policy nonsense. A discussion of the implications for interest group influence, policy creation, and the democratic functioning of school boards concludes the chapter. Particular attention is paid to how school superintendents interested in improving school board policymaking should respond to district characteristics, norms, and processes that result in ineffective school politics.

COBB COUNTY AND THE ADOPTION OF
SCIENCE TEXTBOOKS

Cobb County is one of metropolitan Atlanta, Georgia's wealthiest and most conservative school districts. The median income of its 608,000 residents is $58,000. In the last presidential election, 60% of its residents voted Republican (Cobb County Board of Elections and Registration,

2002). Six of the seven school board members are Republicans. The county is also the home of some of Georgia's most conservative politicians, including former Speaker of the U.S. House Newt Gingrich and former U.S. Representative Bob Barr.

The Cobb County School System is the 28th largest district in the United States, the second largest in Georgia, and one of 11 districts located in the Atlanta metropolitan area. It has a student population of 96,000 that grows, on average, 2,700 students a year. Eighty-one percent of its students pursue some form of post-secondary education. The system includes 103 schools with plans to build 12 more in the next few years. The system employs 12,000 people, approximately 8,000 of whom are classroom teachers.

This district has had a long history of controversy over the teaching of evolution. In 1979, the county adopted a policy on the subject that stated,

> The Cobb County School District acknowledges that some scientific accounts of the origin of human species as taught in public schools are inconsistent with the family teachings of a significant number of Cobb County citizens. Therefore, the instructional program and curriculum of the school system shall be planned and organized with respect for these family teachings. The Constitutional principle of separation of church and state shall by preserved and maintained as established by the United States Supreme Court and defined by judicial decisions. (Cobb County School District, 1979, OCGA, 20-2-50; 20-2-57; 20-2-59)

At the same time, the county also adopted regulations to guide the implementation of this policy. These regulations stated:

- The curriculum would be organized so that no student was compelled to study the origin of human species.
- The origin of human species would not be taught at the elementary or middle school levels.
- The study of the origin of human species would not be required for graduation.
- Elective opportunities to investigate theories of the origin of human species, including creation theory, would be available.
- All high school courses offered on the origin of human species as electives would be so noted in curriculum catalogs and course listings (Cobb County School District, 1979, OCGA, 20-2-50; 20-2-57; 20-2-59).

These policies remained in place in the spring of 2002, when the system began the process of adopting new science textbooks as required by state law every six years (Cobb County School District, 1999, OCGA 20-2-1010).

The district followed an adoption process that included appointing a committee of school personnel to review and rate science texts. Following the review, a citizen advisory committee was convened to assess the textbooks recommended by the internal committee. After that assessment, district administrators chose a set of science texts and placed them on display for 15 days. At the end of this period, the board was to vote to adopt the texts.

However, the week before the adoption vote was to take place, the board received a letter from county resident, Marjorie Rogers, objecting to the chosen textbooks and threatening to file suit to halt adoption. In this letter, dated March 13, 2002, Ms. Rogers raised five objections to the texts:

1. I object to the proposed textbooks in that they do not teach scientific fact, but rather promote the philosophy of naturalism under the guise of "science".

2. I object to adoption of the proposed texts insofar as they present untrue, unproven, or highly speculative comments dogmatically as if they were certain knowledge.

3. I object to adoption of the proposed texts insofar as they present ... "evidence" for evolution which is either untrue or unproven.... Many textbooks contain the UNPROVABLE ASSUMPTIONS that life arose from non-living material, and that all life forms came from a "simple" single-celled organism. No one has ever observed this happening. No lab experiments have confirmed that life could have arisen by chance. Therefore, it should not be presented in textbooks as fact or science. It is a BELIEF.

4. I object to the adoption of the proposed textbooks insofar as they confuse the concept of micro-evolution with macro-evolution, and mislead students to believe that these concepts are the same and that the former provides support for the latter.

5. I further object to the adoption of the proposed textbooks insofar as they violate the Cobb County regulations—IDBD Theories of Origin.

This letter, in effect, reminded board members of the 1979 regulations governing theories of origin.

Board members and administrators in charge of the adoption now scrambled to head off court interference. They consulted attorneys who informed them that the old regulations were in violation of current state and federal law. This now left them with two problems—how to get text-books adopted and how to rewrite the Theories of Origin policy.

The board decided to tackle the more pressing problem of the text-book adoptions first. To that end, they considered some of the remedies suggested by Marjorie Rogers in her letter:

1. The provision of supplemental material to students that presents alternate arguments and views on evolution;
2. The placement of a disclaimer in each textbook that highlights the theoretical nature of evolution;
3. The placement of stickers throughout the books in the sections containing objectionable material. For example, "Darwin's univer-sal tree of life is inconsistent with the fossil record of the Cambrian explosion and with recent molecular evidence." (from letter dated March 13, 2002)

They did not consider her suggestions to ask for the textbook publishers to eliminate sections involving evolution or that the district glue offensive pages together.

Then in late March, the board held a meeting at which they were to adopt the new science textbooks and also an insert for the textbooks. The board met before a packed house of approximately 150 people to take action. They began their meeting by taking public comment on the issue. Approximately 30 people signed up to address the board with each being given one minute to speak.

The majority of speakers urged the board either not to adopt the pro-posed texts or to delay action on the issue. Many made personal state-ments about their beliefs on the subject. But overwhelmingly, these statements were against evolution with only two speakers supporting the textbook adoption. The statements made included:

- Scientists believe evolution to be passé that there must be a creator behind organisms.
- I don't want anyone taking care of me in a nursing home to think I came from monkeys!
- We have taken God out of school and because of this we have Col-umbine.
- We need to teach creationism if we teach evolution.
- We believe the Bible is correct in that God created man.
- I don't expect the public school system to teach only creationism, but I think it should be given its fair share.

Many of the speakers identified their church affiliations. Marjorie Rogers, who also addressed the board, presented them with a petition of 2,318 signatures urging the board to adopt accurate textbooks. She claimed that the petition was circulated in Bible study classes at various churches.

At the end of the public comment, a motion was made to adopt the recommended textbooks. Following this was a motion to include an insert in the texts:

> This textbook contains material on evolution. Evolution is a theory, not a fact, regarding the origin of living things. This material should be approached with an open mind, studied carefully, and critically considered.

After the meeting, Joe Redden, Superintendent of Schools, claimed that the insert was not a disclaimer but merely reinforced what the texts already convey. He stated, "The books do not present Darwin's theory, the theory of evolution, as fact."

Despite this statement, the move was met with displeasure by many present. Marjorie Rogers claimed she was only "partly satisfied with the disclaimer." She also stated she would ask the board to more clearly define alternative explanations for the origin of life and to establish an elective science course that would explore the controversies surrounding the issue. Others felt the board had overreacted to pressure from evangelical parents. One parent claimed, "In an attempt to placate the fundamentalists, they have insulted the intelligence of our children." Another said, "I'm shocked Cobb County is handling it this way."

Unfortunately for the Cobb Board, this displeasure meant the issue was far from over. Within weeks, the American Civil Liberties Union, on behalf of Jeffery Selman, a Cobb parent, filed suit to have the insert removed. In referring to his suit, Selman claimed, "The side for scientific education was asleep. We felt safe. This is the 21st century, for crying out loud. We can't go back to this" (MacDonald, September 7, 2002). A spate of news coverage followed both the adoption and the filing of the suit. And soon after, another petition began circulating among parents that demanded the board maintain "traditional academic standards and integrity in the sciences."

Within this climate, the board still needed to take action on their Theory of Origins policy. In late August, they proposed to change the policy so that evolution would not be banned from the lower grade levels and discussion of "disputed views" would be allowed. The board voted to allocate 30 days to consider such a change. This 30-day period only further instigated those on either side of the dispute and provided additional time for other interests to enter the fray.

In early September, John Calvert and William Harris, co-directors of Intelligent Design Network, held a seminar sponsored by the North Georgia chapter of the American Family Association. The seminar drew about 40 people to the Cobb County Civic Center. The purpose of the seminar was to expose Cobb County advocates to the arguments of intelligent design[4] and introduce the "wedge strategy."

The "wedge strategy" is attributed to Phillip Johnson, a retired University of California-Berkeley law professor who began the intelligent design (ID) movement with his 1991 book, *Darwin on Trial*. According to Johnson's (2000) book *The Wedge of Truth*, the "wedge strategy" outlines a five-year plan involving three ingredients: a) scientific research, writing, and publicity about ID; b) publicity and public opinion in favor of ID; and c) cultural confrontation and renewal. According to Johnson, "The 'Wedge of Truth' ... enables people to recognize that 'In the beginning was the Word' is as true scientifically as it is in every other respect" (Griffis, 2002, p. 37). And, it "seeks nothing less than the overthrow of materialism and its cultural legacies" (Griffis, 2002, p. 37).

In addition to the introduction of the "wedge strategy" in Cobb County, the National Academy of Sciences asked 30 scientists and physicians in Georgia to lobby the county to remove the textbook inserts. According to board member Betty Grey, the scientists and physicians began contacting board members individually by letter, email, and phone. Two days later, a group of 28 professors calling itself Georgia Scientists for Academic Freedom, petitioned the board and advised that "careful examination of evidence for Darwinian theory should be encouraged." Following this, a group of other Georgia professors submitted sets of petitions reinforcing the importance of evolution in science education.

The issue had quickly become the most polarized debate ever faced by the board. They became inundated with individual correspondence on the issue. The school superintendent, Joe Redden, received 39 emails during a two-week period about the board's actions. Board member, Betty Grey, said she received 173 email messages in one day. Additionally, the *Atlanta Journal and Constitution* provided forums for those interested in expressing their views on the topic.

The forums drew significant participation on both sides of the issue. Some of the comments made include:

- I do not want my child subjected to a curriculum that ignores the key scientific principles which govern our universe.
- I personally think that it is abundantly clear that the hypocritical religious tyrants who believe in the non-scientific ideas of creationism will not be satisfied until their fanciful, nonsensical opinions

are forced upon all of society to the exclusion of all other contrary evidence.

- I have already had to remind teachers and a principal to keep their religious views in check. I don't want my child to have any more potential opportunity to have Christian views shoved down his throat.
- Why should we fear this [policy] so strongly? I would only say that those that are so adamantly opposed to any view but their own, are pushing their own "religion."
- I for one don't want my child being told day after day that they are nothing more than a step on the evolutionary ladder towards some higher being and that this is the only explanation of our existence.... May God bless you all in your pursuit of truth and happiness (*Atlanta Journal and Constitution* Forums: Teaching the Origins of Life, September 26, 2002 and Reaction to Cobb School Board Decision, September 28, 2002)!

When the board finally met to vote on a policy change, board chair, Curt Johnston, began by stating,

> We seem to have been caught in the middle of a dispute between various parties who apparently want to use our curriculum to promote their own views. Much of what has been said in the media regarding our decisions has been misleading, so we wanted to take a moment to clear the air.... We felt the need to revise the policy because the existing policy could be read to restrict the teaching of evolution or to require teaching creationism.... To the parents and the citizens of Cobb County ... we are willing to listen, but we are not willing to cater to any particular viewpoint where genuine doubt exists, be it scientific or religious. (Johnston, September 27, 2002, Atlanta Journal and Constitution Online)

Following the statement, the board voted unanimously to adopt a policy that reads:

> It is the educational philosophy of the Cobb County School District to provide a broad based curriculum; therefore, the Cobb County School District believes that discussion of disputed views of academic subjects is a necessary element of providing a balanced education, including the study of the origin of species. The subject remains an area of intense interest, research, and discussion among scholars. As a result, the study of this subject shall be handled in accordance with this policy and with objectivity and good judgment on the part of teachers, taking into account the age and maturity level of their students.

Rather than clarify the board's position on the teaching of evolution and creationism, the resulting policy appeared to create more confusion. Asked to explain the board's intentions, Chair Curt Johnston responded, "Just what the policy says, no more, no less." Further, Johnston wasn't sure whether the new language allowed creationism to be discussed. Lynn Searcy, another board member commented, "The policy, the language of the policy, speaks for itself." According to Glenn Brock, the board's attorney, the language of the policy was carefully chosen with the purpose of keeping the school district within legal bounds.

Coverage of the vote by the *New York Times* stated, "Georgia School Board Requires Balance of Evolution and Bible" (Zernike, 2002), whereas the *Atlanta Journal and Constitution* stated, "School Board Chief Says New Policy Reflects 'Diversity of Opinion' but Doesn't Promote Specific Views" (Johnston, 2002). Others appeared as confused as the journalists. One high school parent stated, "This policy is still not clear. It appears to be intentionally unclear in an attempt to circumvent the laws of our country" (MacDonald, 2002). A biology teacher in the county said, "It doesn't say anything. I don't think it will have any impact whatsoever on my personal teaching" (Taylor, 2002). Another science teacher said he and his peers "were experiencing a mixture of frustration, embarrassment and disappointment." He went to say, "They made teaching science very, very difficult" (Taylor, 2002).

PERSONALISM AND INTEREST GROUPS

Mawhinney (2001) states that much of interest group theory is predicated on the concept that "a free and active group system was critical in a democracy" (p. 189). For example, David Truman (1971) believed interest groups to be at the center of politics. Truman argued that the complexity of government provided a multiplicity of points of access to governmental decisions. And, "this diversity assures various ways for interest groups to participate in the formation of policy, and this variety is a flexible, stabilizing element" (p. 519). These scholars believe the diversity among interests is evidence of a capacity for obtaining broad representation of the beliefs and values of U.S. citizens (Mawhinney, 2001).

In addition to this representative function, many political scientists also believe interest groups serve other important functions in our democracy. Mansbridge (1992) claims

> Decisionmakers, including citizens and their representatives, use the information and insights that interest groups feed into the deliberative process to decide what is best for them individually and narrowly, what is best for

the larger groups of which they are a part, what is best for the nation as a whole, and, on the basis of all these considerations, how they want the polity to act. (p. 35)

Wuthnow (1991) also states that these interest groups contribute to the cultural health of our society. And Putnam (1995) argues that these groups, focused on representation of their interests, develop skills of communication and collaboration. These skills then contribute to strengthening our social connectiveness. Thus, these scholars believe that interest groups, through their deliberative function and social aspects, serve to strengthen our society and the conduct of democracy.

However, much of the work of these scholars is predicated on the notion that interest groups do in fact operate as groups. That is, these scholars see interest groups as organizations allowing people to work together to advance collective beliefs.[5] The organization, in the view of these scholars, acts to represent its members in the policymaking process. Recent evidence suggests that this is not how interest groups currently operate.

Since the late 1980s and early 1990s, interest groups have shifted their organizational lobbying capacity from centralized, lobbyist-oriented offices, to field-based operations (Goldstein, 1999; Opfer, 2001). Political parties, groups, and campaigns now mobilize *individuals*. As Goldstein argues,

> The growth of the mass media has made it easier for representatives and constituents to communicate with each other, and technological advances have made it feasible for groups to generate, virtually instantaneously, thousands and even hundreds of thousands of letters, faxes, phone calls, and telegrams when an issue or bill comes to a head (p. 24).

Rosenstone and Hansen (1993), in a 30 year time series study of Roper survey data, demonstrate that the organizational strategies of interest groups play a crucial role in determining individual participation in politics. As they conclude, "The strategic choices of political leaders—their determination of who and when to mobilize—determine the shape of political participation in America" (Rosenstone & Hansen, 1993, p. 36). This shape of political participation is increasingly more individualistic.

Verba, Schlozman, and Brady (1995) found that the proportion of Americans making issue-based contact with national policymakers doubled, from 11% of the population in 1967, to 22% of the population in 1987. Additionally, Goldstein (1999), in an analysis of National Election Study data, found that more individuals are contacting Congress to convey their feelings on issues and that this contact has been sharply increas-

Table 4.1.   Percentage of Respondents, by Religious Tradition that have Heard a Sermon or Participated in a Church Discussion Group on a Political Issue during a 12-month Period

Evangelical (%)	Mainline Protestant (%)	African American Protestant (%)	Catholic (%)	Jewish (%)	Other (%)
59	64	70	59	64	62

Source: Wuthnow and Evan (2002).

ing since the early 1990s. *Individuals* are now more likely to participate when *interest groups* recruit and mobilize them to participate.

Religious interests play a key role in mobilizing individuals for political participation. Wuthnow and Evans (2002) show that many clergy feel it is appropriate to engage directly in political activities and encourage participation from the pulpit and by arranging special forums, Sunday school classes, or seminars at which key political issues are discussed. As Table 4.1 indicates, the percentage of parishioners who have heard sermons or participated in church discussion groups on key political issues is significant across faith traditions.

Many of the congregants, targeted by clergy, do then engage in political activities. Table 4.2, based on findings from Wuthnow and Evan's (2002) study, show that close to one third of all respondents claimed to have contacted an elected official within a 12 month period. Additionally, one third of respondents in evangelical and mainline protestant traditions indicated they would like to see religious leaders forming political movements. And, more than 50% of respondents in both of these traditions would like to see people from their tradition have more influence in shaping opinion on important social issues. Thus, not only are interest groups in general turning to more individualistic forms of political participation, religious interests appear particularly suited, both in belief and structure, to pursue grassroots tactics.

Table 4.2.   Percentage of Respondents Who Contacted an Elected Official in the Previous 12 Months, by Tradition

Evangelical (%)	Mainline Protestant (%)	African American Protestant (%)	Catholic (%)	Jewish (%)	Other (%)
30	32	22	27	67	27

Source: Winthrow and Evan (2002).

The Cobb County evolution case indicates that a byproduct of this grassroots, individual participation is a politics of personalism. Cupitt (1999) defines personalism as "the conviction that persons and personal relations have somehow *got* to be the ultimate" (p.22, emphasis in original). Those who ascribe to this conviction "want if they can to bring everything down to persons, personal experience, personal qualities and personal relationships. Anything else tends to strike [them] as 'abstract' and boring" (Culpit, 1999, p. 22). Personal beliefs about how the world came into being became the standard by which political actors influenced the Cobb County School Board and also judged the decisions made. Rarely did interest group actors show respect for, or even acknowledge, the viewpoint or democratic aspirations of others. That is, they seldom mentioned a wider impact of the textbook adoption and subsequent "Origins" policy than on their own child, and when they did it was with a vague reference to "the children" or "we". In essence, they lacked a grammar of democracy that acknowledges the impact of education policy on all children in a school, district, state, or nation.

This personalistic aspect of the Cobb County case is not unique. Thirty-seven years ago, Rieff (1966) warned that the U. S. was undergoing a cultural revolution—a widespread turn to psychological thinking and corresponding abandonment of morality and public virtue. More recently, Cupitt (1999) has contended that the rise of personalism coincides with the celebrity culture of postmodernity. "In Britain and the United States it is today notoriously difficult to interest the public in any idea at all except *via* a personality—and that includes political ideas" (p. 24). The focus then by Cobb County interests on the personal aspects of policymaking may be part of a larger trend toward a personalism orientation. People with such motivation became more politically involved in order to vocalize and attain their personal needs.

This personalism by interest groups has serious implications for school board policy making and democracy in general. Fiorina (1999) argues that while the mobilization of individuals increases the participatory nature of our democracy, it "increasingly has put politics into the hands of unrepresentative participators—extreme voices in the larger political debate" (p. 409). No matter what the sample studied—state convention delegates, national convention delegates, financial contributors, campaign activists, or candidates themselves—individual participants come disproportionately from the extremes of the opinion distribution (see, i.e., Brown, Powell, & Wilcox, 1995; Erikson, 1990; McCann, 1996; Miller & Jennings, 1986).

Not only do the activists take extreme positions, they also take these positions on issues that the majority does not care about. Verba and Nie (1972) and Verba, Scholzman, and Brady (1995) report that participants care about different issues than nonparticipants. And, because politicians today are more accessible due to e-mail, fax, voicemail, etc., committed activists have less need to broaden their appeals in order to mobilize a mass following than was previously necessary.

School board members may be especially susceptible to personalistic appeals within this accessibility context for two reasons. First, voter turnout is so low in most board elections that every vote counts.[6] In this context, a pulpit appeal for or against a school board member, made in a few large-sized congregations could determine the outcome of a school board election. Second, the nature of school board business—education—requires responsiveness on the part of board members. Delay in responsiveness could mean disadvantaging a student or students.

Communitarian scholars have long argued that groups based only on a junction of personal preferences will amount simply to a collection of individuals pursuing private ends. Their members will only practice personal gratification and not act for a common good. Rieff (1966) claims that personalism corrodes any sense of obligation that emanates from outside the self. Thus, democratic participation becomes simply another "personal experience" that one could take or leave. For educational policymaking, the implication is that if the issue under discussion has no personal bearing, attention and action will not result. People become concerned, not with the public good and social policy aspects of education, but only with the individual impact. They ask, "What role should schools play in helping me?" and never ask "What role should schools play in helping us?"

Personalism impacts not only commitment to democratic ideals but also to democratic institutions themselves. Lichterman (1996) argues, "Personalism upholds a personal self that lives with ambivalence towards, and often in tension with, the institutional or communal standards that surround it" (p. 6). It becomes less important whether policies violate the separation of church and state or impinge on the rights and beliefs of others. Personalistic actors are concerned with achieving their own visions even at the expense of others. They are willing to rely on "wedge" strategies and "overthrow … cultural legacies" to obtain their own ends. Institutions serve utilitarian functions only. People use schools and school boards for their own ends; schools and school boards do not exist to support communities.

Further, personalism reproduces itself. In Wuthnow's (1991) study of volunteerism in the U. S., he concluded that personalism limits the bonds of obligation that volunteers could produce with those they help and society in general. Practicing compassion because it feels good did not promote a sense of community but simply more individualism. Protesting for or against the teaching of evolution may result in individual satisfaction through participation and perhaps the resulting outcomes, but it will not lead to a collective sense of efficacy and investment concerning the school curriculum.

The activism undertaken by personalistic motivations in individuals is usually short-lived and results in shifting public attention to issues. Bellah, Madsen, Sullivan, Swidler and Tipton (1985), in their study of individualism and commitment, suggested that if activists did not define their commitments in terms of communal obligations, those commitments had a precarious basis and did not last long. Personalism might justify impulsive protest but such a political commitment easily fades, only to reemerge in some other short-lived personal enthusiasm. Thus, while interests in Cobb County may have taken intensive action at the time of the textbook and policy adoption, the chance that any would continue to remain engaged in order to determine the impact on actual classroom practice is unlikely.

POLICY NONSENSE

Beyond the impact of personalistic interests on democratic ideals and institutions, the actions of these activists have more immediate and observable impacts on the policy that emerges from the conflict. The fragmentation of the policymaking process due to individual, personalistic participation does not result in cohesive policy. The personalistic politics that were evident in Cobb County created polarized policy positions and compromise was not evident. As a result, the Cobb County Board crafted a policy of nonsense. As Bruce Alberts, president of the National Academy of Sciences, commented to the board, "You're just taking the guts out of biology to the point where it makes no sense" (MacDonald, 2002).

The *American Heritage Dictionary of English Language* provides five definitions for nonsense, three of which apply to the Cobb County policy:

1. Words or signs having no intelligible meaning;
2. Subject matter, behavior, or language that is foolish or absurd;
3. Matter of little or no importance or usefulness.

In the first instance, the board endorsed neither evolution nor creationism. They crafted a policy that embodied this contradiction and the result was a message that conveyed no meaning—board members were unsure of the policy's potential impact, journalists conveyed contradictory accounts of the policy's meaning, and observers believed it said nothing.

In the second instance, the board's actions appeared foolish or absurd. Many interests on both side of the issue suggested:

- It will make the community look bad.
- They've made a mockery of science.
- Of course there isn't such thing as evolution—the Neanderthal school boards in Georgia prove it.
- Will the Cobb County approach inspire students, confuse them, or just generate more apathy about their education?
- While the Cobb County School Board is at it why not declare that the earth is at the center of the Universe and that the sun revolves around the earth.
- Cobb County really looks backward now!
- Hats off to the Cobb County School Board for finding yet another way to cripple their students with ignorance.

Thus, not only was the policy without meaning and contradictory, many believed the passage of the policy to be both frustrating and embarrassing.

Finally, the Cobb County policy is nonsensical because it is counterproductive to a desired end. Curt Johnston, board chairman, claimed, "Our teachers are nervous about what they can talk about. This will clarify things." In reality though, the resulting policy was of little guidance to teachers. It states that the policy relies on "objectivity and good judgment on the part of teachers." Thus, teachers were left wondering what they should be teaching in regards to evolution and creationism. As the *Atlanta Journal and Constitution* concluded, "Faced with equally impassioned pleas to allow creationism to be taught in the classroom or to ban it, the Cobb County school board chose to do neither" (Taylor, September 23, 2002).

CONCLUSIONS

The Cobb County School Board faced a multitude of individuals, mobilized by interest groups, who were concerned with how evolution and creationism should be taught. These participants acted, not to advance a collective belief or out of obligation to education for the whole, but out of individual compulsion or personalism. The conflicting and contradictory nature of the interests did not (a) provide information to improve decision-making (Mansbridge, 1992), (b) increase collaboration (Putnam, 1995), or c) contribute to the cultural health of Cobb County (Wuthnow, 1991). The interests involved did not exert a positive influence on policy-making by the board as some research has surmised they might. Instead, they created a paradoxical and contradictory situation that resulted in policy nonsense.

Participatory democratic institutions can be expected to have salutary consequences only if those engaged are representative of the interests and values of the larger community. When engagement is largely dominated by minority viewpoints, problems of unrepresentativeness arise. How might school superintendents counteract these personalistic tendencies by policy actors so that the resulting board political processes and policies are more representative? Ironically, Fiorina (1999) suggests that the answer is actually more civic involvement; to raise various forms of civic engagement to levels where extreme voices are diluted. Thus school superintendents should attend to district characteristics and processes that limit participation and focus on ways to channel participation in useful ways.

To increase participation, superintendents might first consider whether there are kinds of political engagements that depend upon and reinforce individuality rather than just accommodating it or reining it in. Lichterman (1996) has claimed that "Personalism develops in a kind of community ... in which people create and practice norms of highly individualized expression" (p. 7). If this is the case, superintendents must assess the political arrangements of school boards that reinforce these norms of individualized expression.

Hess and Leal (2001) suggest that opportunities to participate are partly the consequence of community characteristics and may have developed over the years with little planning and coordination. For fear of being overwhelmed by interests, large districts have, for example, limited involvement to only a few access points. Also, Southern districts have traditionally been more hierarchical and less participatory than the national norm. While these districts may have changed enrollment practices to address their past history of limiting access to some populations, they may not have addressed the institutional structures put in place to limit interaction with their communities (Plank & Ginsberg, 1990). In contrast, districts with large percentages of African Americans and those with lower student teacher ratios tend to offer community members more access to decision—making (Hess & Leal, 2001).

Chubb and Moe (1990) propose that school districts have developed rigidly controlled processes to resist interest groups. In essence, as interest group pressure has increased in districts, districts have developed institutional arrangements that limit community access to decision—making. There may be two institutional arrangements that reinforce individualized expression in school board processes. The first, and most obvious, is the structure of the public comment period at meetings. Many boards allot specific time periods for public comment. In Cobb County, they allot 30 minutes. Individuals sign up to speak and the allotted time is divided among those who sign up. The result of this arrangement is a succession of individuals given little time for substantive input. The arrangement reinforces individual communication and provides no forum for collaborative or joint input—a group representative gets the same time as an individual unless group members all sign up and turn over their time to their representative. Further, the amount of public comment allowed in any one board meeting limits the amount of participation by the public. This time limit becomes especially problematic when contested issues arise.

Second, the use of e-mail and phone calls to contact board members increases the individuality of public sentiment. Board members are available by e-mail and phone in order to appear responsive to their constituents. However, these forms of communication also effect the perceptions of the board members themselves. They come to weigh the importance of an issue based on the number of e-mails and phone calls rather than the content of those messages. E-mails and phone calls get characterized as "for" or "against." For example, when Superintendent Joe Redden was asked to characterize this kind of contact, he claimed it was "almost evenly divided, pro- and anti-evolution." And Chairman Curt Johnston said, "I'm just weighing [them]." Thus, these forms of communication do not provide information useful to the policy deliberation but are only individual "votes" on the policy itself. School superintendents need to evaluate how their district's characteristics and processes may support or impede active political participation by community members.

In addition to district characteristics and institutional norms that encourage personalistic politics, school superintendents must also examine the costs of participation for the average parent or citizen. The demands on time and energy required for participation are sufficiently severe that those willing to pay the costs are disproportionately of extreme viewpoints. Fiorina (1999) argues that to combat this, we must lower the costs of participation. The current structure of school board meetings require those interested in participating to leave their children at home, come to a weeknight board meeting, and sit for hours in order to speak for one minute. School superintendents concerned with improving board policy processes must attend to the ability and willingness of the average citizen to participate within this structure. This may mean reconsidering when people are allowed to participate, the forms of participation, the timing of participation, and the amount of time given to participation.

Further, superintendents must help board members understand the motives of those who try to influence them. Board members must recognize that there is nothing wrong with those who do not participate; rather, there is something unusual about those who do. Fiorina (1999), referring to the Chicago machine's attitude toward self-selectors, claims that activists are all too often people "nobody sent" (p. 416). Given the increasingly individualistic nature of interest group influence and the personalistic tendencies of this type of participation, it is essential that board members recognize that the moderate center is not well-represented in contemporary politics. The average citizens are frustrated with government because they too often see the participants locked in a battle over unattractive and unrealistic alternatives. The result is unnecessary conflict, animosity, delay, gridlock, and policy nonsense. Board members must be educated by superintendents to resist the temptation to acquiesce to what Ehrenhalt (1998) termed "quarrelsome blowhards" in order to truly represent the nonparticipating majority.

NOTES

1. See for example Mansbridge, 1992; Mawhinney, 2001; Putnam, 1995; Truman, 1971; Wuthnow, 1991.
2. See for example Berry, 1989; Fiorina, 1999; Heclo, 1989; Knoke, 1990; Lowi, 1969; Wilson, 1990.
3. See for example Goldstein, 1999; Opfer, 2001.
4. According to the website for the Intelligent Design Network, Intelligent Design is a scientific disagreement with the claim of evolutionary theory that natural phenomena are not designed. ID claims that natural laws and chance alone are not adequate to explain all natural phenomena. Evidence that is empirically detectable in nature suggests that design is the best current explanation for a variety of natural systems, particularly irreducibly complex living systems. Intelligent Design is an intellectual movement that includes a scientific research program for investigating intelligent causes and that challenges naturalistic explanations of origins which currently drive science education and research.
5. David Truman's (1971) widely cited definition of interest groups makes this assumption clear. He defines an interest group as "any group that, on the basis of one or more shared attitudes, makes certain claims upon other groups in the society for the establishment, maintenance or enhancement of forms of behavior that are implied by the shared attitudes" (p. 21).
6. According to the Secretary of State's election data for Georgia, voter turnout in school board elections has averaged 8-11% in the last two election cycles. While this can mean a win by as much as 7,000 votes in Cobb County, the number of votes needed to win can decrease to under one hundred in city or small county districts. For example, the largest margin of victory by a Marietta City School Board member (located in Cobb County) in the 2002 election was 200 votes. It is also important to note that one of the churches involved in the Cobb County evolution policy debate, Johnson Ferry Baptist, has more than 5,000 members.

REFERENCES

Arocha, Z. (1993). The religious rights march into public school governance. *The School Administrator, 50*(9), 8-15.

Forum: Reaction to Cobb School Board decision. (2002, September 28). *Atlanta Journal and Constitution.* Retrieved September 30, 2002, from http://www.accessatlanta.com/ajc/metro/cobb/opinion/decisionforum.html

Forum: Teaching the origins of life. (2002, September 26). *Atlanta Journal and Constitution.* Retrieved September 30, 2002, from http://www.accessatlanta.com/ajc/metro/cobb/opinion/oldforums/0902evolution.html

Bellah, R., Madsen, R., Sullivan, W., Swidler, A. & Tipton, S. (1985). *Habits of the heart.* Berkeley: University of California Press.

Berry, J. (1989). *The interest group society.* Glenview, IL: Scott Foreman.

Bjork, L., & Lindle, J. (2001). Superintendents and interest groups. *Educational Policy, 15*(1), 76-91.

Brown, C., Powell, L., & Wilcox, C. (1995). *Serious money.* Cambridge, England: Cambridge University Press.

Cobb County Board of Elections and Registration. (2002). *Election results and statistics.* Retrieved October 26, 2002, from http://www.cobbelections.org

Cobb County School District. (1999). *Regulations for textbook selection and adoption, OCGA 20-2-1010, Revised November 10, 1999.* Retrieved April 17, 2002, from http://www.cobb.k12.ga.us/~boardpolicies/ifaa_r.htm

Cobb County School District. (1979). *Regulations for theories of origin policy. OCGA, 20-2-50; 20-2-57; 20-2-59, adopted December 12, 1979, revised April 28, 1983, August 8, 1984, August 9, 1995.* Retrieved on April 17, 2002, from http://www.cobb.k12.ga.us/~boardpolicies/idbd_r.htm

Cupitt, D. (1999). The new labour project: Modernization and personalism. *Political Theology, 2*(1), 19-26.

Danzberger, J. (1994). Governing the nation's schools, the case for restructuring local school boards. *Phi Delta Kappan, 75*(5), 367-373.

Ehrenhalt, A. (1998, January). The increasing irrelevance of Congress. *Legislative Studies Section Newsletter, 16.*

Erikson, R. (1990). Roll calls, reputations, and representations in the U.S. Senate. *Legislative Studies Quarterly, 15,* 630.

Feuerstein, A., & Opfer, V. D. (1998). School board chairmen and school superintendents: An analysis of perceptions concerning special interest groups and educational governance. *The Journal of School Leadership, 8*(4) 373-398.

Fiorina, M. (1999). Extreme voices: A dark side of civic engagement. In T. Skocpol & M. Fiorina (Eds.), *Civic engagement in American democracy.* Washington, DC: Brookings Institute Press.

Glass, T., Bjork, L., & Brunner, C. C. (2000). *The 2000 study of the American superintendency: A look at the superintendent of education in the new millennium.* Arlington, VA: American Association of School Administrators.

Goldstein, K. (1999). *Interest groups, lobbying, and participation in America.* New York: Cambridge University Press.

Griffis, K. (2002, May 22-28). God vs. Darwin: Cobb County shows why mixing science, religion and politics is a really bad idea. *Creative Loafing, 31*(2), 35-39.

Heclo, H. (1989). The emerging regime. In R. Harris & S. Milkis (Eds.), *Remaking American politics*. Boulder, CO: Westview Press.

Hess, F. M., & Leal, D. L. (2001). The opportunity to engage: How race, class, and institutions structure access to educational deliberation. *Educational Policy, 15*(3), 474-490.

Intelligent Design Network. (2003). *Intelligent design*. Retrieved September 29, 2003, from http://www.intelligentdesignnetwork.org

Johnson, P. (1991). *Darwin on trial*. Downers Grove, IL: InterVarsity Press.

Johnson, P. (2000). *The wedge of truth*. Downers Grove, IL: InterVarsity Press.

Johnston, C. (2002, September 27). School board chief says new policy reflects "diversity of opinion"' but doesn't promote specific views. *Atlanta Journal and Constitution Online*. Retrieved September 30, 2002, from http://www.access atlanta.com/ajc/metro/cobb/0902/27johnston.html

Knoke, D. (1990). *Organizing for collective action*. New York: Aldine de Gruyter.

Lichterman, P. (1996). *The search for political community: American activists reinventing commitment*. Cambridge, England: Cambridge University Press.

Lowi, T. (1969). *The end of liberalism: Ideology, policy, and the crisis of public authority*. New York: W. W. Norton.

MacDonald, M. (2002, September 7). Cobb dads enter fray over evolution in schools. *Atlanta Journal and Constitution Online*. Retrieved September 30, 2002, from http://www.accessatlanta.com/ajc/metro/cobb/0902/08parents.html

MacDonald, M. (2002, September 20). Group of Georgia science profs urges Cobb to allow other origin of life views. *Atlanta Journal and Constitution Online*. Retrieved September 30, 2002 from http://www.accessatlanta.com/ajc/metro/cobb/0902/21evolution.html

MacDonald, M. (2002, September 26). Cobb vote on evolution in spotlight. *Atlanta Journal and Constitution Online*. Retrieved September 30, 2002 from http://www.accessatlanta.com/ajc/metro/cobb/0902/26evolution.html

Mansbridge, J. (1992). A deliberative theory of interest representation. In M. Petracca (Ed.), *The politics of interests* (pp.32-57). Boulder, CO: Westview.

Mawhinney, H. (2001). Theoretical approaches to understanding interest groups. *Educational Policy, 15*(1), 187-214.

McCann, J. (1996). Presidential nomination activists and political representation: A view from the active minority studies. In W. Mayer (Ed.), *In pursuit of the White House*. Chatham, NJ: Chatham House.

McCarthy, M. (1996). People of faith as political activists in public schools. *Education and Urban Society, 28*(3), 308-326.

Miller, W., & Jennings, M. K. (1986). *Parties in transition*. New York: Russell Sage.

Opfer, V. D. (2001). Beyond self-interest: Education interest groups in the U.S. Congress. *Educational Policy, 15*(1), 135-152.

Plank, D. N., & Ginsberg, R. (Eds.). (1990). *Southern cities, southern school: Public education in the urban South*. New York: Greenwood.

Putnam, R. (1995). Bowling alone: America's declining social capital. *Journal of Democracy, 6*, 63-78.

Rieff, P. (1966). *The triumph of the therapeutic: The uses of faith after Freud*. London: Chatto and Windus.

Rosenstone, S., & Hansen, J. (1993). *Mobilization, participation, & democracy in America*. New York: Macmillan.

Stake, R. (1995). *The art of case study research*. Thousand Oaks, CA: Sage.

Taylor, M. (2002, September 23). Cobb board to clarify how origin of life can be taught. *Atlanta Journal and Constitution Online*. Retrieved September 30, 2002, from http://www.accessatlanta.com/ajc/metro/cobb/0902/23evolution.html

Taylor, M. (2002, September 28). Cobb teachers ponder new evolution rule. *Atlanta Journal and Constitution Online*. Retrieved September 30, 2002, from http://www.accessatlanta.com/ajc/metro/cobb/0902/28teachers.html

Truman, D. (1971). *The governmental process* (2nd ed.). New York: Knopf.

Verba, S., & Nie, N. (1972). *Participation in America*. New York: Harper and Row.

Verba, S., Schlozman, K., & Brady, H. (1995). *Voice and equality*. Cambridge, MA: Harvard University Press.

Wilson, G. (1990). *Interest groups*. Oxford, England: Basil Blackwell.

Wuthnow, R. (1991). *Acts of compassion: Caring for others and helping ourselves*. Princeton, NJ: Princeton University Press.

Wuthnow, R., & Evans, J. (2002). *The quiet hand of God: Faith-based activism and the Public role of mainline protestantism*. Berkeley: University of California Press.

Yin, R. (1989). *Case study research: Design and method*. Newbury Park, CA: Sage.

Zernike, K. (2002, August 23). Georgia school board requires balance of evolution and Bible. *The New York Times Online*. Retrieved September 30, 2002 from, http://www.nytimes.com

CHAPTER 5

A-PEERANCES CAN BE DECEIVING

Superintendents, School Boards, and the Transformation of Intentions

Peggy L. Placier, Douglas R. Hager, and Angela M. Hull

School reformers rarely find that reform implementation completely fulfills their original hopes. In our study, we examined the sponsors' intentions for, and subsequent local reactions to, a report comparing school districts in Missouri. Since 2000, the annual Public Education Evaluation Report (PEER) has presented data on Missouri districts grouped according to percentages of low-income students, per-pupil expenditures, and enrollment. For each group, the report displays scores on the Missouri Assessment Program (MAP) as well as dropout, graduation, mobility, and attendance rates. The PEER sponsors hoped that it would propel community action for school improvement. In this study, we explored how superintendents and school boards transformed those intentions. Moreover, our findings challenged the popular perspective that the public reporting of school performance will foment school accountability by transferring the impetus for change from school leadership to the lay public.

The Politics of Leadership: Superintendents and School Boards in Changing Times, 95–115
Copyright © 2005 by Information Age Publishing
All rights of reproduction in any form reserved.

THEORETICAL FRAMEWORK

According to Dorn (1998), implementation of accountability systems, including the public reporting of performance data, has altered the relationship between school administrators and their communities. Rather than affirming the expert claims of superintendents, statistics are now often used to question and even counter said claims. To date, however, this aspect of the accountability policy context has received relatively limited attention (see Dorn, 1998; Starr, 1987). The aim of our study was to examine this relationship in the micro-level context of a school district.

To achieve our aim, we applied a sociological framework called the transformation of intentions (Hall, 1995; Hall & McGinty, 1997; Placier, Hall, McKendall, & Cockrell, 2000). This framework, articulated by Peter M. Hall (1995), is well-suited to the study of policy processes in which persons at one place and time intend to influence the actions of persons at another place and time, but the ensuing process is nonlinear, ambiguous, and contingent on unforeseen or uncontrollable factors. Policy, as Hall (1995) defines it, is a process, rather than a concrete text. Typical policy discourse divides the process into stages such as "formation" or "implementation," implying that policy is a thing made in one place and time and transmitted elsewhere to be practiced. Hall (1995) and others have argued, rather, that policy is *constituted* when actors representing multiple, perhaps divergent or conflicting, interests and roles interact under conditions of uncertainty and ambiguity (Estes & Edmonds, 1981). Policy is a process of the transformation of intentions.

The transformation of intentions, in the usual sense, occurs when actors aim their actions at a problem for announced purposes, such as transforming an intention to reduce dropout rates into an "at risk" program. In other cases, intentions may be implicit, covert, or unannounced; but one can observe their symbolic representations in policy processes. Transformation can be a *double entendre* in which some actors' intentions subvert or resist others' intentions. New or previously unrecognized intentions may emerge, or actors may have intentions for policy other than the resolution of problems, such as advancing their careers, reputations, or influence (Hall & McGinty, 1997; Placier et al., 2000), or mitigating possible negative consequences of externally mandated policies and/or programs (Scribner, Hager, & Warne, 2002).

Nevertheless, the indeterminacy of the policy process should not be exaggerated, because it usually occurs in an organizational context entailing established institutional conventions, structural linkages among policy actors and organizations, and unequal distribution of power. Education reform is generally a top-down phenomenon in which policy initiators have advantages based on their structural positioning. For instance, legislators have legal authority to enact policies that affect teachers, even though teachers may attempt to reinterpret, resist, or avoid them.

As we found, superintendent-school board relationships are quite interesting with regard to the transformation of intentions, because these relationships are so complex. The literature often focuses on tensions surrounding the unclearly differentiated roles and powers of superintendents and boards (Ferguson & Nochelski, 1996; Feuerstein & Opfer, 1998; Grady & Bryant, 1989, 1991; Hentges, 1986; LaRocque & Coleman, 1993; Newman & Brown, 1993; Tallerico, 1989; Zlotkin, 1993). External policy initiatives, introduced into the context of these relationships, reveal the dynamics of local school governance (Hentges, 1986; Newman & Brown, 1993; Tallerico, 1989).

DESIGN AND METHODS

We linked three different investigations into one study that followed the PEER process through time. We began with a history of the policy originators' intentions for PEER and the process of its construction. Next we analyzed responses to a superintendent survey administered several months after the first annual PEER's release. The survey responses, in turn, allowed us to target specific districts and to generate questions for qualitative case studies of how superintendents and school boards responded to PEER. This chapter includes one case study.

PEER Development Process

Data sources for this segment were texts generated during construction of the first PEER in 1999-2000, that expressed the intentions of its sponsor, the Partnership for Outstanding Schools (the Partnership). The Partnership contracted with the Consortium for Educational Policy Analysis (CEPA) at the University of Missouri-Columbia to develop the report. At the time, two of the co-authors worked with CEPA. The third co-author worked in public relations for the Partnership. However, both CEPA and the Partnership have since been dissolved. We have conducted our study of the effects of PEER independent of these organizations.

Superintendent Survey

CEPA mailed a survey to all Missouri superintendents ($N = 522$) approximately six months after release of the first PEER. The instrument included 25 Likert-type and 14 open-ended items. We analyzed written responses to these open-ended questions:

1. What do you understand to be the primary purpose(s) of PEER?
2. Given your answer, has PEER accomplished this (or worked toward this)?
3. In what ways has PEER been used in your district?
4. Who (e.g., school board members, parents, business leaders, etc.) has used PEER?

The number of returned surveys was 215 (41%). Some were returned with no responses on the open-ended items; 174 were usable for our study. Of these, 11 respondents did not identify their districts, but we can say that superintendents from districts with lower than average percentages of students eligible for the federal free/reduced lunch program (FRL) were over-represented. Few superintendents of small, rural K-8 school districts responded. Therefore, the respondents did not mirror the distribution of districts in the state as a whole. Another limitation of the survey was that, despite reassurances of confidentiality, superintendents knew that CEPA had worked on PEER, which may have made them cautious in their responses or disinclined to respond at all.

Qualitative Case Studies

Responses on the survey were brief and did not give us a thorough sense of the superintendents' thinking or social contexts; therefore, we followed up the survey with district case studies. We identified districts based on the survey responses (positive or negative). From these, we selected 10 that represented a variety of social contexts and that were accessible. We mailed information about the study and informed consent forms to superintendents and school board presidents, and began the study with those who volunteered in response either to this mailing or to follow-up telephone calls. We used snowball sampling; for example, during the first interviews we asked interviewees for suggestions of other districts that might inform our study. From these, we purposefully sampled districts that would provide comparisons and contrasts with the initial set, and invited them to participate.

In this chapter, we focus on one district, Railton, in order to detail the micro-level processes at work in transforming the intentions of PEER. The case study was constructed from several data sources. We interviewed the superintendent and school board president, using an interview protocol focusing on the local context, superintendent-board relationships, perceptions and reactions to PEER, and ideas about school reform. About 60 minutes in length, the interviews were audiotaped, transcribed, and coded for thematic analysis using a constant comparative method. We also collected local news reports, websites, and other district documents. In addition, we collected descriptive statistics on the district and its community.

POLITICAL CONTEXT OF PEER

In the wake of *A Nation at Risk* (National Commission on Excellence in Education, 1983), policies mandating "accountability" became the zeitgeist of public education reform. By the 1990s, a dramatic shift toward performance-based education evaluation began to spread across the country (Ravitch, 1995). The shift was strengthened by the Improving America's Schools Act of 1994 (U.S. Department of Education, 1994), which linked improved student performance with accountability. By 2000, some form of accountability system was in place in all 50 states (Goertz, Duffy, & LeFloch, 2001). Salient features of most policies were increased testing and public reporting of district and school performance data (Goertz et al., 2001; Linn, 2000). In 2001 many of these accountability mechanisms became federal law via the No Child Left Behind Act of 2001 (NCLB) (U.S. Department of Education, 2001).

Missouri's Excellence in Education Act (1985) mandated regular state evaluations of districts and a yearly multiple-choice achievement test. After years of testing, however, there was little improvement in many districts, and educators disparaged the test as an outmoded way of assessing learning. The accountability system that followed, the Outstanding Schools Act (OSA) (1993), was ostensibly inspired by a court judgment that the state's school finance system was unconstitutional. On the heels of this judgment, newly-elected Democratic Governor Mel Carnahan invited the head of the National Business Roundtable to meet with Missouri policymakers and business leaders to outline legislation folding school finance revisions into a systemic reform package. This group's positions mirrored the agenda of the Clinton administration's neoliberal education policies (Fowler, 1995; Smith & Scoll, 1995). The OSA required the State Board to adopt academic performance standards for Missouri students, dubbed the "Show-Me Standards" after the state's nickname (Placier, Walker, & Foster, 2002). The standards were in turn linked to performance-based assessments, the MAP.

The OSA explicitly forbade the State Board or Department of Education from using the MAP to compare schools and districts, although in other states such comparisons were required by similar legislation. This provision, supported by the state superintendent organization, frustrated advocates of a market view of accountability, in which parents as consumers should be able to compare school performance. Because state achievement data are publicly available, however, this did not preclude other organizations from comparing schools. And in fact, that is what happened with PEER.

FINDINGS

Intentions for PEER

The Partnership for Outstanding Schools (the Partnership) was a business-educator coalition funded by businesses and grants, founded with the purpose of advocating for implementation of the OSA. Some Missourians were skeptical about impending reforms, particularly the new funding formula, increased corporate taxes, and growing state control. The Partnership's mission was to "create support for locally-controlled education reforms" that would fulfill the intentions of the OSA. Eventually, the fervor around the OSA died down, and the Partnership needed to consider a change in its activities. Its president, a business leader and State Board member, learned that other states had reports comparing the achievement of districts and schools. He traveled to Texas, where he heard glowing reports about this process. The Partnership and CEPA, supported by funds from three private foundations, contracted to develop a similar report using the MAP.

In the terms of our theoretical framework, the Partnership's stated intentions, a continuation of its intentions for the OSA, were to improve achievement in order to provide both greater opportunities for all students and a better workforce for Missouri employers. They planned to transform these intentions into a report comparing district performance. In a cover letter enclosed with the first PEER, the Partnership stated that they "envisioned PEER activating school/community dialogue opportunities." The Partnership reasoned that "the Department cannot compare school districts, leaving the resulting state report card to be nothing more than a compilation of 'phone book' style information." Therefore, the Partnership sought to develop a fair and informed comparison process that would be accessible to the general public.

In essence, this was the Partnership's theory about the value of district comparisons: If parents and community members heard that their district was performing poorly in relation to similar districts, they would arrive at the district's doorstep demanding change. The local media would play an essential part, and the Partnership hired a public relations consultant to frame the message. A communication tool kit advised PEER advocates to avoid loaded terms such as *competition, comparison,* and *report card,* as well as *state department, the state,* and *state board of education,* and to emphasize that this was a private report "intended to further community-based public education support and reform." The Partnership recognized that as a private organization (albeit including a State Board member and education administrators), they were performing what was, in other states, a *governmental* function. As the PEER cover letter stated, "Other states use the same concept for their accreditation processes, and their student achievement steadily rises." The tool kit also expressed the hope that PEER would be a catalyst for collaboration among school districts.

The CEPA staff began a review of the research on factors influencing achievement. They held focus groups of superintendents, Partnership members, and State Department representatives, who debated the variables to use for groupings. Everyone agreed that percentage of students eligible for FRL (a stand-in for family income) should be one of the variables, because of its significant association with test scores. It was finally decided to use per-pupil expenditures (PPE), a more disputed explanatory factor, as a second variable, and district enrollment (size) as a third. CEPA obtained the necessary data from the State Department. A cross-tabulation between FRL and PPE resulted in the initial groupings; within each group, districts were ordered by size, and then subgrouped into sets of 10-16. Districts within a subgroup could be scattered geographically or located in variable economic/demographic contexts.

As this work proceeded, the Partnership began a campaign to win advanced support for PEER. They successfully solicited endorsements from groups such as Associated Industries of Missouri, the Chamber of Commerce, and the Missouri Parent Teacher Association (PTA). They did not solicit educator group endorsements, but focused meetings with educators on keeping them informed. In fact, it was believed that the state superintendent group, led by a powerful and opinionated executive director, would never have endorsed PEER. As a consequence, the Partnership devoted more public relations efforts than originally planned to regional superintendent groups. In these meetings, even superintendents from high-performing districts gave PEER a negative reception. It was apparent that PEER ran counter to local ways of comparing themselves. They also questioned the validity of MAP as a means of comparison, and associated PEER with the state accountability system. Superintendents who thought PEER might be a fair and helpful approach often did not speak up. Instead, they made private comments to CEPA or Partnership representatives.

After PEER was released in spring 2000, CEPA and the Partnership received mixed local reactions. A superintendent wrote to CEPA that "We will use this report for all of our school improvement efforts." Superintendents in one PEER group related that they would be meeting to discuss collaboration. A local PTA reported that PEER would help them engage parents and public, and a Republican representative on the House Education Committee said that PEER was useful in her work. Local chambers of commerce expressed strong interest in PEER. CEPA and the Partnership also received a variety of complaints from superintendents, but it was hard to tell whether they spoke for a vociferous minority or expressed a more widespread feeling. CEPA administered a superintendent survey in order to better understand their reactions, as well as the local uses of PEER. Had PEER fulfilled its sponsors' intentions, at least in some districts?

How Superintendents Perceived the Partnership's Intentions

Of the 174 respondents, a majority (69%) said that PEER had positive purposes. Of these, most saw the purpose as creating fair comparisons, by matching similar districts. Other positive purposes mentioned less frequently were to provide information to the public, to improve accountability, to promote collaboration among similar districts, to motivate public involvement, or to provide a baseline for measuring improvement. Only 30 (17%—the rest did not respond or were "unsure") thought PEER was negatively motivated, but these reactions were often strong. Some denounced the practice of comparing districts, circumventing the intentions of the OSA. A few saw threatening or crass financial, personal, or political, intentions, e.g., "Political bickering and to create jobs that are useless," "Pressure public education! "Advocate for Vouchers!"

In light of these responses to the first question, responses to the second question, "Given your answer, has PEER accomplished this (or worked toward this)?" were complex. Many superintendents who considered PEER to be well-intended nevertheless did not think it *fulfilled* those intentions. Some said that fair district comparisons were a good idea, but PEER excluded many important variables or employed inaccurate data. Some doubted the validity of MAP. Some felt their district's group was not locally meaningful. Others saw negative unintended consequences of PEER: "It has only alienated schools," "It caused undue worry and pressure." Of those who thought that PEER was negatively motivated, some sardonically claimed it *was* successful in achieving its intentions, e.g.,

"PEER is doing a wonderful job," "It has accomplished job security for someone."

While the Partnership expressed the intention for PEER to be used as a tool to guide school improvement, 47% of those who responded said there had been no (40%) or very minimal (7%) use. Add the non-responders, several unclear or "don't know" responses, as well as four negative comments about the report, and we can infer that there was limited use of PEER in ways the Partnership intended. One noted, "It has probably not been used to the full extent due to apprehension by administrators." Uses mentioned by the remaining 44 superintendents were: comparisons with other districts, reform or school improvement processes, communicating with the public ("Some bragging"), or discussions with the board and staff. Five said they used PEER to generate support for levy and bond issues.

When the survey asked "who had used" the PEER report, the importance of school boards emerged. While the Partnership had intended *all* community members to use PEER, most superintendents mentioned only administrators and school boards. Only 24 mentioned parents or the public. Twenty-seven percent said that there were *no* users of the report: "It was presented and then pitched!" "I gave it to the board, but they didn't 'use' it." One said, "I provide more meaningful interpretations," implying that a superintendent can better explain data to the board and public (Dorn, 1998). Another noted that "PEER is a duplication of effort and waste of paper. School districts that are interested in improvement already have the information." These short responses gave us only hints of what we might learn through more in-depth research. To find out more, we had to go into the field.

RAILTON SCHOOL DISTRICT:
PUT YOUR BEST FACE FORWARD

Railton is a small rural town that, although somewhat down-at-the-heels, has not given up. While farming is still part of its culture, family farms are declining, and the region has lost population. As the business section of the newspaper enthusiastically reports, the Chamber of Commerce hopes to diversify the economy by promoting Railton as a location for business and industry. Downtown storefronts are occupied by modest, locally-owned small businesses, and a rapidly expanding community college is a resource for employers seeking hirees with technical or health skills. However, Railton's county ranks very poorly on an annual state report of risk factors for children, with high rates of births to teen mothers and juvenile law violations. According to the 2000 Census (U.S. Census Bureau, 2000), nearly one fourth of Railton adults lack high school diplomas or General Education Development (GED) certificates, and the unemployment rate is much higher than the state average.

We collected news stories about Railton schools for the year surrounding release of the first PEER, and found that school board meetings and other district events were front-page news. Most stories were upbeat, focusing on facilities, awards, special events, music, and above all, sports. The reports boasted that, thanks to voter support of bond issues as well as state and federal support, the district had recently constructed three new schools, a central office, and an early childhood center. The board consistently voted to upgrade facilities and buy new equipment. The superintendent stressed the district's solid financial footing. Reporters did not speculate about what happened in closed school board sessions, or delve into why people were fired or resigned.

Before PEER came along, however, Railton educators were concerned about MAP scores. The state had made accreditation more contingent on increasing percentages of students at the proficient and advanced levels on the MAP. A rare negative story in 1999 reported that the assistant superintendent disclosed to the board that Railton students were not making hoped-for improvements. His explanation was that students were not prepared for the open-ended, problem-solving items on this new style of performance-based exam. The reporter contextualized this by noting that Railton's problems were shared by other districts in the nation, quoting a U.S. Department of Education representative's comments on low NAEP scores.

In the first issue of PEER released in April 2000, Railton was grouped with 9 other districts, all of which were somewhat higher than the state average for FRL percentage and PPE. The districts varied in enrollment (1,100-4,500), with Railton's 2,000 students placing it near the middle. Nine districts, including Railton, were situated in small towns in rural counties. Two were adjacent to military bases that brought more ethnic minority families into their communities. The anomaly was one urban district with 87% minority enrollment. In Missouri, such districts are stigmatized as having little in common with predominantly white districts.

Readers of PEER were meant to compare student outcomes within groups. At the time of the first PEER, educators were still becoming familiar with MAP, and no district in Railton's group performed very well. However, in subsequent PEERs, while all the districts in its group have improved over time, Railton has lagged behind state averages in most content areas.

Superintendent-Board Relationships in Railton: Working as a Team

The current school board president had nothing positive to say about the "dictator" superintendent and ineffectual school board in office at the time of the first release of PEER. A mother of three, she ran for the board in 1999 because she felt "compelled" to do so. Neither the administration nor the board, she said, were "interested in public comments or parent concerns" or even in children. They were "jumping on any new band-wagon," adopting programs "that had not proven to work through research." Based on her children's experiences, she was not willing to go along "blindly" with their decisions. She had "begged" them to pilot reforms, with parent choices about participation, but "got deaf ears." She had even complained to the State Department of Education. When she joined the board, she said, "the superintendent at the time, I'd never forget, he was in my face with his finger, 'I'm sick of you, and you're not making changes.'" She said she bit her tongue at board meetings for a time, but with patience and hard work, "I feel like now we're headed in the right direction."

Another community complaint about the previous superintendent, according to the board president, was that he did not live in the district and had no ties to Railton. He took early retirement in 2000, and some of his administrative team also left. The board hired a superintendent from a smaller district in the same PEER group. In the news story about his selection, he cited his record of leadership awards, state accolades, and a winning bond issue. According to the board president, he and other administrators they hired "seem more attentive to concerns, to the community," taking a more "trusting," "team" approach. The superintendent moved to Railton and participated in many community organizations.

The superintendent's perspective complemented that of the board president. Part of the way through our interview, however, the superintendent was called away to another meeting, and turned the interview over to the assistant superintendent, who was knowledgeable about PEER and was in charge of communicating with the board and media about district data. The two had come to Railton together and worked as a team.

Although he remarked that "you're supposed to say this wherever you go," the assistant superintendent declared that this board was the best he had ever seen. They may have been latecomers in this regard, he said, but they were currently "extremely focused" on student achievement. However, he said, the board did not micromanage. His position on superintendent-school board relationships was to "focus on what [the board] needs to know."

We get that information to them, and they ask questions, and of course what they want is results. And I like a board that is focused on results, because those are the ones that let you do your job and step back.... So we have a school board that knows what their role is, and that's refreshing.

Board meetings, he exclaimed, typically lasted "anywhere from twenty minutes to a half hour." The board president concurred, saying that even if the board and administration argued behind closed doors, when they faced the public, they would appear to be "on the same page."

Some districts, the assistant superintendent said, were still in the dark about data and technology. He was excited about creating quantitative reports using a new state internet access system. During the interview, he reached for a thick notebook of data he had formatted and shared with the board, observing that "it's probably more than they can handle, and they are very interested in it, and some of the board members read that stuff from cover to cover, some don't." He liked to present the board and school principals with "data information," interpreted and in context, rather than raw data.

Both the assistant superintendent and the board president were pleased to describe recent improvements in the district, even if scores did not match rising state expectations. Putting the best face on the situation, the advantage of a district with "challenges," the assistant superintendent said, was that it was easier to make gains than in a "successful" district. Both expressed the belief, however, that further gains depended on more parent support. According to the assistant superintendent, the "blue collar workers" in the community "value their schools" and "value their kids;" but they did not know how to help their children, especially in reading. The district offered parenting classes, and a business partner provided children with free books, but something more was needed. The board president noted that "parent accountability" was crucial, but she was not sure how to accomplish that in a district with so many "high needs" children and uninvolved parents. Parents who contacted her seemed concerned about sports, relying on the board to make curriculum decisions. Others were simply apathetic.

PEER Came to Railton: But Who Knew?

In 2000, there was *no* local newspaper coverage in Railton of the first PEER, even though a news release was sent to all local media. The school board president thought that she had heard about PEER at a school board association meeting.

I found out my administration had this but they had not given it to the board. The [then-assistant superintendent] didn't want to give it to me.... But I finally got it, but he's like, "Don't let anyone else see this," you know, "I understand you want to see it." ... That was his reaction.... We didn't do well ... so needless to say he didn't want to get this in the wrong hands.

Later, she remembered looking at PEER with the current superintendent, comparing Railton with his previous district. He shared the second edition of PEER with the board, and they had a chance to ask questions.

The assistant superintendent reinforced the board president's views of the change in administrative approaches, saying, "we are very open and honest with the board and we share everything that comes, good news and bad news, we don't keep any secrets." He was also confident that he knew ways to share information that would not alarm the board.

I never used the word "negative" with them, or "concerned" or anything like that. We always look at strengths and challenges ... but I did tell them that here are a couple of areas that we really have some challenges in, because we are behind in these scores. But you keep it positive, and of course we were new so ... they knew we were setting goals.

In seeming contradiction to her earlier demand to see PEER, the board president was now cautious about public access, because of potential negative interpretations.

if you had press that were watching you like a hawk, it was a real bandwagon for them to jump on. And I just didn't feel like it was a real valid report to put a lot of stock in ... like it put us in the light we needed to be in. I think you need to be more positive than negative when you're going to the public at all costs. I'm not saying lie to them, but there are ways to say things and there are ways not to say things, and this was so black and white, clear cut, there's no explanation basically.

Through her four years on the board, she had come to share the former administration's viewpoint about communicating with the public about district performance.

Intentions of PEER: They Meant Well, But ...

Asked what he thought the Partnership had intended, the assistant superintendent first gave a skeptical response, but then gave the Partnership the benefit of the doubt.

I figured somebody was trying to make some money somewhere down the line ... what I thought they were trying to achieve was, give a vehicle districts could use to set realistic goals by being able to compare themselves to other districts that were similar socioeconomically.... And I was excited when it came out, because it I thought it was leveling the playing field.

The school board president said she had "mixed feelings." She granted "that their overall purpose was probably good, to get districts to improve and to ... compare apples to apples." However, she immediately added, "I don't think that's what happened." She thought that money the Partnership spent on PEER would be better spent on something useful, such as providing districts with information about "things that work." Both leaders had the impression that PEER had been a very expensive project.

The interviewer explained that the Partnership had intended PEER to inspire community involvement. Had this occurred in Railton? Not according to the assistant superintendent. He said that the only person "activated" by PEER was the president of the Chamber of Commerce, who

asked a lot of questions...we had some really good conversations. But as far as mobilizing the community, that it didn't do. (Interviewer: Why?) People lead hectic lives, and they leave to the school district what the school district needs to do and they'll get stirred up over an issue or something, but usually those issues are, unfortunately, athletics, or discipline and things like that, and not academic.

The board president, while convinced that "parents are the key to raising education standards," reflected that

the [state] report card is mandated to be distributed and I don't think I've ever had a phone call from a patron that read it, really read. Which to me is not good, I mean they should be more interested in it, but it's just, parents are busy, you know, sports is a big focus and I think that they just think, "Oh, they're handling that, we pay them to do that, not the board, the administration."... I don't know what to do with people, they just don't seem to care. That's probably a strong statement, but I don't know what else to say.

Why did PEER fail to fulfill its sponsors' intentions in Railton? The board president suggested four possibilities. First, district comparisons did not make sense, as "apples to apples." She said, "All I wanted to do was pick Railton's scores out ... quite frankly I didn't care about anyone else's." She was baffled by the grouping of an urban district with Railton. Second, she questioned MAP's validity: "You can make numbers mean anything ... there can always be room for error in any instrument." Third, she was concerned about external interference, because getting information out to the public is more a district's responsibility ... be kind of protective of your turf, and when somebody outside your district tries to tell other people if your district is doing well enough, you are like, "Well, who are you, and who gave you the authority, and how did you get this information about our district?"

Finally, the report was confusing. "To me there was a lot of explaining that needed to be done" to explain how the districts compared.

I remember as a parent, before I got on the board, if I heard something like that, I mean I would be devastated, "My goodness, they're doing this bad!" I probably wouldn't hear anything else.

Uses of PEER? Not Really

Not surprisingly, when asked whether they had used PEER as a basis for planning, these leaders said it played a very minor role. The assistant superintendent said

I don't find ourselves sitting down and comparing our scores with (another district). I find us comparing our scores with what we have done in the past, state averages, and what the top district in the state is doing ... I don't care what socioeconomic population or funding they have, if they are doing it, we can do it, and that's what we look at ... when the PEER report came out I thought we would make comparisons more valid, and I don't anymore. I just think we need to shoot for the top.

In addition, he said, it had become much more important to attend to *state* mandates and data. He said that PEER came along about "ten years too late." It had been replaced by state data systems that superintendents could access directly and interpret for the board.

The board president said, "I saw it as one indicator, I didn't see it as all-inclusive ... I see it as a stepping-stone. I mean I did see it as that...obviously we did need to make improvements." However, now that improvements were in progress, she said, "I don't have to look at this anymore." She said that she found her conversations with other board members at state meetings much more informative than PEER.

DISCUSSION

How were superintendents and school board members in Railton able to transform the Partnership's bold intentions? They used at least two strategies. First, they understood that they did not *have* to do anything in response to PEER. Structural power in this case was on the side of the policy implementers (Hall, 1995). The Partnership depended upon the voluntary efforts of local community actors, over whom it had no authority, to fulfill its intentions (Hall, 1995). Therefore, an obvious strategy was to avoid local media coverage and other ways of disseminating PEER to the community, in order to mitigate possible negative effects of an external threat to the district's positive image (Hentges, 1986; Scribner et al., 2002 Tallerico, 1989). Local reporters covered only what the board and administrators openly discussed or released, without probing further. They kept the focus on good news, and did not seem knowledgeable about state and national education policy.

According to the board president, the former assistant superintendent attempted to conceal PEER from the board until she, at that time an assertive, critical new member, demanded to see it. However, after four years on the board, she agreed with administrators that showing PEER to Railton's blue collar citizens might alarm or confuse them unnecessarily (although this contradicted her judgment of them as apathetic). According to Tallerico's (1989) classification of school board members, board service had transformed her from a restive vigilant to a proactive supportive position. Only the Chamber of Commerce president inquired about PEER, probably because the state Chamber publicized the report among its members. But after a conversation with the assistant superintendent, he apparently did not instigate the hoped-for community dialogue. The Partnership may not have believed it possible for a district to *completely* avoid PEER, but in Railton that is what happened.

A second strategy, useful in case someone *did* gain access to PEER, was to cast doubt on its credibility and usefulness. When asked about the intentions behind PEER, the assistant superintendent's first response was that it was probably a way for someone to make money. Railton's school board president defined PEER as just "one indicator," and not a valuable one at that. She considered other districts in Railton's PEER group to be incongruous, and both leaders named districts that they considered to be better references for comparison. She also considered MAP to be invalid, a position voiced by many educators around the state, as the serious consequences of MAP scores were becoming more evident. National experts (Elmore, 2002; Linn, 2000) have also questioned the validity and reliability of tests used in accountability systems.

Why did Railton leaders use these strategies? Three explanations, grounded in other research as well as our theoretical framework, seem plausible in this case. First was the changing political context of accountability, in which state policy mechanisms (especially after NCLB) have more powerful effects on local action than a report published by a private organization. With tighter linkages, the state's power to regulate local education actors became less ambiguous and negotiable (Hall, 1995). In this context, PEER seemed redundant, given the state's display and release of district data. Yet, even in the case of state accountability, Railton's leaders seemed able to avoid local fallout. A search of recent news articles showed that there had been no coverage of "Adequate Yearly Progress (AYP), a provision of NCLB, even though this issue prompted front page stories in other communities and was a major cause of concern in the state capital. State Department data showed that most Railton schools did not make AYP. Therefore, our findings about the (non)effects of PEER seemed to apply to state data reporting, as well. If state leaders intended state report cards or AYP figures to raise public awareness in Railton, they seemed unaware that the local media might not receive, ask for, or search for these figures. They seemed to overestimate public access to or understanding of web-based data reports in low income communities.

During the same week that AYP was *the* school news in other communities, Railton's superintendent and board were pictured on the front page of the newspaper, because the district had joined nearly 200 others in a lawsuit against the state based on financial inequities. Railton's working class and business property owners paid a relatively high tax rate, yet Railton had fallen behind in PPE, because state funding had not followed the formula adopted after the OSA. Railton's school board opened the 2003-04 school year with painful program and staff cuts. District leaders seemed to be saying to the state: If you are going to hold all districts accountable to the same standards, you must give us adequate resources.

A second set of explanations for transformation of the Partnership's intentions for PEER can be found in the district's political culture. One political interpretation of local resistance to accountability is to characterize it as a revival of democratic localism (Waite, Boone, & McGhee, 2001). However, it would be difficult to characterize Railton's culture as democratic. The rural, working class community context may have been conducive to strong administrative or professional control of most education decisions (Ferguson & Nochelski, 1996). The norms and conventions of the district and community favored administrative control rather than the community involvement that the Partnership had envisioned. A strong district administration can effectively limit the power of local interest groups and external interference in school board decisions (Hentges, 1986). Moreover, superintendent communication style has been shown to increase the likelihood of receiving school board support on those matters that are primarily internal to the district, such as issues regarding the curriculum or school programs (Petersen & Short, 2002). Another aspect of the district culture was the shared belief that most Railton parents were apathetic, probably unable to comprehend PEER or other data, and in most cases not even concerned about academics. This is similar to Lareau's (2000) findings on relationships between educators and working class parents, and suggests potentially productive links between her cultural capital analysis and district policy research.

In terms of levels of concern, leaders assumed that parents were focused on their own children, not the aggregate of all district students reported in PEER or the state report card. In fact, concern for her own children's education was the board president's motivation for running for office. Once her immediate concerns were resolved, she supported the administration. Leaders could quite honestly boast to the community about steady improvement, moreover, without mentioning unfavorable comparisons with the state average or other districts.

Leaders also promulgated the notion that their community was unique, what anthropologists call an emic or particularistic perspective. The board president felt that it was not legitimate for outsiders who knew nothing about Railton to categorize and match it with other districts. As she said, leaders should protect their turf when faced with such threats. CEPA researchers and the Partnership, from their detached etic perspective, saw Railton from a statewide, macro level standpoint, based on objective data obtained from the state. Howley (1998) argues that state accountability systems based on a macro perspective destroy local meanings of achievement in rural areas, and we might extend that argument to reports such as school report cards or PEER that ignore aspects of local contexts that cannot be easily quantified or compared.

Another district norm was "know your role"—reduce the ambiguity of district policy-making by clarifying each person or group's official duties (Hall, 1995). This, in fact, was the central theme of the state school board association's board member training sessions, which Railton's board had attended. The assistant superintendent was pleased that the board had taken this motto to heart. The "know your role" norm reinforced strategies that the administrators used to minimize the effects of PEER. Board members were not supposed to micromanage. The superintendent and assistant superintendent felt that it was their role to interpret achievement data. They viewed PEER, as an external report, as an attempt to preempt their role of mediating between data and the board. Dorn (1998) argued that statistical reports might undermine the authority of superintendents. However, these leaders believed that they could create their *own* reports as local policy tools, using the state's data access system and adding their interpretations.

Studying PEER provided us with a window into superintendent-school board relationships in this district. We obviously cannot generalize from this case, but two important findings about those relationships and accountability policy surfaced in our study. First, the intentions of external reformers can be radically transformed within the dynamics of those relationships, based on local norms and conventions. Second, this case provides an interesting counterexample to the perspective that accountability via the public reporting of data has decreased the authority of superintendents and increased community members' demands on and involvement in their schools (see Dorn, 1998). While this may hold true for many schools, this study revealed important differences in local control and decision-making in schools and communities that seem to expand Dorn's perspective. Indeed, the intentions of the school board president and school district administrators in this town, as well as the tacit affirmation of support for the superintendent from local news media and civic leaders, exemplified the import of these differences.

Accordingly, our findings affirm the traditional view of the superintendent as expert, even in the age of accountability policy, as decisions continue to be made without much public participation, and school performance is primarily talked about in terms dictated by school leadership. Therefore, while published test scores and AYP have supposedly been used in many communities to hold school administrators accountable and even question their leadership, there is evidence that this is not going on in all communities. Since our study was conducted, however, NCLB's consequences for low achievement have been implemented. We would have to revisit this community to find out if local conventions are sufficiently strong to resist a policy backed by both state and federal power. In terms of the preparation of future school superintendents, we would not recommend, based on our findings, that they be taught to believe that it is a good thing to take advantage of a complacent or uninformed community in order to avoid both external and local accountability. In a democratic society, they should be taught to engage community members in dialogues about the kinds of accountability they want.

As we continue our case study research, we will add to our knowledge of how superintendents and school board members, along with other community members, respond to external, privately sponsored initiatives such as PEER. An initially unplanned but very important outcome of the study will be greater understanding of superintendent and school board responses to state and federal accountability policies within the community context.

REFERENCES

Dorn, S. (1998, February 1). The political legacy of school accountability systems. *Education Policy Analysis Archives, 6*(1). Retrieved September 18, 2002, from http://epaa.asu.edu/epaa/v6n1.html

Elmore, R. F. (2002). Testing trap. *Harvard Magazine, 105*(1). Retrieved September 18, 2002, from http://www.harvard-magazine.com/on-line/0902140.html .

Estes, C., & Edmonds, B. (1981). Symbolic interaction and social policy analysis. *Symbolic Interaction, 4*(1), 75-86.

Excellence in Education Act, 83d Missouri General Assembly, 1st Sess. ' Ch. 160 et seq (1985).

Ferguson, J. M., & Nochelski, P. S. (1996). The power of letting go. *American School Board Journal, 183*(4), 37-39.

Feuerstein, A., & Opfer, V. D. (1998). School board chairmen and school superintendents: An analysis of perceptions concerning special interest groups and educational governance. *Journal of School Leadership, 8*(4), 373-398.

Fowler, F. C. (1995). The neoliberal value shift and its implications for federal education policy under Clinton. *Educational Administration Quarterly, 31*(1), 38-60.

Goertz, M. E., Duffy, M.C., & LeFloch, K. C. (2001). Assessment and accountability systems in the 50 states: 1999-2000 (CPRE Research Report Series RR-046). Philadelphia: University of Pennsylvania, Consortium for Policy Research in Education.

Grady, M. L., & Bryant, M. T. (1989). Critical incidents between superintendents and school boards: Implications for practice. *Planning & Changing, 20*(4), 206-214.

Grady, M. L., & Bryant, M. T. (1991). School board presidents describe critical incidents with superintendents. *Journal of Research in Rural Education, 7*(3), 51-58.

Hall, P. M. (1995). The consequences of qualitative analysis for sociological theory: Beyond the micro level. *The Sociological Quarterly, 35*(2), 397-423.

Hall, P. M., & McGinty, P. J. (1997). Policy as the transformation of intentions: Producing program from statute. *The Sociological Quarterly, 38*(3), 439-467.

Hentges, J. T. (1986). The politics of superintendent-school board linkages: A study of power, participation, and control. *ERS Spectrum, 4*(3), 23-32.

Howley, C. B. (1998, Feb. 25). *Distortions of rural student achievement in the era of globalization.* Athens OH: Rural Center Appalachia Educational Laboratory. (ERIC ED419634).

LaRocque, L., & Coleman, P. (1993). The politics of excellence: Trustee leadership and school district ethos. *Alberta Journal of Educational Research, 39*(4), 449-475.

Lareau, A. (2000). *Home advantage* (2nd ed.). Lanham, MD: Rowman & Littlefield.

Linn, R. L. (2000). Assessments and accountability. *Educational Researcher, 29*(2), 4-16.

National Commission on Excellence in Education. (1983). *A nation at risk: The imperative for educational reform.* Washington DC: U.S. Department of Education.

Newman, D. L., & Brown, R. D. (1993). School board member role expectations in making decisions about educational programs: Do size of school and region of country make a difference? *Urban Education, 28*(3), 267-280.

Outstanding Schools Act, 87th Missouri General Assembly, 1st Sess. ' Ch. 160 et seq. (1993)

Petersen, G. J., & Short, P. M. (2002). An examination of school board presidents' perceptions of their superintendent's interpersonal communication competence and board decision making. *Journal of School Leadership, 12*(4), 411-436.

Placier, M., Hall, P. M., Benson McKendall, S., & Cockrell, K. S. (2000). Policy as the transformation of intentions: Making multicultural education policy. *Educational Policy, 14*(2), 259-289.

Placier, M., Walker, M., & Foster, B. (2002). Writing the show-me standards: Teacher professionalism and political control. *Curriculum Inquiry, 32*(3), 281-310.

Ravitch, D. (1995). *National standards in American education: A citizen's guide.* Washington DC: Brookings Institution Press.

Scribner, J. P., Hager, D. R., & Warne, T. R. (2002). The paradox of professional community: Tales from two high schools. *Educational Administration Quarterly, 38*(1), 45-76.

Smith, M. S., & Scoll, B. W. (1995). The Clinton human capital agenda. *Teachers College Record, 96*(3), 389-404.

Starr, P. (1987). The sociology of official statistics. In W. Alonso & P. Starr (Eds.), *The politics of numbers* (pp. 7-57). New York: Russell Sage Foundation.

Tallerico, M. (1989). The dynamics of superintendent-school board relationships. *Urban Education, 24*(2), 215-232.

U.S. Census Bureau. (2000). *Census 2000.* Retrieved June 10, 2004, from Office of Social and Economic Data Analysis: http://oseda.missouri.edu/2000_census/index.html

U.S. Department of Education. (1994). *Improving America's Schools Act.* Retrieved June 10, 2004, from http://www.ed.gov/legislation/ESEA/toc.html

U.S. Department of Education. (2001). *No Child Left Behind Act of 2001.* Retrieved June 10, 2004, from http://www.ed.gov/policy/elsec/leg/esea02/index.html

Waite, D., Boone, M., & McGhee, M. (2001). A critical sociocultural view of accountability. *Journal of School Leadership, 11*(1), 182-203.

Zlotkin, J. (1993). Rethinking the school board's role. *Educational Leadership, 51*(2), 22-25.

CHAPTER 6

WHEN GENERALS (OR COLONELS) BECOME SUPERINTENDENTS

Conflict, Chaos, and Community

Bonnie C. Fusarelli

Within the last decade, in an attempt to improve often dismal school system performance, several states passed laws changing certification requirements for superintendents, effectively permitting anyone, however trained, to become superintendent of a school system (Fusarelli & Petersen, 2002). Influenced by neo-conservative attacks questioning the efficacy of university-based preparation programs (Hess, 2003; 2004), state policymakers are revising licensing criteria and administrator certification requirements, shifting from input models (e.g., academic credits and certification) to output-driven models (e.g., competencies and performance). Several states, including Michigan, Tennessee, and Illinois, have either partially or totally eliminated requirements for superintendent preparation and several others, including Colorado, Florida, Kentucky, and Washington, have lowered the barriers for entry of non-educators into the superintendency. For example, in Tennessee, superin-

The Politics of Leadership: Superintendents and School Boards in Changing Times, 117–134
117

tendents need only citizenship and a college degree (in any field of study) (Kowalski & Glass, 2002). Further, emergency certification for persons from non-traditional backgrounds in the form of waivers is permissible in almost every state.

In part, the changes reflect a response to a perceived leadership shortage or crisis in America's schools. The movement toward alternative certification for school administrators also reflects the neo-conservative attack on public education—that schools are failing, have been failing for decades, and that new thinking and new leadership are required (Hess, 2004). Cronin and Usdan (2003) trace the evolution of this "new politics of education" (p. 183). They argue that many of the current calls for reform in school governance have their roots in the civil rights movement of the 1960s.

In the mid 1960s, the composition and role of school boards shifted away from a corporate model of "establishment" members who acted as trustees for the community at large and were focused on the "4 b's (boards, budgets, buildings, and buses)" (Cronin & Usdan, 2003, p. 182). Cronin and Usdan (2003) explain that minority groups who were historically neglected by unresponsive school boards demanded access to governing the institutions that played such vital roles in the lives of their children. Many of the new board members saw themselves as representatives of "specific racial, geographic, or educational constituencies" (p. 182). Because their own children often attended public schools, these new board members were more willing to delve into school issues at the building level, thus challenging "the traditional board-superintendent relationship and its demarcation line between administration and policy" (Cronin & Usdan, 2003, p. 182). The corporate paradigm of school board service was no longer operative and there was a shift away from the 4 b's to the "4 r's (race, resources, relationships, and rules)" (Cronin & Usdan, 2003, p. 182).

By the 1980s, a weak national economy, coupled with reports such as *A Nation at Risk* (National Commission on Excellence in Education, 1983) led to increased criticisms of the educational system and generated momentum for standards-based school reforms. The passage of the *Goals 2000: Educate America Act of 1994* ushered in a new era of standards and accountability. Cronin and Usdan (2003) explain that this "new politics of education, in essence preempted the traditional school leadership" (p. 183). As business leaders questioned the adequacy of the school leadership structure, new models of leadership began to emerge, including calls for mayoral involvement and the employment of untraditional leaders as superintendents.

Today, state policymakers are increasingly skeptical about the utility and effectiveness of traditional administrator preparation, arguing that corporate or military leadership skills are appropriate and transferable to the public school system (Tucker, 2003). Many policymakers believe that training in business, politics, or the military is sufficient preparation to lead school districts—an implicit attack on the knowledge base in educational administration and a subject of intense debate within the field itself (Donmoyer, Imber, & Scheurich, 1995).

As a result, "School boards around the country have been hiring a new breed of superintendent—military generals, a federal prosecutor, a health care executive, an investment banker and former corporate executives" (Geiger, 2002, p. 1). Although this movement remains small (about 1% nationwide), these non-traditional leaders are becoming increasingly common in large, urban school systems. Currently, three of the largest districts in the country—New York City, Los Angeles, and Chicago—with over three million students combined, are being led by superintendents with no significant educational background, no advanced training in educational administration, and no certification as a school administrator. A recent survey by the Council of the Great City Schools (CGCS) found that about 15% of CGCS superintendents come from non-traditional backgrounds (CGCS, 2003). Moreover, the movement is filtering down into medium-sized school districts, as this case study illustrates.

To date, little research has been done on the effectiveness of non-traditional superintendents (military officers, businesspeople, lawyers, and others) leading school systems. Empirical questions such as, "What happens when an individual unfamiliar with the education culture and workings of school boards is chosen to lead a school district?" have not been addressed in the literature, beyond a few anecdotal case studies (Fusarelli & Petersen, 2002, p. 287; Stanford, 1999). The trend of hiring non-educators to run school systems reflects the belief that schools need people with "management skills of a scope and scale that might be found in individuals from outside education," according to Judy Seltz, director of planning and communications for the American Association of School Administrators (AASA) ("Can Non-Educators Lead Our Schools?", 2000, p. 2). In his assessment of the performance of non-educators leading school systems, Paul Houston, executive director of AASA, remarked that the performance record of non-traditional superintendents from outside the field is mixed, with a few well-publicized successes and some failures—particularly an inability to raise student achievement and close the achievement gap (The Council of State Governments, 2004).

SCHOOL BOARD/SUPERINTENDENT CONFLICT

Americans are generally ambivalent toward educational experts and expertise. Danzberger (1994) claims that "this profound ambivalence accounts for much of the motivation to elect lay people to make local education policy and for the expectation that they will act as buffers between citizens and the possible 'excesses' of professional educators" (p. 368). The governance system for public schools is complex and even at the local level, the school board is not the only local institution whose decisions determine what will or will not occur in schools (Danzberger, 1994). Teacher and administrator unions, principals and teachers in individual schools, and, increasingly, planning or governing bodies in individual schools (such as site-based decision-making committees) all make decisions or share authority once lodged with the school board (Danzberger, 1994).

Many superintendents believe that school governance would be healthier if boards were restricted to a broad policy role that limited them to developing the budget, setting goals, ensuring accountability, assessing the superintendent's performance, and planning for a successor to the superintendent (Carter & Cunningham, 1997). The literature on school board and superintendent relationships highlights the tension between boards and superintendents and the political nature of school boards (Feuerstein & Opfer, 1998; Tallerico, 1989). Feuerstein and Opfer (1998) note that research on school boards suggests "this tension is due in part to the disequilibrium between lay control and the power of professional expertise and also to the ambiguous nature of policy making and administrative functions in educational governance" (p. 374). Greene (1992) found that school boards operate from a political/self-interest model rather than a community/public-good model. Board members engage in school management by responding to demands by individual parents rather than deferring to decisions from within the schools. Over the last 30 years, school boards have become increasingly politicized and more involved in the daily operations and administration of their school districts, making it more difficult for superintendents to provide strong leadership for school improvement (Björk, Bell, & Gurley, 2002). Recently, in Washington, DC, two of the leading candidates for superintendent withdrew from consideration, citing concerns over governance, control, and authority issues (Blum, 2004). When a policy or practice is unsuccessful, boards and superintendents often blame each other, resulting in a lack of clear accountability. In response, a growing number of policy activists advocate eliminating school boards altogether (Danzberger, Kirst, & Usdan, 1992; Finn & Keegan, 2004).

Danzberger (1994) explains that school boards frequently appear dysfunctional because individual board members lack a common definition of the board's role and are, therefore, incapable of charting a clear direction for their school systems. Frequent turnover in board membership further exacerbates the problem, as does the impact of turnover in the superintendency (Fusarelli, Cooper, & Carella, 2003; Glass & Björk, 2003; Natkin et al., 2002). Frequent board and superintendent turnover inhibits strategic planning and implementation of systemic reform initiatives.

The adoption and implementation of new policy is often a hotly contested process. Several factors, including community context and the issue being contested, strongly affect the nature of educational politics and policy outcomes (Feuerstein & Opfer, 1998). In other words, "the extent to which a community seeks to control educational policy making and to influence professional educators depends upon the community type and the issue at stake" (Burlingame, 1988, p. 440). As the case study below illustrates, communities in which the local school board seeks to control policymaking, micromanage district affairs, and interfere with the superintendent's leadership create conditions ripe for superintendent turnover and school systems in constant turmoil.

Research on superintendents and school boards finds that district leaders' success in managing and implementing change is dependent upon the relationships they have established with their board of education (Carter & Cunningham, 1997; Feuerstein & Opfer, 1998; Kowalski, 1995, 1999; Petersen & Short, 2001). Fusarelli and Petersen (2002) note that, "patterns of board-superintendent interactions follow fairly well established patterns of behavior along a continuum from amicable support to outright hostility" (p. 288). Poor relationships between the superintendent and the board make it difficult for a district to achieve its goals. Fusarelli and Petersen (2002) reviewed the salient literature and noted that,

> a precarious relationship [between a superintendent and his/her school board] deters school improvement (Danzberger, Kirst, & Usdan, 1992), affects the quality of educational programs (Boyd, 1976; Nygren, 1992), increases conflict over district instructional goals and objectives (Morgan & Petersen, 2002; Petersen, 1999), weakens district stability and morale (Renchler, 1992), negatively influences the superintendent's credibility and trustworthiness with board members (Petersen & Short, 2001), impedes critical reform efforts such as district restructuring (Konnert & Augenstein, 1995), and collaborative visioning and long-range planning (Kowalski, 1999), as well as eventually resulting in an increase in the 'revolving door syndrome' of district superintendents (Carter & Cunningham, 1997; Renchler, 1992). (p. 283)

Many of these negative consequences of poor relations between the board of education and the superintendent were evident in Bowie County.

THE SETTING

The Bowie County School District[1] is a medium-sized district serving a small southern city and the surrounding county. Unlike much of the state,

Bowie County has a stable population base, experiencing little growth during the 1990s; the county's population grew only 0.6% from 1990-2000, compared to 9.6% growth statewide (U.S. Census Bureau, 2001). The growth rate in the last 10 years is considerably lower than neighboring counties, most of which are experiencing rapid growth. The county's ethnic and socioeconomic demographics are comparable with statewide demographics. With four elementary schools, one middle school, and one high school, the district enrolls over 2,600 students and employs a staff of 450. Its annual budget is approximately 17 million dollars. State accountability results place Bowie County in the lowest 40% of districts statewide.

Since passage of a major school reform initiative over a decade ago, the state has been engaged in comprehensive educational reform. The initiative redistributed school leadership through the mandated installation of local decision-making councils that have legal authority over school matters. The reforms prompted revisions in the preparation and induction of new school leaders through creation of a regulatory agency responsible for the certification of teachers and administrators (Browne-Ferrigno, Rinehart, & Fusarelli, 2003). The reform act empowered the state regulatory agency to determine preservice preparation requirements for aspiring principals and inservice professional development for certified school personnel (Pankratz & Petrosko, 2000). The agency changed (some would argue weakened) the requirements for both principal and superintendent certification and licensure and established new, alternative routes to school leadership. In 2001, Bowie County Schools hired Frank Ford, the first non-educator to be a superintendent under the revised requirements for school administrators. The district was selected for this case study because the school board took the unusual step of hiring a non-educator as superintendent.

METHODS AND DATA SOURCES

The research presented in this chapter is drawn from an analysis of multiple interviews with key stakeholders and newspaper accounts of events in the Bowie County School District. Semi-structured interviews lasting 50-80 minutes each were held with the superintendent, the assistant superintendent, the high school principal and vice-principal, three of the applicants who sought Ford's position after he resigned, and four school board members. Several of the participants were interviewed on more than one occasion. The researcher also spent seven days observing in the district, attending school-related functions, and talking to district-level employees. In keeping with established methods of qualitative research, the researcher kept detailed field notes and a methodological log of ideas that informed her understanding of the situation (Bogdan & Biklen, 1992; Lincoln & Guba, 1985). The researcher shared her insights and solicited feedback from key participants.

Due to its long history of conflict between the community, school board, and superintendent, and its proximity to one of the state's leading newspapers, the district has received an unusual degree of media coverage, providing the researcher with an extensive documentary database upon which to draw. To triangulate the data, 81 articles were collected from the local press that mentioned the school district or Superintendent Ford.

FINDINGS OF THE CASE STUDY

The Narrative

Frank Ford, a retired Army colonel, was the first superintendent in the state to be certified under a program that encourages people from nontraditional backgrounds to enter the field of education. In his first position, Ford was appointed as state manager to oversee the state's takeover (due to failing standardized test scores and fiscal irregularities) of a county school system. He was accused of overhauling the schools "military style" – which Ford considered a compliment. He claimed to be "decisive, quick-acting, and mission focused." As the state manager, Ford's fast moving approach to school reform was attacked by professional educators and the community at large. He drew similar criticisms in Bowie County. As will be discussed in a subsequent section of this chapter, these criticisms negatively impacted Ford's relationship with district educators and the board of education.

Prior to legislative passage of a major school decentralization bill in 1990, conflict between the superintendent and the school board in Bowie County was minimal, with several superintendents enjoying long tenure. However, when the decentralization bill passed, the district's 14-year veteran superintendent, Steven Biddings, resigned, citing the new approach to school leadership mandated by the reform as the main impetus for his departure. By all accounts, Bidding was an autocratic, but well respected, leader who resigned because he claimed that his style of leadership would not work well in the new context of distributive leadership initiatives such as site-based decision-making councils. Since Bidding's departure, the leadership of Bowie County Schools has been in continual flux with over six superintendents in the past 14 years.

After Ford was appointed superintendent, conflict arose almost immediately between the school board and the superintendent over his leader-

Table 6.1.   Superintendent Tenure—Bowie County School District

Superintendent	Length of Tenure
Anna Manning	August 2003–present
Frank Ford	August 2001–January 2003[a]
Sam Best	April 2001–August 2001[b]
John Cutter	Summer 2000–April 2001
Sam Best	1995–Summer 2000
Larry Smith	August 1990–1995
Steven Biddings	1976–1990

[a]Ford resigned in January 2003 but was rehired as a "consultant" for the remainder of the school year.
[b]Sam Best retired in April 2001 but was reappointed as Acting Superintendent after Cutter was released.

ship style. However, this conflict cannot be attributed solely to a clash between the cultures of the military and education. The district had a history of conflict between the school board and administrators, dating back to the passage of the statewide school decentralization reform initiative described earlier. Ford's immediate predecessor, John Cutter, was a highly respected, veteran educator who garnered national awards as a principal and as superintendent. Yet Cutter ruffled some board members' feathers with a management style the board described as "rigid." Board member Mr. Smith claimed, "His way of thinking was, 'Hey guys, this is what I'm gonna do, and that's it.'"

The Bowie County school district's recent history is full of emotionally charged conflict between community members, the school board, and administrators. Community members, parents, superintendents, board members, faculty, and staff—virtually everyone with a stake in the school system—have been in a near-continuous state of sparring and fighting over the last several years. For example, the same week Superintendent Ford was asked by a parent to resign, two board members unexpectedly resigned from the school board, including the board chair, a veteran of 17 years on the school board. One of the board members who resigned, Ms. Odel, an 11-year veteran of the board, stated that "the community has lost faith in me." The state was forced to appoint two board members to replace those who had resigned. Unfortunately, the board resignations were not unusual. The board has a long history of in-fighting and as a result few people have been willing to run in Bowie County school board elections. In 1998, for example, just two weeks prior to the filing deadline, no one had applied to be on the ballot for two vacant school board seats. In most recent school board elections, the candidates for the various slots were generally running unopposed.

Making the situation more problematic, these conflicts do not revolve around any one central issue. Several distinct issues have served as lightning rods for school-community conflict, including an increasingly tough fiscal situation, proposed budget cuts, declining test scores, public mistrust, weak rapport between parents, district officials, and board members, high administrative turnover, and unpopular budget proposals, especially those from Superintendent Ford.

During Ford's administration the State Attorney General found that the school board violated the state's open meetings law when it conducted a series of three un-posted special meetings over a seven-month period, including hosting a work session in the basement of the board chair's home. In addition, the board's chair was found to have violated the law by not responding quickly enough to an open meetings complaint. The Assistant Attorney General also determined that the board had "misstepped when it failed to give newly appointed members the agenda of a special meeting until they arrived for the meeting. The board should also have included agendas in its posted notices of special meetings." In response to the Attorney General's findings, the board chair stated, "I am so sick and tired of answering charges that have no foundation. We never violated [the open meetings act]. It was pure oversight and accidental. Somebody was assigned to the task and goofed in doing it."[2]

Around this same time, the state Office of Education Accountability found irregularities in job postings and hiring; four coaches were hired using irregular practices. There was innuendo that board members were directly involved in the interviewing and hiring of coaches – a clear violation of the state's site-based management law. The school district later voided the contract of the high school baseball coach, Mr. Jones, and reopened his position after acknowledging he was hired illegally over the summer. Jones filed a lawsuit against the district, arguing that he was unlawfully terminated. This was one of many lawsuits that kept the district in a state of constant turmoil.

Contributing to the turmoil was the long-held practice by the board of pre-writing the minutes of their public meetings. This practice resulted in many community members feeling left out and not represented by the board members. According to one interviewee, much of the district's business has traditionally been conducted by the board behind closed doors. Two other interviewees claimed that much of the board's business was done informally and that board members had been known to meet in restaurants and other locations in a nearby city (presumably to avoid notice) for informal meetings. One such meeting was held with a job interviewee, Dr. Knight, after Ford resigned. Dr. Knight claimed to have felt uneasy, like something wasn't right with meeting in such a clandestine manner. After the meeting, Knight called an attorney who specialized in educational law in the state to inquire about the meeting's legality. Ultimately, Dr. Knight was not selected to succeed Ford, a decision he saw a fortuitous because of the discord in the district. One of the areas he saw as most contested was that of educational priorities for the district.

Bowie County has a history of conflict over the district's educational priorities. For example, prior to Ford's tenure, parents, students, and current and former staff criticized the decision to create a new position of district-wide athletics director at an annual salary of $53,500. At the time, Kate Jones, a former high school athletic director, expressed concerns about the decision in light of other staff lay-offs (due to a projected budget shortfall). She stated, "We spent several board meetings talking about cutbacks, and then we hire someone who will incur $53,500 from the general fund." The superintendent at that time, Sam Best, who resigned in April 2001, acknowledged that he clashed with the school board because he thought the high school coaches were overpaid. At the time, the head football coach, Harry Duddle, was paid thousands of dollars more than any other teacher in the district and more than some elementary school principals, although his contract was not out of line with other head football coaches in the area.[3] As a supplement to his salary, Duddle received approximately $6,000 per year to supervise the weight room. Superintendent Best said he wanted to bring coaches' salaries "back to reality," citing as a problem the fact that some high school assistant coaches were paid a stipend of more than $3,000 per year, while academic department heads received less than $800.

Best also questioned the amount of extended days allotted to administrators and some staff, including Coach Duddle's wife, Jackie Duddle, who worked as a teleconferencing and computer lab coordinator in the district. Jackie Duddle was paid for 26 additional days outside of the school year, which she claimed were used for meetings, planning programs, scheduling, and training. Interestingly, after Best resigned, the board voted to cap coaching salaries and trimmed the number of extended paydays for district employees. Superintendent Best claimed that he had urged the board months earlier to implement these policies and the board had agreed, but because "a couple of personnel determined they wouldn't be getting money increases," the board failed to follow the superintendent's recommendations. Best lasted only ten months as Bowie County superintendent. Some faculty members and parents charged that he was asked to leave because of his commitment to academics over athletics. But board members said they simply took him up on his third threat to quit. When some parents accused the board of pandering to athletics, board member Mr. Dowd said, "I don't know what planet that came from."

As a result of these conflicts (and others to numerous to mention), superintendent turnover in Bowie has been extraordinarily high—six superintendents in the past 14 years. The turnover in the superintendency is only one indicator of the administrative turmoil in the school district. In the district's lone high school, five principals left or have been removed within the past eight years. Four of the principals lasted only one year each.

Amid all this turmoil, in an attempt to improve student achievement and turn the district around, the board of education hired a non-educator (Frank Ford) in 2001. However, conflict between the superintendent and the school board continued unabated and, after barely completing first year at the helm, Superintendent Ford was already seeking positions elsewhere. Ford was a finalist for a superintendency in a northern state but was not selected. In addition, Ford applied for a superintendency in a district in the eastern part of the state but withdrew his application when he learned he was a finalist for the other position. Publicly, however, Ford claimed he withdrew his application to the district within the state because of his "renewed confidence in his school board."

Ford's decision to actively seek another superintendency in the midst of his first year in Bowie County rankled some parents. Ford had previously commented at a school board meeting that "[I] did not come here to fail. I came here to graduate with the Class of 2014. That's when we will have reached proficiency. Then I will be done." A former state legislator said, "I was amazed with his failure to be honest with this community. He's done immeasurable damage to our school system." A parent stated, "I think a lot of citizens in Bowie County would be happy to see him leave." Ford ultimately resigned mid-year during his second year as superintendent. However, he was hired as a consultant by the district to serve as superintendent for the remainder of the school year.

A Clash of Leadership Styles and Cultures

From the beginning of his tenure, there was an on-going clash of leadership styles between Frank Ford, members of the community, and the school board. Only five months into his superintendency, concerned citizens created an accountability group called The Citizens for Accountability in Bowie County Schools. Ford had been superintendent for less than a year when the group asked him to resign—partly in response to his proposed budget cuts. He refused. Two board members, Mr. Koch and Ms. Calhoun, publicly stated that they wanted Ford to resign. One parent, Jim

Dennis, said Ford exercised a "military style of leadership" in handling the district's budget woes. During Ford's first year in office, the district faced an anticipated $500,000 shortfall due to cuts in state education funding. In response, Ford proposed cutting 27 teacher aides and an assistant principal's position. His rationale was to cut personnel down to the minimal level necessary to remain accredited—a strategy he had previously used as a state takeover manager. His proposal drew sharp criticism from parents and teachers. Critics from within the school system charged that making such cuts in a small town where everyone knows everyone else was very difficult. The elementary school principal, Anna Manning, reported that she cried when she told her staff that they may receive pink slips. She explained: "I know their families and I felt like I was the one taking the food off their tables." Ford reprimanded Manning for her emotional response and he allegedly countered "Don't look at faces, look at spaces"—a response that was not well received because it conflicted with the cultural norms of the community. Ultimately, the school board approved a measure to reduce the number of teacher aides from 28 to 11 over 3 years by attrition.

Parents were also upset over Superintendent Ford's proposal to eliminate drivers' education, over a number of "special meetings" held by the board that were not advertised (including one meeting at a school board member's home), and over a drop in student academic performance on the state standardized tests. Although Ford attempted to respond to these issues, his failure to understand local politics and his strong resistance to compromise ultimately doomed his administration.

The issues of parent and community discontent were a source of distraction for Superintendent Ford, but even more time-consuming were the numerous lawsuits with which Ford was involved during his first year as superintendent. These suits ranged from charges that Ford and the board violated open meeting policies to more serious allegations of malicious conduct. Critics of Ford claimed that he was on a mission to fire anyone who disagreed with him and that he burdened teachers and school administrators he didn't like with demands for "show cause" letters. Skeptics claimed that he wanted to eliminate his critics and fill the vacancies with young, inexperienced people because they cost less to hire and were impressionable and more easily molded into compliant employees. One interviewee claimed that Ford was aggressive in trying to get his way and that, in at least one case, he attempted to influence a school council's decision to hire an assistant principal (at the elementary school where Manning was principal). Ford did not want the assistant principal position filled and was accused of threatening school-based decision-making council members. He allegedly warned them that if they hired the assistant principal, he would require each council member to answer for their actions in a public hearing.

One of the more controversial issues Ford faced involved the annual review of the elementary school principal, Anna Manning. Manning, an outspoken critic of Ford, was given an unsatisfactory annual performance evaluation even though her school's performance on state standardized exams had improved every year. Manning hired a lawyer and appealed her evaluation. Ultimately, it was determined that Ford failed to comply with procedural rules and Manning's evaluation was changed to a satisfactory review.

One result of this conflict was that teachers and parents began to question Ford's leadership and, as stated previously, The Citizens for Accountability in Bowie County Schools gained members and became even more outspoken in its criticism of Ford. Supporters of Ford claimed that The Citizens for Accountability was created to discredit him and position Anna Manning to take over the superintendency. Ultimately, Ford did resign and Manning was appointed the new superintendent. Manning was one of four finalists to replace Frank Ford and her appointment was not without controversy.

Superintendent Manning Takes Control

Questions about conflicts of interests and accusations of back-room dealings clouded Manning from the beginning of her application process. One issue was that three of the five members of the school board had ties to Manning's husband. One board member worked in the same bank as Manning's husband and had been involved in a business venture with him. Another board member was part of the same business deal. The third member worked for the same bank (in a different branch) and once worked with Anna Manning in the schools. Although no one publicly accused the board of wrongdoing, the board chair received more than 60 unsigned letters alleging, among other things, that Anna Manning was a lock for the superintendent's job because of the links between her husband and the three board members. Manning's response to the allegations was that it's a small town and that, of course, she would have ties to the community and to board members but that that didn't mean the superintendent's search was rigged. Despite the controversy, Manning was appointed superintendent and consequently numerous central office administrators and other school level administrators hired under Ford either resigned or were forced out.

DISCUSSION

This case study highlights the importance of history and context when analyzing clashes between the leadership styles of non-traditional superintendents (non-educators), school boards, and the community. In this case, while the leadership style of Superintendent Ford appears in conflict with some community members' expectations as well as those of the board, the long history of superintendent-school board conflict in this district contributed significantly to the leadership crisis.

The legacy of the state's school reform act and its restructuring of school governance dramatically impacted the role of educational leaders and school boards. Superintendents and school boards lost power and control and some are still struggling to adjust to this model of governance. Bowie County's board has been unwilling to forgo micro-management and this has contributed to the continuing turmoil, conflict, and leadership crisis in the district.

Nevertheless, the blame does not rest solely on the school board. Non-traditional superintendents, such as Ford, appear to be more uncomfortable with the bureaucracy and grassroots politics than superintendents who have risen through the educational ranks. Paul Houston of AASA observed that many non-traditional superintendents find the political aspect of the job very complicated, daunting, and frustrating because outsiders often fail to appreciate the limits to their authority and the need to work with diverse constituencies (Council of State Governments, 2004). This was apparently the case with Ford, who was demonstratively ruffled by efforts to organize protests against his policies. According to several sources, Ford was greatly agitated by criticism and suggestions for improvement from other educational leaders within the system. He viewed the insiders as part of the problem, not as part of the solution. This attitude resulted in a great deal of conflict with career educators who were already skeptical of an outsider's ability to reshape the structure and culture of an institution the leader had no experience operating within.

Equally problematic is that often when boards hire non-traditional superintendents, they are looking for a maverick or a "highly effective medicine man" (Cronin & Usdan, 2003, p. 177)—someone to come in from the outside and shake up the system. However, research to date has not confirmed that non-traditional superintendents are any more unconventional than their traditionally trained peers (Public Agenda, 2003). Possibly, selection committees operate with a bias against anyone with extremely radical ideas or who support greater consumer choice. Thus, the non-traditional superintendents may not be as unconventional as their backgrounds may make them appear (Public Agenda, 2003). Most often, the conventions they embrace are "a technocrat's convention that systems and 'systemic' thinking can solve problems" (Public Agenda, 2003, p. 51). This appears to be the case with Ford who failed to introduce new, radical approaches to reform, but instead focused on cutting expenses to more effectively manage the district's budget.

IMPLICATIONS FOR PRACTICE

When school boards seek out non-traditional superintendents, it is often in an attempt to find a heroic leader who can salvage a failing system. However, it appears that it is not the fact that individuals are educational outsiders that makes the difference, but rather that they have the inter-personal qualities, political acumen, and leadership skills required to lead a school district and work with a school board. Successful school leaders are able to bring often-divided boards, communities, parents, and staff together around a core vision of school improvement (Stanford, 1999). Superintendents unwilling or unable to accurately read the organizational culture of the school system and surrounding community, and unwilling to invest time cultivating relationships with key stakeholders, are unable to lead because, quite simply, no one will follow them. Ford failed to build a rapport with educators and the broader community and, as a result, when he made unilateral decisions to cut staff, his decisions were challenged and scrutinized. He was viewed as uncaring and unsympathetic to the needs of individuals who had lived and worked in the community their entire lives.

Successful non-traditional superintendents surround themselves with trained people from within the educational establishment. Usually, their number two person is a traditional educator. This was not the case with Ford who hired non-educators for central office staff and a non-traditional high school principal (from the business world). He effectively increased the number of educational outsiders and this was not well received by many of the district's teachers and administrators.

As a former military officer, Ford may have been well-trained and skilled at battle. While some schools and school districts resemble battle-fields, Cronin and Usdan (2003) remind us that successful school leadership requires a talent for figuring out ways to improve classroom and student performance. Ford failed to do this. In the end, it was his inability to work within the culture of the community and the school board that led to ineffectual leadership, near-constant conflict, and his resignation.

It appears that the Bowie County school board created a recipe for failure in hiring an outsider to instigate reform in a close-knit community. The board attempted to rectify the problem with their choice for Ford's replacement. Anna Manning, the new superintendent, is a career educator who came up through the educational ranks in the Bowie County school system. The board hopes that she will be more sensitive to the community's needs, more attuned to the culture of the school district and surrounding community, and that her experience in the system will help her steer the district onto a course of continual reform and improvement. However, the tumultuous experiences of other traditionally-trained superintendents and the activism of the board in micromanaging school policy suggests that Manning's reign will not be without problems. It remains to be seen if the controversy surrounding the hiring of Manning will ultimately limit her ability to take charge of the school system.

NOTES

1. A pseudonym. Consistent with qualitative research methodology, some of the personal details and geographic locations have been changed to protect the identity of the superintendent, other interviewees, and the community. All names used in this case study are pseudonyms.
2. This board member stated her intention not to seek re-election in Fall 2002.
3. Duddle quickly transformed a perennially losing football team into a state champion, a feat considered one of the biggest upsets in that state's high school football history.

REFERENCES

Björk, L. G., Bell, R. J., & Gurley, D. K. (2002). Politics and the socialization of superintendents. In G. Perreault & F. Lunenburg (Eds.), *The changing world of school administration* (pp. 294-311). Lanham, MD: Scarecrow Press.

Blum, J. (2004, May 21). D.C. superintendent search hurt by oversight dispute. *Washington Post.* Retrieved July 1, 2004, from http://www.washingtonpost.com/wp-dyn/articles/A43638-2004May20.html

Bogdan, R. C., & Biklen, S. K. (1992). *Qualitative research for education* (2nd ed.). Boston: Allyn and Bacon.

Boyd, W. L. (1976). The public, the professionals, and educational policy: Who governs? *Teaches College Record, 77*(4), 539-578.

Browne-Ferrigno, T., Rinehart, J. S., & Fusarelli, B. C. (2003, November). *The Kentucky principalship: Redesigned by ISLLC standards, assessed by educational practitioners, influenced by policy and context.* Paper presented at the Annual Meeting of the University Council for Educational Administration, Portland, OR.

Burlingame, M. (1988). The politics of education and educational policy: The local level. In N. J. Boyan (Ed.), *Handbook of research on educational administration* (pp. 439-454). New York: Longman.

Can Non-Educators Lead Our Schools? (2000, June 16). *Education World.* Retrieved June 29, 2004, from http://www.educationworld.com/a_admin/admin175.shtml

Carter, G. R., & Cunningham, W. G. (1997). *The American school superintendent: Leading in an age of pressure.* San Francisco: Jossey-Bass.

Council of State Governments. (2004, January 16). *AASA Director Paul Houston talks about the "Politics" and the "politics" of school leadership.* Retrieved June 29, 2004, from http://www.csg.org/CSG/Policy/education/Dr.+Houston+interview.htm

Council of the Great City Schools. (2003, October). Urban school superintendents: Characteristics, tenure, and salary. *Urban Indicator, 7*(1), 1-7.

Cronin, J. M., & Usdan, M. D. (2003). Rethinking the urban superintendency: Nontraditional leaders and new models of leadership. In W. L. Boyd & D. Miretzky (Eds.), *American educational governance on trial: Change and challenges* (pp. 177-195). Chicago: University of Chicago Press.

Danzberger, J. P. (1994, January). Governing the nation's schools. *Phi Delta Kappan, 75*(5), 367-374.

Danzberger, J. P., Kirst, M. W., & Usdan, M. D. (1992). *Governing public schools: New times, new requirements.* Washington, DC: Institute for Educational Leadership.

Donmoyer, R., Imber, M., & Scheurich, J. J. (Eds.). (1995). *The knowledge base in educational administration.* Albany: State University of New York Press.

Feuerstein, A., & Opfer, V. D. (1998). School board chairmen and school superintendents: An analysis of perceptions concerning special interest groups and educational governance. *Journal of School Leadership, 8,* 373-398.

Finn, C. E., Jr., & Keegan, L. G. (2004, Summer). Lost at sea. *Education Next, 4*(3), 15-17.

Fusarelli, L. D., Cooper, B. S., & Carella, V. A. (2003). Who will serve? An analysis of superintendent occupational perceptions, career satisfaction, and mobility. *Journal of School Leadership, 13*(3), 304-327.

Fusarelli, L. D., & Petersen, G. J. (2002). Changing times, changing relationships: An exploration of current trends influencing the relationship between superintendents and boards of education. In G. Perreault & F. Lunenburg (Eds.), *The changing world of school administration* (pp. 282-293). Lanham, MD: Scarecrow Press.

Geiger, P. E. (2002, February). When superintendents become the generals. *The School Administrator.* Retrieved September 25, 2002, from http://www.aasa.org/publications/sa/2002_02/colGeiger.htm

Glass, T., & Bjork, L. G. (2003). The superintendent shortage: Findings from research on school board presidents. *Journal of School Leadership, 13*(3), 264-287.

Greene, K. R. (1992). Models of school board policy-making. *Educational Administration Quarterly, 28*(2), 220-236.

Hess, F. M. (2003, Fall). Lifting the barrier. *Education Next, 3*(4), 12-19.

Hess, F. M. (2004). *Common sense school reform.* New York: Palgrave Macmillan.

Konnert, W. M., & Augenstein, J. J. (1995). *The school superintendency: Leading education into the 21st century.* Lancaster, PA: Technomic.

Kowalski, T. J. (1995). *Keepers of the flame: Contemporary urban superintendents.* Thousand Oaks, CA: Corwin Press.

Kowalski, T. J. (1999). *The school superintendent: theory, practice, and cases.* Upper Saddle River, NJ: Prentice-Hall.

Kowalski, T. J., & Glass, T. E. (2002). Preparing superintendents in the 21st century. In B. S. Cooper & L. D. Fusarelli (Eds.), *The promises and perils facing today's school superintendent* (pp. 41-59). Lanham, MD: Scarecrow Press.

Lincoln, Y. S., & Guba, E. G. (1985). *Naturalistic inquiry.* Beverly Hills, CA: Sage.

Morgan, C., & Petersen, G. J. (2002). The role of the district superintendent in leading academically successful school districts. In B. S. Cooper & L. D. Fusarelli (Eds.), *The promises and perils facing today's school superintendent* (pp. 175-196). Lanham, MD: Scarecrow Press.

National Commission on Excellence in Education. (1983). *A nation at risk.* Retrieved June 29, 2004, from http://www.ed.gov/pubs/NatAtRisk/risk.html

Natkin, G., Cooper, B., Fusarelli, L. D., Alborano, J., Padilla, A., & Ghosh, S. (2002). Myth of the revolving-door superintendency. *The School Administrator, 59*(5), 28-31.

Nygren, B. (1992). Two-party tune up. *American School Board Journal, 178*(7), 35.

Pankratz, R. S., & Petrosko, J. M. (Eds.). (2000). *All children can learn.* San Francisco: Jossey-Bass.

Petersen, G. J. (1999). Demonstrated actions of instructional leaders: An examination of five California superintendents. *Education Policy Analysis Archives, 7*(18). Retrieved June 29, 2004, from http://epaa.asu.edu/epaa/v7n18.html

Petersen, G. J., & Short, P. M. (2001). School board presidents and the district superintendent relationship: Applying the lens of social influence. *Educational Administration Quarterly, 37*(4), 533-570.

Public Agenda. (2003). *Rolling up their sleeves.* New York: Author.

Renchler, R. (1992). Urban superintendent turnover: The need for stability. *Urban Superintendents' Sounding Board, 1*(1), 2-13.

Stanford, J. (1999). *Victory in our schools.* New York: Bantam Books.

Tallerico, M. (1989). The dynamics of superintendent-school board relationships: A continuing challenge. *Urban Education, 24,* 215-232.

Tucker, M. (2003, Fall). Out with the old. *Education Next, 3*(4), 20-24.

U.S. Census Bureau. (2001). Retrieved September 7, 2002, from http://quickfacts.census.gov/qfd/states/21/21017.html

CHAPTER 7

POLITICAL AND APOLITICAL SCHOOL BOARD AND SUPERINTENDENT TURNOVER

Revisiting Critical Variables in the Dissatisfaction Theory of American Democracy

Thomas Alsbury

As early as the late 1800s and early 1900s, educational administrators have been aware of the effects of politics on the efficient and effective operation of schools. Wirt and Kirst (1992) suggested that local school politics indeed influences the relationship between school officials and the community. A governance theory crafted by Lutz and Iannaccone (1978), purported that community dissatisfaction eventually leads to school board member and superintendent turnover, and this turnover, if frequent, may adversely influence stability and continuity of purpose within the staff, especially in an environment of change (Fullan & Miles, 1992). Presently, a national call for school reform and legislated accountability measures have increased the need for local administrators and

The Politics of Leadership: Superintendents and School Boards in Changing Times, 135–155
Copyright © 2005 by Information Age Publishing
135

school board members to anticipate and better understand community conflict and the effect upon the school organization.

SCHOOL GOVERNANCE THEORIES

Theorists have formulated several explanations and models to best describe the political mechanisms operating within local school boards and central office administration. Theories include the Continuous Participation Theory (Zeigler & Jennings, 1974), the Decision-Output Theory (Wirt & Kirst, 1992), and the Dissatisfaction Theory of Democracy (Iannaccone & Lutz, 1970). Mitchell (1978) indicated that these theories represented three "different concepts of democracy with different tests for its reality" (p. 76).

Continuous Participation theorists note that findings of low voter participation in school board elections, limited variety in political platforms, internal recruitment of replacement board members, and uncontested board seats (Zeigler & Jennings, 1974) indicate that schools don't function as particularly democratic entities despite the local election of school board members (Mitchell, 1978). Because school board members do not represent nor are endorsed through the vote of a majority constituency they fail to fall under the scrutiny of true democratic controls.

The Decision-Output Theory (Wirt & Kirst, 1992) examines relationships between the inputs (demands and resources) on a school governance system and the outputs (programs and policy) of that system. While the Theory agrees that while a locally elected board system appears to provide citizens the option of influencing their school, "The promise of referendum control by citizens [in school governance] ... has not been matched by reality" (Wirt & Kirst, p. 222). Iannaccone and Lutz (1994), in delineating the differences in their Dissatisfaction Theory conclude, "While conceding that citizens are occasionally able to compel their will at referenda, Decision-Output Theory still views local educational governance as undemocratic" (p. 40).

Iannaccone & Lutz (1970), conversely, describe local school governance as a democratic process where citizens periodically reach a point of sufficient dissatisfaction and selectively defeat school board members for the purpose of changing the direction of the school district. They contend that following a change in the membership in the school board through election defeat or forced resignation or retirement, the superintendent is often replaced, leading to policy change within the district. This is a frequently observed sequence of events since superintendents generally lack tenure protection and are vulnerable to replacement. Despite the positive intention of the local electorate, frequent turnover in the leadership may lead to discontinuity in organizational goals, policy, and procedures, and may negatively affect the entire organization (Grady & Bryant, 1989). In addition, rapid turnover of top school officials can impede the achievement of positive school reform (Olson, 1995).

The governance theories presented above, reflect three distinct philosophical assumptions when determining whether a local system is governed democratically. The Continuous Participation Theory defines the level of democracy as congruent with the level of public participation in school governance. The Decision-Output Theory defines democratic governance as the congruity between public demands on the school and the schools delivery of those demands. Lutz and Wang (1987) indicate that the Dissatisfaction theory defines democracy as the freedom to participate when school patrons decide to do so. The unique perspective among organizational theories defines and measures democracy based on the *opportunity* to change a school system, rather than on how frequently citizens choose to act. It is a theoretical focus on "liberty of opposition seen in the capacity to unseat those in office" (Lutz & Iannaccone, 1978, p. 131) that makes the Dissatisfaction Theory unique among school governance theories.

DISSATISFACTION THEORY OF AMERICAN DEMOCRACY

Iannaccone and Lutz (1970) purport that their Dissatisfaction Theory of Democracy is the most accurate in describing the chain of events that occur within a school governance system. The Theory describes a political cycle that includes community dissatisfaction, school board turnover, superintendent turnover and school policy change. Iannaccone and Lutz (1994) note the importance of collecting data on these four major components of the Theory over a long period of time, since the public act to change their school's governing body sporadically and only after reaching sufficient dissatisfaction. The Dissatisfaction Theory describes a chain of events that begins with the public reaching a critical level of dissatisfaction, followed by a dramatic increase in their involvement in school elections. When involvement reaches the necessary level, one or more school board members are replaced, leading to pressured turnover of the superintendent within three years. Generally, the new superintendent brings with him/her a change of school policy that more closely matches the most recent community concerns. Studies confirming significant relationships between the components of this ordered chain of events has met with varying success. It has been suggested that the ability to demonstrate a significant relationship between incumbent school board defeat and superintendent turnover is "central to this theory [Dissatisfaction Theory] and has been developed as a broad indicator of the flow of changed ideological and value commitments from the citizens to the school management system" (Mitchell, 1978, p. 76). Consequently, many studies have focused on measuring the relationship between the rates of incumbent school board and superintendent turnover, with initial studies supporting the Dissatisfaction Theory (Ledoux & Burlingame, 1973; Lutz & Iannaccone, 1978; Mitchell & Thorsted, 1976). Conversely, more recent studies been less supportive of the Theory (Hosman, 1990; Weninger & Stout, 1989), with some suggesting that an expansion of traditionally identified variables may be necessary to more adequately detect the four distinct components predicted by the Dissatisfaction Theory (Ledoux & Burlingame, 1973).

Expanding the Definition of School Board Turnover

The link between school board member defeat and superintendent turnover is the most widely studied and one of the few directly measurable components of the Dissatisfaction Theory. Nearly every study from 1966 to the present has failed to adequately define school board turnover, presuming that all turnover is equivalent to election defeat. Researchers explain that board members, who detect community disapproval, simply resign or retire to avoid the embarrassment of an upcoming election defeat, thereby justifying the use of all turnover data in studies of the Dissatisfaction Theory (Mitchell & Thorsted, 1976; Rada, 1984). In opposition to this presumption, surveys by the National School Board Association indicate that board members resign or retire for personal, financial, or moral reasons rather than political conflict or pressure from the community (Erickson & Keirnes, 1978; Mitchell & Spady, 1983). In reviewing the methods of most quantitative studies on the Dissatisfaction Theory, it appears that researchers have used yearly lists of school board members to detect turnover leaving them no means to determine the reasons for school board turnover.

Since the Dissatisfaction Theory centers on a sufficiently disgruntled community taking action by defeating a school board member it could be suggested that using *all* turnover data may significantly influence any subsequent correlation measure between school board and superintendent turnover and thus the conclusions of such studies. This is especially important since school board and superintendent turnover frequently occur in the absence of community dissatisfaction and thus do not reflect the episode described by the Theory (Mitchell & Thorsted, 1976). Mitchell (1978) said, "Future work needs to be done on the possibility that a more refined operational definition of *incumbent defeat* could be generated" (p. 89). Mitchell (1978) went on to conclude that "the impact of these refinements in the definition of incumbent defeat could alter significantly the picture of the relationship between incumbent defeat and superintendent turnover" (p. 89).

A need existed, therefore, to conduct a study of superintendent and school board member turnover, including a distinction between voluntary and involuntary turnover of board members. Since Iannaccone and Lutz's (1970) terminology for school board defeat was not clearly delineated, there was a need to provide a more uniform definition for *political* and *apolitical school board turnover,* and school board member *defeat,* further operationalizing Dissatisfaction Theory. In addition, there was a need to include qualitative data collection methods in studying school districts that do not seem, in light of the quantitative data, to follow the chain of events described in Dissatisfaction Theory.

METHODS

Quantitative Study Phase Return Rate

Quantitative and qualitative study methods were employed in two phases of the project. In the first phase of the study, a double post-card survey was mailed to all superintendents (296) in a state in the Northwest region of the United States, with 176 surveys returned representing a rate of 59.5%. All returned surveys were used in the study and were determined using chi-square analysis to have a high level of representation based upon district size, organizational structure, and geographic distribution. The return rate was a sufficient number, given the representativeness of the data, for the analysis techniques used in this study (Gliner & Morgan, 2000).

The little-used double postcard survey is comprised of a double postcard upon which the survey is printed. On this double postcard survey, superintendents were asked to respond to five general questions including the trend in student enrollment, community population, and socioeconomic changes. The survey asked for the year of each school board turnover from 1993-2000; whether the turnover was a retirement, resignation, or defeat; and the reason for the turnover. The section requesting school board turnover data used a modified forced choice design, which allowed the respondent to select from a number of pre-determined options and to add independent responses if desired. The available choices for why school board members resigned or retired included the following: (a) too time consuming, (b) satisfied all her/his goals, (c) personal or family health, (d) served long enough/someone else's turn, (e) public pressure, (f) dissatisfied with school programs, (g) time wasted on unimportant matters, (h) interferes with personal business, (i) state/federal reform movement, (j) conflict with other board members, (k) teacher unions, (l) moved out of town or voter district, and (k) other. Respondents could select multiple responses and could add additional items under "other."

The Chi-square Test for Independence and the Bonferroni t statistic were used to test for a significant relationship between superintendent and school board member turnover. The level of statistical significance for the study was established at .05 with a corrected alpha level factor of .033 from the Bonferroni t formula results, to avoid Type I error common for multiple chi-square testing using the same data.

Defining Political and Apolitical School Board Turnover

School board member and superintendent turnover data were disaggregated and analyzed comparing all school board turnover to all superintendent turnover, and *politically motivated* school board turnover to all superintendent turnover. The data on the reasons for school board member turnover were operationally defined as political or apolitical turnover as shown in Table 7.1. In this study, *apolitical* school board turnover was designated as resignation or retirement, under indicated survey options a, b, c, d, and l. *Politically motivated* school board turnover was designated as defeat, or resignation or retirement when options e, f, g, h, i, j, k, and/or appropriate reasons noted under option m, "other," were selected. To

Table 7.1.   Operational Designations for Determining Political and Apolitical School Board Member Turnover

Politically Motivated Turnover (Survey Options Selected)	Apolitically Motivated Turnover (Survey Options Selected)
(e) Public pressure	(a) Too time consuming
(f) Dissatisfied with school programs	(b) Satisfied all her/his goals met
(g) Time wasted on unimportant matters	(c) Personal or family health
(h) Interferes with personal business	(d) Served long enough/Someone else's turn
(i) State/Federal reform movements	(l) Moved out of town or voter district
(j) Conflict with other board members	(m) Other
(k) Teacher Unions	
(m) Other	

maintain a conservative approach, the selection of a single politically motivated reason for board turnover was characterized as equivalent to defeat in this study. The choices provided on the survey regarding why school board members retired or resigned were taken from national school board surveys and research studies conducted on the reasons for school board resignation and retirement (Erickson & Keirnes, 1978; Robinson & Wood, 1987). It is important to note that however conservative the definition in this study, even reported apolitical turnover could mask pressured retirement or resignation. However, because the survey was confidential and board member names were not shared, and there was an allowance for multiple responses, there would be little reason for the superintendent to refrain from an honest assessment. It is likely that they would have known about any political motivations for a school board turnover. In addition, conservative options for politically motivated turnover were used to help ensure more accurate reporting and the ability to detect hidden political pressure. For example, selection (g) time wasted on unimportant matters, as a reason for retirement or resignation may not represent community dissatisfaction or an ensuing politically motivated turnover, but board change indicated under this option on the survey would have been designated as equivalent to defeat in this study.

QUANTITATIVE RESULTS

The study investigated the existence of a statistically significant relationship between school board member and superintendent turnover when delineating between all school board turnover and politically motivated turnover and defeat. In the study, analyses were conducted for superintendent turnover 1-, 2-, 3-, and 4-years after each of the school board elections were held in 1993, 1995, 1997, and 1999. Previous research indicates that it may take up to four years to observe a superintendent change after board member turnover has occurred (Lutz & Iannaccone, 1978). At the time of the study, most superintendents received three-year contracts so it is reasonable to expect a gap of at least three years before a resulting change in the superintendent; even if the contract was non-renewed after the first year. Also, research has suggested that it may take three to four years for new school board members to become comfortable with their position and able to gain other board members' support to non-renew a superintendent, or they may need the confidence of a re-election win before presuming that they have a community mandate to take action (Mitchell, 1978).

Chi-square measuring for a relationship between *all* school board turnover and superintendent turnover up to four years after a school board election resulted in a non-significant result ($\chi^2 = 1.79$, $df = 2$, $p = 0.4077$). Chi-square measuring for a relationship between *politically motivated* school board turnover and superintendent turnover up to four years after a school board election resulted in a significant result ($\chi^2 = 10.75$, $df = 3$, $p = 0.0132$). It can be clearly seen that delineating for politically motivated school board member turnover had a noticeable impact on the results in this study. This finding provides a note of caution regarding the limitations of statistical research in examining a myriad of variables likely to impact school governance. Researchers have the challenge of collecting and analyzing numerous uncontrollable variables, in an effort to discover those that measure the presence or absence of a connection between the cogent components of a particular governance theory. In studies of the Dissatisfaction Theory distinguishing between political and apolitical turnover appears to be a critical variable missed in previous studies. Additionally, inconsistent results from studies attempting to empirically evaluate the Dissatisfaction Theory using quantitative data highlights the importance of exploring, through qualitative methods, what is happening in school district governance. However, even when controlling for political and apolitical school board turnover, 21 districts produced quantitative data that did not appear to support Dissatisfaction Theory.

QUALITATIVE RESULTS

Selecting Districts for Qualitative Study

In his study, Freeborn (1966) called districts whose quantitative data relationships did not seem to support the Dissatisfaction Theory, "deviant cases," and suggested that further ethnographic data may need to be collected to explore the discrepancy. This study, shared Freeborn's (1966) assessment, and defined a "deviant case" as a district with frequent school board turnover but no ensuing superintendent change as would be predicted by the Theory. It should be noted that a "deviant case" is defined based upon quantitative school board member and superintendent turnover data that does not *appear* to support the Theory, but upon further investigation may follow the Theory's predicted sequence of events. Mitchell (1978) explained that school board member and superintendent turnover can occur in the absence of community dissatisfaction, and recommended that "other important sources of variance in incumbent defeat and superintendent turnover be measured" (p. 79). As recommended by Freeborn (1966) and Mitchell (1978), this study probed further into these "deviant" districts using qualitative research methods.

Introduction of the Adams District

The districts in this portion of the study were unique in context, but met the selection criteria as a "deviant" district. The choice to report exclusively on the Adams district in this chapter was prompted by space restrictions and the desire to fully explore the contextual dynamics important in a qualitative analysis. Additionally, it can be reported that although the data were varied and unique in the remaining districts, and beyond the scope of this chapter, similar conclusions supporting the use of the Dissatisfaction Theory resulted.

Qualitative data were collected using semi-structured open-ended interviews of the superintendent, the assistant superintendent, the district business manager, the superintendent secretary, and the current school board members (Patton, 2002). The purpose of the interviews was to gather information about the district from 1980 to 2000 in regard to demographics; socioeconomic changes; population changes; enrollment changes; voting patterns; community dissatisfaction; school board and superintendent turnover and reasons for the turnover; gender on the school board; voting patterns on the school board; school policy change; and other elements that might reflect changes in the community, voter participation, school board, superintendent, or school policy. Transcriptions from the audio recordings were highlighted and analyzed for emerging themes. Triangulation of interview data and document collections covering events from 1980 to 2000, included the minutes from school board meetings, budgets, memos, facilities documents, local newspaper letters to the editor, and school news articles.

The Adams School District fit the criteria as a "deviant case" with ten incumbent school board turnovers but no superintendent turnover during the 1993-2000 study period. This number of school board changes was nearly double the average school board turnover in the study. The absence of superintendent turnover following multiple school board turnovers would appear, on its surface, to fail to support a key tenet in the Dissatisfaction Theory: the effect of school board turnover on superintendent change. Documentary data were collected for a period of 1980-2000 in addition to the interview data. For purposes of confidentiality, this system was called the Adams School District and some district demographics are excluded here.

The Adams Community, School District, and Superintendent

District Profile

The Adams School District is located in Adams, a rural, remote community with some logging and farming. The economic health of the community relies on a military base, and related service jobs supporting the military personnel. Recently, the community has attracted retirees who enjoy the remote setting and the beautiful surroundings that offer outdoor activity.

In the 1970s, the community was much smaller and described as being "conservative and closely knit." After the expansion of the military base in the 1980s, the community grew rapidly, nearly doubling in size to its current population of about 20,000. The school had maintained a free and reduced lunch count of around 15%, with increases starting in 1995 leading to a current level of 30%.

In 2000, there were about 6,900 students accommodated by one high school of about 2,000, two middle schools of around 700 each, and six elementary schools with a collective enrollment of 3,500. From 1993 to 1999, the school board, comprised of five members, had ten school board member turnovers, but currently is described as "very stable" by school personnel and board members.

Dr. Miller was appointed to the post of interim superintendent in June 1993, and then continued in the position. The outgoing superintendent left when "budget problems pressured him to resign." Within the first few months of his superintendency, Dr. Miller had made several important changes in the school district due to the budgetary crisis. These involved staff and program reductions.

Changes in the Community Values and Levels of Dissatisfaction

Changes in the community values can be indicated by changes in assessed valuation of property within the school district, changes in school enrollment as hypothesized by Iannaccone and Lutz (1970), changes in socioeconomic status of the community or school population, and changes in external resources. The assessed valuation in the district increased by 50% around 1980, due to the expansion of the local military base. In 1991, the base underwent a reduction in activity and personnel and assessed valuation declined approximately 18% but has increased steadily since then, keeping pace with normal inflation rates. One notable trend was a substantial increase in subsidized housing from 1995 to 2000. Respondents reported that increased low-income housing probably resulted from an increase in number of lower paid jobs starting in 1995. Currently, these homes have begun to attract low-income families from surrounding areas needing hard-to-find subsidized housing, causing a slower assessed valuation growth.

Student enrollment changed over the history of the Adams School District with dramatic increases in 1980 and a 30% reduction in 1991, as a result of military base expansions and declines. The socioeconomic status of the district also changed as a result of changes in military base personnel. Before1980, the community was comprised of lower middle class blue-collar laborers, followed by a significant increase the number of highly paid officers from 1980 to 1995, and then a subsequent return to lower paid enlisted personnel that continues to date. Federal Impact Aid amounting to approximately 22% of the district's revenue budget declined from 1995 to the present and created a diminished need for local levies and lower than average tax rates.

Change in Citizen Participation in School Board Elections

The level of citizen participation in school board elections have often been measured by comparing voter participation rates before and during increased school board or superintendent turnover. Dissatisfaction Theory would predict that a dissatisfied community would likely become more active at election time in an effort to change their school board composition. Other indicators of community participation may include (a) changes in the number of candidates running for school board seats; (b) changes in the number of votes received by incumbents versus the total votes cast in the election; (c) the number of resignations and board appointments to unexpired terms; (d) the number of primary elections; (e) the number of board positions open during the election year; and (f) any unique voter circumstances impacting voting patterns in the community, such as "director" district status.

These data were collected in Adams from 1980 to 2000 and revealed several key changes in community involvement over the district's history. From 1980 to 1986 there was little community participation followed by one vacated board seat and one contested position, including an incumbent and two challengers, from 1986 to 1987. Triangulated interview and document data indicated that these school board changes emanated from community dissatisfaction and resulted in an altered school board position on several policy topics. In 1992, three board positions were up for election, with one incumbent school board member running against a single opponent and two vacated positions refilled by unopposed candidates. The perspective candidates all ran on platforms opposing the existing school board policy and activities, and there was general dissatisfaction from school personnel directed toward the school board and superintendent. From 1993 to 2000, there were nine school board member changes reported as political motivated by the existing school personnel and school board members.

Another important contextual variable in school board elections is the presence or absence of "at large" versus "director district" elections. In the Adams School District, an "at large" voting district, opponents running for vacated or incumbent board seats could choose to run for any seat. Other "director" districts in this State require the school district to be mapped into geographic sections, and attach each board seat to a particular region from within the district, allowing only citizens living in those areas to run for the seat. It is easy to imagine that in "director" districts, there may exist board candidates who better reflect the community's values but would be disallowed from running for a vacated board position. Conversely, other board seats may be difficult to fill or filled by an uncontested candidate, leading to a board composition that does not accurately reflect community values.

Adams School District is a reflection of how unique contextual variables, not easily measured quantitatively can greatly alter our understanding of the level of community influence on local school governance. For example, from 1989 to 1992, while there were multiple changes in the school board, three out of the five board members remained constant, allowing for little change in the board policy disposition. Additionally, during the 1995 election, two antagonists inexplicably chose to run against strong incumbent opponents when they could have filed for board seats that were vacated and run unopposed. The fact that they did not run for the open seats allowed board stability to continue. If both candidates had chosen to run for the unopposed seats, they likely would have been elected, and the board and superintendent may have been pressed into change. Adams school staff and existing school board members could not explain why the opponents did not run in vacated seats.

Change in School Board Positions

Dissatisfaction Theory suggests that if voters are dissatisfied and begin to run against and vote against incumbent board members, old board members are defeated or pressured to resign, and new board members with new values take their place. Data collected to indicate this change include change in the number of incumbent board member defeats; change in the type of board member, for example gender, or socioeconomic composition; and special circumstances concerning the personalities of defeated, resigning, or retiring board members and newly elected board members.

It is predicted by Dissatisfaction Theory that an increase in incumbent *defeat* (not merely apolitical turnover) indicates community dissatisfaction with the existing school board and its values. From 1993 to 2000, nine school member turnovers occurred in Adams. Of these, three board members resigned to care for ill family members, two had job changes requiring a move, one died of cancer, one resigned due to a job change that increased her work hours, one was defeated after choosing not to campaign, and one chose not to run because he was at odds with the other board members. Evaluating other variables, data indicated no discernable change in gender rates or socioeconomic characteristics of the board members from 1980 to 2000.

Another key piece of qualitative data identifies which board members chose to retire or resign, and who replaced them. It is very possible that sometimes turnover on the board is due to bad luck or timing, rather than community dissatisfaction. For example, in Adams, one member who was appointed and then won the seat turned out to be an antagonist; a fact unknown by the voting public or the board members until after the election. During this board member's tenure, he created negativity and conflict on the board and voted to non-renew the superintendent's contract each year. The superintendent noted that if there had been more than one antagonist on the board, he would have resigned his position. After this board member's four-year term, he chose not to run. Two years before this board member's re-election date, a friend with similar antagonistic feelings ran for a school board seat. However, instead of running in a vacated position, this opponent chose to run against the board president who was very popular in the community. The opponent received only 30% of the vote. An unknown individual with views favorable to the current board ran unopposed in the vacated seat. Most school personnel believed that if this antagonist had run in the vacated position he would have won the seat, and both antagonists would have served on the board at the same time. This occurrence would not have been a statement of dissatisfaction by the community as much as timing and happentance. However, it well may have compelled the superintendent to resign his position.

Changes in the Superintendent and School District Policy

Dissatisfaction Theory predicts that the result of school board member defeat(s), will lead to a change in the superintendent, within three years of the board turnover, followed by policy revisions by the new board and superintendent to better match the community's demands. As we review the history of superintendent in Adams, we start with Dr. Nice who served from 1970 to 1986 and retired, being replaced by an interim superintendent, Dr. Jones who retired at the end of 1987 and was replaced with another interim superintendent, Dr. Smith. Dr. Smith was an administrator from the Adams central office who agreed to serve for one year and belay his planned retirement so the district could conduct an extensive national superintendent search. As a result of the search, Dr. Anderson was hired and served from 1987 to 1993. Dr. Miller, the new assistant superintendent, was hired in 1988 from outside the district. In 1993, Dr. Anderson resigned, due to budgetary problems, political pressure, and a recent change of three school board seats representing two defeats at the polls. Dr. Miller was hired for one year as interim superintendent and then was officially appointed to the position in 1994.

Dr. Miller began his tenure, in 1994, by eliminating four administrative, teaching, and support staff positions. Budget problems forced Dr. Miller to cut instructional aide time, increase class sizes, add extra-curricular student fees, and reduce the length of the school day. All of these policy changes spoke to concerns of the staff and community, as determined through triangulation of data from documents, interviews, and board minutes. At the time of the study, Dr. Miller remained as superintendent despite 10 school board member changes.

Data Analysis

Qualitative data provide valuable insight into the governance events occurring at the Adams School District that would not have surfaced through quantitative analysis alone. Using numerical data concerning the high school board member turnover in isolation might lead one to predict, based upon Dissatisfaction Theory that the superintendent should have been replaced between 1993-2000. Adams, contains contextually unique variables, as do every school district, that may influence study conclusions on the reliability of Dissatisfaction Theory. Indeed, superintendent turnover, in Adams, occurred in 1986, 1987, and 1993, during times of lower school board member turnover. However, when analyzed through the lens of the qualitative data, the political chain of events seems to support Dissatisfaction Theory in its basic theoretical premises.

Table 7.2 provides a chronology of events as they occurred in Adams compared against the four major study variables or events described by Dissatisfaction Theory. Table 7.2 shows that Adams experienced changes in community values during three time periods in 1980, 1991, and 1995; and one change in citizen participation in 1992. It also shows four periods with distinct changes in the school board configuration and three periods of superintendent change. In Adams, there is superintendent turnover without school board turnover from 1980 to 1991 and school board turnover without superintendent turnover between 1993 and 2000; these data do not distinguish between political and apolitical board turnover and fail to support Dissatisfaction Theory. However, if we distinguish between political and apolitical board turnover, and evaluate changes in Adams based upon the four major changes predicted by Dissatisfaction Theory, support for the Theory emerges. When controlling for politically

Table 7.2. Chronology of School Governance Events in Adams as Identified by Dissatisfaction Theory Variables

	Changes in Major Study Variables			
Year	Community Values	Citizen Participation in Election	Board Values	District Policy
1980	Military base expansion Enrollment increase Assessed value increase			
1986			2 new board members-vacated seats/apolitical turn-over	16-year supt. retires/interim replacement
1987				Interim replacement retires Outside superintendent hired
1988				
1989				
1991	Military base decline Enrollment decline Assessed value decline			
1992		Increased voters More challenges Closer vote count	3 antagonists join board political turnover	
1993				Supt.forced to retire/inside interim
1994				Interim becomes supt.-inside
1995	Military base changes Socioeconomic decline Federal aid decline		4 apolitical turnover	
1998			4 apolitical turnover 1apolitical turnover	
1999				
2000				

The shaded region represents a period where each of the four theoretical variables of the Dissatisfaction Theory were evidenced leading to forced superintendent turnover in 1993.

motivated school board turnover, Adams remains seemingly peaceful throughout the study period, with the exception of 1991 to 1994, where three board changes are purposeful and community-driven. Only during this time period, do we observe changes in community values, as evidenced by military base, enrollment, and assessed value decline, followed by an increase in voter participation in the local school board elections. During this time period, voters successfully defeated three incumbent board members and placed three opposing viewpoints on the board, representing the first board majority change in Adams. Within two to three years of the school board change, the superintendent was forced into retirement and the new superintendent effected major changes in the school policy. When the data from the Adams School District includes the seminal components of Dissatisfaction Theory and only politically motivated board turnover, the series of governance events described by the theory is evident, as shown in the highlighted portion of Table 7.2.

It may be beneficial to discuss school board and superintendent turnover that occurs outside of the highlighted section of Table 7.2. An important difference in school board and superintendent turnover occurring outside of the highlighted region of Table 7.2 is the apolitical nature of the turnover and the lack of any data suggesting increased community dissatisfaction. Dissatisfaction Theory does not preclude the possibility of frequent random and apolitical school board member and superintendent turnover, because it does not emanate from community dissatisfaction. Dissatisfaction Theory contends that community's whose values and expectations have become incongruous with the school board will, when their dissatisfaction has reached and adequate level, change school leadership through school board member defeat. This is seminal to the theory's claim of democratic governance and this sequence of events can be seen occurring in Adams between 1991 and 1993. Previous studies of governance theories have focused on the collection of quantitative data over short snapshots of time that disregard the reason for school board turnover and include random apolitical board turnover, not reflecting community dissatisfaction, and not relevant to the political chain of events Dissatisfaction Theory describes.

Luck also played a role in the governance events occurring in Adams. In one incident, school board turnover failed to occur because an opponent chose to run against a popular incumbent rather than an open board seat. In another incident, four years of board turmoil occurred when an appointee turned out to be an antagonist in disguise. In Adams, as in many other smaller communities, numerous school board seats may be vacated due to job changes or illness, and filled by unopposed and unknown candidates. These new board members do not necessarily carry a mandate from the community for change. This occurrence of random board change happens more frequently in director districts where the candidate's physical address pre-selects who can run for particular school board seats. These random, unpredictable, and quantitatively immeasurable events can cloud or extend the time span of the events predicted by Dissatisfaction Theory. In fact, the theory would contend that if a board member won a seat through appointment or uncontested election and was antagonistic toward the existing board and the community, that member should be removed from the board in a subsequent election. Thus, the democratic process presumed to be in effect by Dissatisfaction Theory, works to remove randomly appointed or elected antagonists if they don't reflect the community values. In this study, Dissatisfaction Theory accurately predicted the defeat of the randomly-placed antagonist in the next election in Adams.

DISCUSSION

Studies in educational governance have attempted over the years to lend support to a theory that would help school practitioners and policy-makers better understand, describe, predict, and perhaps control administrative turnover and discontinuity of leadership within the local school district (Iannaccone & Lutz, 1970; Wirt & Kirst, 1992; Zeigler & Jennings, 1974). Iannaccone and Lutz (1970) contended that the citizens democratically exercise their control over local school governance by defeating incumbent school board members at the polls when they become dissatisfied enough with the school's policy. Through this change in school board composition, superintendent leadership is altered and school policy changes to more closely match the community's values.

The quantitative phase of this study focused on the relationship between school board member and superintendent turnover. While some research has supported the use of Dissatisfaction Theory in analyzing political conflict, few quantitative studies have been able to verify any single causal factor, or combination of factors, to predict conflict (Lutz & Wang, 1987). Through quantitative and qualitative data analysis, this study supports making a distinction between political and apolitical school board member turnover, identifying an important variable absent in previous studies of this kind.

In this study, data supported the continued use of Dissatisfaction Theory when a distinction was made between political and apolitical school board turnover. The originators of Dissatisfaction Theory noted the inability of researchers to identify key variables and provide wholistic analysis of events in school districts. Iannaccone and Lutz (1994) said, "early research on the Dissatisfaction Theory did not attempt to probe empirically the full range of the theoretical argument" (p. 42). Others have suggested that gathering a combination of varied and interrelated factors unique to each community may be important to reach a clearer explanation of the data on school board and superintendent turnover (Ledoux & Burlingame, 1973). This study's use of qualitative as well as quantitative data and the more clear definition of school board turnover speaks to concerns voiced about previous research methods, and lends support to Dissatisfaction Theory.

Like in previous studies, quantitative data from Adams, like the high number of school board member turnovers (10 from 1993-2000) would seem to suggest community dissatisfaction and lead to a prediction of superintendent change within three years, according to Dissatisfaction Theory. However, when analyzing qualitative data over a 20-year time span, the political chain of events in Adams appears to follow Dissatisfaction Theory in its basic theoretical premises, as shown in Table 7.2. Notably, Lutz and Iannaccone (1970) developed the Dissatisfaction Theory as a result of a case study involving a single school district. It was the analysis of numerous qualitative variables that emerged through their case study that allowed them to detect some of the major theoretical components functioning in the school district governance. In this study, additional qualitative analyses were conducted on other randomly selected districts and yielded similar support for Dissatisfaction Theory. It is the movement away from case study analysis and toward quantitative evaluations of Dissatisfaction Theory that may have led to a misunderstanding of the theory's foundational variables and an inability of past researchers to recognize the occurrence of the events predicted by the theory.

Some researchers have questioned whether the Dissatisfaction Theory is still useful today, in light of changing community involvement in local school politics. After conducting studies of school governance in urban settings, Lutz and Merz (1992) suggested that an increase in community diversity, population movement, and fragmentation may eliminate the likelihood of shared community values. Since Dissatisfaction Theory presumes that communities act at the polls when the school board does not share the common community values, does the absence of shared values negate the occurrence of the events predicted by the theory? The specific qualitative analysis of events in urban districts was outside the focus of this study. However, through the use of qualitative data analysis and a clear delineation of politically motivated school board turnover, Dissatisfaction Theory still described the political events in Adams and in the other "deviant" school districts in the study. Unlike most recent studies, this study lends support to Dissatisfaction Theory and the presumption of a democratic influence on school governance, and supports further studies to confirm the findings in this State.

IMPLICATIONS FOR PRACTICING SUPERINTENDENTS

The results of this study may be useful to prospective and practicing superintendents in terms of understanding the political dynamics of their district, by providing them the ability to better predict the level of community dissatisfaction and protect the security of their administrative position. If Dissatisfaction Theory indeed describes the events likely to occur in a district, superintendents would be wise to continue to monitor community change variables used in this study including changes in their community's economic status, socioeconomic ratios, assessed valuation, student enrollment, and in- and out migration. Since school boards tend to function with little community involvement under normal circumstances, it is likely that school board and community values may become less congruous over time, especially as the community undergoes change. Prospective and practicing superintendents should be trained to observe and measure these community change variables and understand the importance of engaging in processes that allow for continual two-way communications between the school board and their community. According to Dissatisfaction Theory, failure to attend to these data, will likely result in the removal of the superintendent, and discontinuity in school leadership.

This study also suggests that superintendents need not be as concerned about apolitical school board turnover, even in relatively high rates. However, school leaders should be aware of politically motivated school board resignation and retirement as well as outright defeat, even in the case of a single board change. According to Dissatisfaction Theory, this likely indicates a schism between community and school board values. Because of this, superintendents would be well advised to frequently assess community attitudes toward the district, develop effective plans to respond to the publics concerns, and work on fostering an open, arena style school board, even though a closed, elite leadership style may seem more expedient and initially supported. This would be especially true following a politically motivated school board turnover.

Superintendents should also be aware that dissatisfaction grows over time and a politically motivated school board defeat is probably symptomatic of a large amount of community dissatisfaction. Administrators can keep track of the level of community dissatisfaction by monitoring the number of voters, number of challengers, and the closeness of the vote count between incumbents and challengers during school board elections. Dissatisfaction Theory suggests that citizen participation will increase as dissatisfaction increases. While the community may not garner enough votes to change the school board in a particular election, increases in these electoral rates may indicate rising dissatisfaction that the superintendent may want to address.

Finally, superintendents looking for prospective positions may be well advised to evaluate the school district based upon the four Dissatisfaction Theory variables; community values, citizen participation, politically motivated board change, and superintendent turnover rates. Understanding where the district is in the chain of events described by the Dissatisfaction Theory may assist the superintendent in avoiding a district with the history of a highly unstable administrative and/ or board composition or at least will help them understand what they may encounter. For example, if a district had just experienced a majority change in the school board and that change was apolitical, the superintendent would not need to assume that there was a community concern that needed to be addressed. However, if that same board change had been politically motivated, the incoming superintendent would need to understand that this was an indication of a community's desire to change the direction of district policy and would be well advised to pursue opening communication avenues, working toward an arena or open board style and be prepared to assess, identify, and change key policies or practices in the district that led to the community dissatisfaction. An understanding of Dissatisfaction Theory factors could guide practitioners to more successful and lengthy tenure in their position and possibly provide further continuity of leadership in school districts.

REFERENCES

Erickson, K. A., & Keirnes, B. (1978, December). Former members tell ... why they left the school board. *OSSC Bulletin, 22*(4), 3-35.

Freeborn, R. M. (1966). School board change and succession pattern of superintendents. *Dissertation Abstracts International, 28*(02), 424A. (UMI No. 6709505)

Fullan, M. G., & Miles, M. B. (1992). Getting reform right: What works and what doesn't. *Phi Delta Kappan, 73*(10), 744-752.

Gliner, J. A., & Morgan, G. A. (2000). *Research methods in applied settings: An integrated approach to design and analysis.* London: Lawrence Erlbaum.

Grady, M. L., & Bryant, M. T. (1989). Critical incidents between superintendents and school boards: Implications for practice. *Planning for Change, 20*, 206-214.

Hosman, C. M. (1990). Superintendent selection and dismissal: A changing community defines its values. *Urban Education, 25*, 350-369.

Iannaccone, L., & Lutz, F. W. (1970). *Politics, power and policy: The governing of local school districts.* Columbus, OH: Charles E. Merrill.

Iannaccone, L., & Lutz, F. W. (1994). The crucible of democracy: The local arena. *Journal of Educational Policy, 9*(5), 39-52.

Ledoux, E. P., & Burlingame, M. (1973). The Iannaccone-Lutz model of school board change: A replication in New Mexico. *Educational Administration Quarterly, 9,* 48-65.

Lutz, F. W., & Iannaccone, L. (Eds.). (1978). *Public participation in local school districts: The dissatisfaction theory of democracy.* Lexington, MA: Lexington Books, D.C. Heath.

Lutz, F. W., & Merz, C. (1992). *The politics of school/community relations.* New York: Teachers College Press.

Lutz, F. W., & Wang, L. (1987). Predicting public dissatisfaction: A study of school board member defeat. *Educational Administration Quarterly, 23,* 65-77.

Mitchell, D. E. (1978). Measurement and methodological issues related to research on incumbent defeat and superintendent turnover. In F. W. Lutz & L. Iannaccone (Eds.), *Public participation in local school districts* (pp. 73-99). Lexington, MA: D. C. Heath.

Mitchell, D. E., & Spady, W. G. (1983). Authority, power, and the legitimation of social control. *Educational Administration Quarterly, 19,* 5-33.

Mitchell, D. E., & Thorsted, R. R. (1976). Incumbent school board member defeat reconsidered: New evidence for its political meaning. *Educational Administration Quarterly, 12,* 31-48.

Olson, L. (1995, April 12). Rapid turnover in leadership impedes reforms, study finds. *Education Week,* p. 6.

Patton, M. Q. (2002). *Qualitative research & evaluation methods* (3rd ed.). Thousand Oaks, CA: Sage.

Rada, R. D. (1984). Community dissatisfaction and school governance. *Planning and Changing, 15,* 234-247.

Robinson, N., & Wood, M. (1987, March). *Why school board members choose to seek or not seek re-election: A test of political efficacy and trust theory.* Paper presented at the annual meeting of the American Educational Research Association, Washington, DC.

Weninger, T. A., & Stout, R. T. (1989). Dissatisfaction theory: Policy change as a function of school board member-superintendent turnover: A case study. *Educational Administration Quarterly, 25*(2), 162-80.

Wirt, F. M., & Kirst, M. W. (1992). *Schools in conflict: The politics of education* (3rd ed.). Berkeley, CA: McCutchan.

Zeigler, L. H., & Jennings, M. K. (1974). *Governing American schools.* North Scituate, MA: Duxbury Press.

CHAPTER 8

BUILDING EFFECTIVE SCHOOL SYSTEM LEADERSHIP

Rethinking Preparation and Policy

Michelle D. Young

It has grown increasingly clear that schools must become more successful with a progressively wider range of learners. Our nation's citizens, leaders and businesses continue to look to the United States education system to provide students with the complex skills they need to participate in a knowledge-driven and technology-based society. Although reformers hold diverse perspectives concerning how schools should be supported or goaded to fulfill this responsibility, most now agree that leadership matters and that increasing the expertise and effectiveness of leaders is essential to the success of ongoing efforts to improve PreK-12 education.

The kind of leadership needed to ensure that all students are able to think critically, to solve complex problems and to master essential content areas is a great deal more demanding than that needed to ensure that most students matriculate with a set of routine skills. Moreover the kind of leadership needed to ensure that all teachers are knowledgeable, skillful and able to respond differentially and appropriately in supporting stu-

The Politics of Leadership: Superintendents and School Boards in Changing Times, 157–179

dents' success is much more challenging than that needed to ensure that a certified teacher is assigned to every class.

It is also clear that the capacities that leaders need in order to successfully meet these challenges can only be widely acquired throughout Pre K-12 education by greater investments in leadership preparation and professional development. Moreover, to capitalize on such reform investments, many leaders in the field and higher education believe, there should be a simultaneous and comprehensive restructuring of the systems by which states and school districts license, hire, induct, mentor, and support the professional development of educational leaders (Young & Kochan, 2004).

Unfortunately, amidst the growing certainty that leadership matters, there is much that we do not yet understand about effective leadership preparation. Fundamental to any discussion of leadership preparation is a judgment about what it is that educational leaders must be prepared to do. If leadership is viewed primarily as management of time and resources, then programs should prepare school and school system leaders to be effective managers of time and resources. However, if educational leadership is defined more broadly to include leadership of learning for all students, then preparation must be designed much differently. Leading student learning requires the opportunity to develop a complex set of knowledge and skills that include more traditional areas of study, such as organizational theory, supervision, management, educational finance, and community involvement, but also extend beyond these areas.

Although the role of educational leaders has evolved through a variety of conceptualizations over the years, it is clear that expectations for superintendents have shifted over the last decade from managing school districts in an effort to improve education to playing a direct role in leading learning. Reflecting this shift, scholars of the Superintendency, including Björk (1993), Glass (1992, 1993), Grogan (2003), Murphy and Hallinger (1986), Myers (1992), Paulu (1989), Petersen (2002), Petersen and Barnett (2003), and Cuban (1988), have focused on the superintendent as a leader of learning and instruction.

Current education reforms, most notably the No Child Left Behind Act (NCLB) of 2002, reinforce the school system leader's role in leading learning. NCLB requirements strongly convey an expectation that leaders are ultimately accountable for student learning. The idea of leadership responsibility or accountability for learning, however, did not emerge from NCLB. Rather support has been developing around the notion of leadership for learning for at least a decade. "Embedded within the concept 'leadership for learning' is the expectation that school and district leaders will have a working knowledge of learning, teaching, curriculum construction and alignment" (Björk, Kowalski & Young, in press, p. 3; see also Björk, 1993; Murphy, 1993).

In this chapter, I address the issue of building effective school system leadership through a review of literature on the experiential and knowledge needs of school system leaders as well as the features of ineffective preparation programs. Subsequently, I outline a set programmatic and policy changes that would be needed to create and support the impact of effective superintendency preparation programs on a wide scale. The goal of nation-wide, high quality leadership preparation is one that has never been adopted in this country or elsewhere. Rather, the history of educational leadership preparation in the United States has been characterized by increasingly larger numbers of mediocre programs that provide less than satisfactory preparation (Young, Petersen & Short, 2002). Implementing this goal reflects the objectives of the National Commission for the Advancement of Educational Leadership Preparation (NCAELP) and the aspirations of the University Council for Educational Administration (UCEA), which both support the belief that

> The profession of educational leadership should be grounded on our best understandings of and latest research on student learning and school and school system improvement. We declare that preparation programs need to be built from that foundation; that is, their primary purpose must be to prepare leaders to create schools in which all children are successful. (NCAELP, 2002, p. 1)

Reformed preparation programs and new policy are critical to this goal.

WHERE SHOULD SUPERINTENDENTS COME FROM?

For a school superintendent, successful experience as both a school leader and as an educator is important. Successful experience as a teacher enables a leader to be conversant in the core technology of teaching and learning. Specifically, it ensures that they have developed a foundation of pedagogical and content knowledge as well as an appreciation for the importance of both of these knowledge bases to effective teaching. Successful experience as an educator will also ensure that a leader is more likely to have foundational knowledge in human development, individual learner differences, and assessment.

Success as a school leader is also important preparation for superintendents. Successful experience as a school leader increases the likelihood that an aspiring superintendent will come to his or her preparation program with core knowledge about leadership as well as leadership experience (Glass, 2004). This previous knowledge and experience forms an important foundation for developing the knowledge and skills needed for school district leadership. For example, learning how to positively impact student learning at a district level requires an understanding of how school-based leaders impact student achievement through what they do in the schools. Moreover, this knowledge is rooted in an understanding of how teachers impact student academic knowledge and how school leaders, "know strong instruction when they see it, know how to encourage it when they do not, and know how to set the conditions for continuous academic learning among their teaching staffs" (Stein & Spillane, 2003, p. 30). English (2004a) uses a military example to make this point. English quotes General S.L.A. Marshall who wrote about the importance of officers' being able to do the work of any soldier serving under him or her. Marshall (1996) wrote:

> Ideally, an officer should be able to do the work of any [soldier] serving under him [or her]. There are even some command situations in which the ideal become altogether attainable and a practicable objective. For it may be said without qualification, that if [the officer] not only has this capability, but demonstrates it, so that his [or her soldiers] begin to understand that he [or she] is thoroughly versed in the work problems that concern them, [the officer] can command them in any situation. This is the bedrock of command capacity, and nothing else so well serves to give an officer an absolutely firm position with all who serve under him [or her]. (p. 63)

Additionally, Nestor-Baker and Hoy (2001), who compared reputationally successful superintendents with traditional superintendents, found that prior experience was very important to superintendents' success in their jobs. Specifically, they found that "expert performers" have "larger amounts of if-then scenarios to draw on in navigating the superintendency, allowing them a seemingly intuitive orientation to the tasks at hand" (p. 123).

Even when agreeing that there are desirable knowledge and skills for school district leaders, many people sincerely believe that anyone with successful experience as a manager can be a superintendent or, at least, that having leadership experience in any setting and exposure to relevant knowledge is enough to allow one to lead a district (see, for example: Fordham Foundation, 2003). The evidence suggests otherwise. As English (2004a) explains

> Some ex-generals have shown they can "manage" a school system (for example, Portland, Oregon and Jacksonville, Florida). Some have been flops (Washington, D.C.). Björk, Grogan and Johnson (2003) indicate that former military officers in Kansas City, New Orleans and Seattle found that "their success in achieving specified educational objectives was thwarted by

deeply entrenched social, economic, and political problems" (p. 456). *Manifesto* (Fordham, 2003) admonitions about "opening" the superintendency to non-educators must be viewed with great skepticism, especially so in the high-stakes accountability scenarios which prevail today and require knowledge of curriculum and teaching practices. (p. 76)

Superintendent leadership expertise—what leaders need to be able to know and do—requires a foundation of successful leadership and management experience in educational settings, and this foundation requires further development through engagement with knowledge and practical experiences developed to ensure superintendents' success in their roles as district leaders.

WHAT DO SCHOOL SYSTEM LEADERS NEED TO KNOW AND BE ABLE TO DO?

There has not been a great deal of research on how superintendents have been prepared, and according to Grogan and Andrews (2002) few institutions have developed programs that are specifically for superintendent candidates; rather most institutions have identified a set of courses that are meant to enhance what was learned through a candidate's principalship preparation (Björk & Gurley, 2003). The dearth of comprehensive superintendent preparation programs may be due to the fact that the position of superintendent varies considerably from district to district, depending upon the size and location of district as well as state laws governing the composition and responsibilities of school boards vis-à-vis the superintendent. Indeed, '[t]he enrollment and complexity of a school district often are key factors in determining what superintendents actually do on a daily basis" (Kowalski, 1999, p. 12). As a result, the question, "What do school system leaders need to know and be able to do in order to lead learning?" has not been definitively addressed.

In approaching the above question, scholars of the superintendency often begin by defining the job roles that superintendents are expected to fulfill and by cataloging the characteristics required of individuals fulfilling those roles. Indeed, Kowalski notes that "as far back as the early 1920's, some writers were developing lengthy lists of characteristics perceived to be necessary for a superintendent" (1999, p. 15), and then suggesting the characteristics as a basis for training.

Professional organizations, too, have sought to define the essential job responsibilities and thus knowledge needed by school district leaders. For example, the National School Board Association (NSBA) in cooperation with the American Association of School Administrators (AASA), devel-

oped a list of 18 job responsibilities for superintendents, which emphasized the role of the superintendent vis-à-vis the school board (AASA,
1994). Focusing directly on the needs of superintendents, AASA has led
the field in defining performance-based goals, competencies, and skills
and in using those criteria as a basis for the formulation of recommendations for improving the preparation of aspiring school system leaders
(Hoyle, 1982). Subsequently, AASA funded a number of studies intended
to validate the criteria it had identified, and these studies served as the
basis for formulating the first set of performance standards that broadly
defined a superintendent's practice. The standards included: (1) designing, implementing, and evaluating school climate; (2) building support
for schools; (3) developing school curriculum; (4) conveying instructional
management; (5) evaluating staff; (6) developing staff; (7) allocating
resources and, (8) engaging in research, evaluation and planning (Hoyle,
English & Steffy,1985). In the early 1990s, AASA created the Commission
on Standards for the Superintendency to develop a set of standards that
integrated professional knowledge and research findings on school system leader performance. Eight standards were created; these include: (1)
leadership and district culture; (2) policy and governance; (3) communications and community relations; (4) organizational management; (5) curriculum planning and development; (6) instructional management; (7)
human resources management; and (8) values and ethics of leadership
(Hoyle, 1993). According to Björk, Kowalski and Young (in press) efforts
such as these "have contributed to moving the superintendency towards
standards-based preparation, development, and licensure" (see also
Hoyle, English & Steffy, 1985; Hoyle, 1993; Hoyle, Björk, Collier, &
Glass, 2004).

Goodman and Zimmerman (2004), have forwarded the most recent
work in this area, listing the job responsibilities of the Superintendent as:
(1) serving as chief executive officer of the school board, including making policy and budget recommendations; (2) supporting school board
decision making with data and information; (3) providing continuous
leadership for the school board; (4) providing continuous leadership for
the educational program (i.e., curriculum, instruction, materials, co-cur-
ricula, etc.); (5) managing personnel matters (i.e., hiring, assigning, evaluating, developing, firing, etc.); (6) developing and supporting district-
wide teams of teachers and other staff working to improve teaching and
learning, and supporting local school councils of staff, parents, and students; (7) managing business and financial matters, bids and contracts,
facilities, transportation, etc.; (8) developing and administering the budget; (9) taking care of daily management and administrative tasks (p. 9).
Notably, Goodman and Zimmerman spend a good deal of time in their

work addressing why these job responsibilities should drive the preparation and professional development of school system leaders.

Another recent effort to link a deeper understanding of superintendent practice to what knowledge and skills matter and why they matter, is being undertake by a team of scholars. This group has worked to expand and update Callahan's (1966) four conceptions of the Superintendency: 1) scholarly leader, 2) business manager, 3) educational statesman, and 4) applied social scientist (p. 184). For example, to these four conceptions, Kowalski and Keedy (2004) added effective communicator, and Petersen and Barnett (2003) added instructional leader. This effort is distinctive for three reasons. First, it has taken seriously the powerful socio-political and contextual issues (e.g., NCLB, student migration, poor economy, etc.) that superintendents and their schools and communities face. Second, this effort is informed by a growing body of scholarship on effective superintendents, which highlights how superintendents create high performing districts that support student learning (Petersen, 2002; Skrla, Scheurich & Johnson, 2000). Third, through this effort, scholars have foregrounded, as key job responsibilities, issues of student, teacher and principal performance without loosing the "harsh reality that [superintendent's] traditional duties have become no less important" (Kowalski, 1999, p. 16).

Given these recent iterations of the superintendent's role and job responsibilities, scholars of the superintendency are developing a clearer understanding of what superintendents need to know and be able to do in order to lead learning within their districts. Although few would be willing to suggest one best way to prepare school system leaders, this work provides an important foundation for the knowledge and skills that should be included in school district leaders' preparation.

WHAT DO WE KNOW ABOUT THE
PREPARATION OF SUPERINTENDENTS?

Superintendents generally enter the profession by completing academic degree programs that recommend them for state licensure. However, not all states require either advanced preparation or licensure. Five states—Florida, Hawaii, North Carolina, Tennessee and Wyoming—do not issue licensure for the superintendency and two additional states—Michigan and South Dakota—do not require licensure of either principals or superintendents. In these states, requirements for practice are set within individual school districts. For the most part, these school districts require some form of advanced preparation and usually an advanced degree. In their national study of the superintendency, Glass, Björk and Brunner

(2000) found that only 8% of superintendents reported having only a masters degree, 24% had earned a masters degree but also had additional coursework, 22% had earned a specialist degree, and 45% had earned a doctoral degree.

There are far fewer preparation programs that are designed for the superintendency than there are for the principalship. This of course makes sense given that there are far fewer superintendents than principals nationwide. This fact alone may also account for fewer number of higher education faculty who specialize in the superintendency as well as the lack of research that has been conducted on school system leadership preparation. The research that does exist reveals that most superintendent preparation programs have a common core of management-oriented courses as well as more academic offerings that are discipline-based (e.g., political science, sociology). Additionally, some, though not all, require an internship or practicum experience (Björk & Gurley, 2003).

In 1999, UCEA conducted a study of school and school system leaders, their work, their preparation and the problems they faced. According to this research, superintendents found programs that focused on knowledge and skill development in law, finance, theory, research, systems orientation and organizational development to be valuable, just as they found opportunities to develop leadership skills and engage in problem solving and decision-making valuable (Bratlein & Walters, 1999). Moreover, superintendents reported that their internship and practica experiences complemented their university-based learning experiences. Although these findings are validating, this study also found that areas that were cited as weaknesses in one program were cited as areas of strength in another program, making it difficult to gain a clear picture of the strengths or weaknesses of superintendent preparation programs.

One very interesting finding from Bratlein and Walters study (1999) was that respondents were not exceedingly critical of their programs. The Glass, Björk and Brunner (2000) study similarly found that two-thirds of their superintendent respondents believed their preparation programs to be "good" (p. 127). These findings contradict the prevailing belief that the quality of superintendent and administrator preparation programs is seriously lacking (Farkas, Johnson & Duffet, 2003; Hess, 2004).

The weaknesses that were identified in university-based preparation programs through Glass, Björk and Brunner's (2000) study of the superintendency included: a "lack of hands-on application (19.8 percent); inadequate access to technology (18.9 percent); failure to link content to practice (16.5 percent); and too much emphasis on professors' personal experiences (13.8 percent)" (p. 156). According to Grogan and Andrews (2002), these were the exact same areas of weakness that were identified in non-university based superintendency preparation programs. "It is clear that both university- and non-university based professional preparation programs share similar weaknesses that emerge from similar constraints on the nature of delivery. They tend to be instructor-centered and classroom based" (Glass, Björk & Brunner, 2000, p. 161).

RETHINKING PREPARATION PROGRAMS

The complexities of modern-day education, together with current political realities, government regulations, economic constraints, diverse social issues, and changing technologies make the public school superintendency a challenging and difficult job. Most university programs that offer preparation programs for the superintendency have been caught unprepared to address these issues. Indeed, rather than heralded as places where leaders can go to develop needed knowledge and skills for the superintendency, preparation programs are often criticized for being out of touch with the practical realities of school (Farkas, Johnson & Duffet, 2003; Guthrie & Sanders, 2001).

Weaknesses Identified in Preparation Programs

Although superintendent programs have many strengths (Glass, Björk & Brunner, 2000), there are weaknesses in these programs as well. As indicated above, in many programs candidates are taught from texts with no concurrent opportunity to apply what they are learning. Instead most programs require candidates to complete the bulk of their coursework before they begin their internship. Then during their internships, many candidates encounter ideas that are quite different from those they studied in the university classroom. Moreover, their supervisor or mentor is often selected with no regard for the quality or kind of practice they engage in.

Additionally, through NCAELP the following areas of weaknesses were identified with preparation programs in a more general sense:

- They are based on the one best system model that one size fits all.
- They are too theoretical.
- They are not practical enough.
- They do not adequately recruit or screen candidates, and as a result they overproduce certified individuals who will never (and in too many cases, *should never*) be school or school system leaders.

- They are too focused on inputs (e.g., classes provided, content covered) and not focused enough on outcomes (e.g., what candidates learn as a result of their preparation).
- They are housed in institutions that do not understand what it takes to develop strong learning-focused leaders and therefore *do not support* that effort through resource allocation.
- They are insular (i.e., any leadership programs seem to operate on the assumption that they can do it alone without assistance or input from the field).
- And they are reactive rather than proactive to external forces (policies, standards, etc). (Young, 2004, p. 2)

Regardless of whether or not these critiques are "true" or generalizable to all higher education preparation programs, it is clear that programs need to do a better job of preparing leaders for the responsibilities they face in schools today and tomorrow—to support student learning and meet the challenges of leading within an environment of accountability (Young, 2004, p.3). Fortunately, most professors of educational leadership agree that there are too many ineffective programs currently operating and have repeatedly called for drastic reform and restructuring of educational leadership preparation (see, for example, Capper, 1993; Culbertson & Hencley, 1962; Grogan & Andrews, 2002; Lomotey, 1989; McCarthy & Kuh, 1997; Milstein, 1993; Miklos & Ratsoy, 1992; Murphy, 1992; Osterman, 1990; Parker & Shapiro, 1992; Young et al., 2002).

Elements of Effective Preparation

Over the past two decades, many educational leadership faculty members, in some cases with leaders from their partner school districts, have begun to change their preparation programs. Stimulated by efforts of several national commissions and task forces that focused the nature of leadership and university-based leadership preparation programs many programs have revised the way the next generation of aspiring principals and superintendents will be identified, recruited and prepared (Björk, Kowalski & Young, in press; Crowson, 1988). However, the number of programs claiming to prepare educational leaders is growing, both inside and outside of institutions of higher education, and many of these programs are not adequately preparing school and school system leaders. As a result, in 2001 the UCEA established the National Commission for the Advancement of Educational Leadership Preparation (NCAELP) with the purpose of advancing widespread improvement in leadership preparation.

One of the first things that UCEA did in to support the work of NCAELP was to publish a review of empirical research on the preparation of educational leaders. This monograph, established that the knowledge base for professional preparation in educational leadership is extremely thin.

> That is, in general the field of school administration is weakly informed by empirical research findings, drawn from either quantitative or naturalistic perspectives. A preliminary review for the project described herein, for example, suggests that the bulk of the work on administrator preservice education falls into one or more of four categories: (1) historical scholarship that tracks preparation over time—analysis that is often embedded in the larger development of the field of school administration; (2) scholarship of critique—often the result of holding preparation up to theory-based standards from perspectives that have not been central to the field's development (e.g., ethics); (3) reform reports; and (4) the scholarship of "alternative futures" in preparation. (Murphy & Vriesenga, 2004, p. 6)

The publication of this monograph was quickly followed by the establishment of a taskforce focused on building a knowledge base around leadership preparation as well as the establishment of a peer-reviewed journal focused on the preparation and professional development of school and school system leaders, the *Journal of Leadership Education*.

As scholars in our field seek to build this important knowledgebase, we must learn from their efforts. Based on my work with UCEA and NCAELP, I have developed a clearer understanding about the characteristics of more effective leadership preparation. From my perspective, the following program features appear to be important:

- A common, clear vision of leadership that is anchored to student learning drives the program;
- Strong partnerships with school districts;
- Planned recruitment and selection strategies that are aligned with the programs vision of leadership;
- A core of full-time faculty that, as a group, have contemporary professional experience, research expertise, and excellent teaching skills;
- A core curriculum that is aligned with national standards, is cohesive, reflects the program's vision of leadership, creates strong connections between theory and practice, and supports candidates

understanding of their ethical and moral obligations to create schools that promote and deliver social justice;

- A cohort model;
- Instructional delivery that incorporates elements of adult learning theory, provides opportunities for novices and experts to reflect while-in-action and reflect about action, makes extensive use of case study methods, problem-based learning, action research, and performance assessments, and provides multiple opportunities for candidates to engage in problems of practice;
- Extended clinical experiences that are carefully constructed to create strong connections between theory and practice
- An assessment system that uses formative and summative assessments to measure program effectiveness and candidate learning; and
- Adequate program capacity.

Although this is, admittedly, a long list, each element is important. For example, having an excellent curriculum will have limited impact if program faculty members are inadequate instructors and/or if the program has inadequate resources. With regard to the latter, there has been a history of programs treating leadership preparation programs as "cash cows," while operating those same programs on a shoestring budget and funding programs in other fields. Education programs in general are funded well below the average, usually near the bottom of all university programs (Ebmeier, Twombly & Teeter, 1991; Howard, Hitz & Baker, 1997). Additionally, faculty members in colleges of education consistently receive lower salaries than faculty members in most other fields (NCES, 1997).

When programs lack adequate resources, it is difficult for them to engage in program improvement efforts. Moreover, while state and national accreditation play a role in improving preparation, their impact on preparation programs has been relatively week to date. Few state agencies have the resources or capacity to adequately evaluate programs or to enforce high standards, resulting in the state approval of programs that lack the material and/or intellectual capacity to provide even adequate preparation.

National Professional Standards

The uneven level of quality in preparation programs and use of licensure among the states can be attributed, in part, to the lack of a nationally agreed upon set of professional standards for school district leadership.

Although a number of organizations, as described previously, have developed standards for school system leaders, there is no nationally agreed upon set of standards that all superintendents and superintendent preparation programs are obliged to meet (Goodman & Zimmerman, 2004). Sykes (1991) argued over a decade ago, professionalism must have a normative base that justifies practitioners being given authority over their work. This normative base (or knowledge base) is considered the standard knowledge that all professionals are expected to have. "When members of a professional guild promulgate standards, they express a basic consensus that there is a common set of skills, understandings, and dispositions needed to be a competent member of that profession" (Cibulka, 2004, p. 2). There have been several significant attempts to identify the knowledge base for both school and school system leaders. In the early 1990s the University Council for Educational Administration (UCEA) developed the Knowledge Base Project and in 2000, Division A of the American Education Research Association (AERA), UCEA, and the Laboratory for Student Success (LSS) formed a task force called *Developing Research in Educational Leadership*. Both of these efforts attempted to identify, review and support high quality research in educational leadership. The results from these other similar efforts can inform policy makers, practitioners, and professors concerned with issues related to improving practice and preparation. Moreover, such efforts provide a foundation for the development of national professional standards for the preparation, practice and professional development of school district leaders.

Although, the idea of having a set of national professional standards has developed increasing support over the last decade and has been embraced by many professional associations and political leaders, there continues to be much debate concerning the importance of adopting standards to inform preparation and practice within the educational leadership professoriate. While some hold that the creation of national standards has been a driver of significant reform, others hold that standards result in the standardization of programs (Cibulka, 2004; English, 2004b).

Perhaps both views are valid. On the one hand, the number of educational administration programs continues to grow, as does the variability of their quality. The adoption of a set of national professional standards may provide a mechanism for improving the quality of the experience that these otherwise weak programs could provide. On the other hand if programs seek only to meet the standards, then our profession, I fear, will suffer. Indeed, professional standards should be used as a foundation for the learning of professionals, around which faculty members have a responsibility to build programs based upon the students they serve, their conceptual framework, and the expertise of their faculty (Young, 2004).

The establishment of national standards for the superintendency, I believe, is needed. The current use of the ELCC standards for the preparation of school district leaders is, at best, a weak substitute. The ELCC do not provide adequate direction regarding how school system leaders should be prepared and what they should be able to do and know as a result of their preparation experience. The work of district leaders is substantially different from that of a school leader, and the difference involves much more than scale.

The absence of a set of national professional standards for the preparation and practice of school district leaders has interfered with higher education's ability to develop agreement around the content and margins of a national curriculum for the preparation of school district leaders. Both UCEA and members of NCAELP have highlighted this issue. In the fall of 2002, UCEA hosted a national conversation in Pittsburgh focused on the development of a national superintendent preparation curriculum. Following that meeting, the UCEA Center for the Study of the Superintendent invited scholars from Tennessee, Missouri, California, Ohio, and Kentucky and representatives of AASA to meet with exemplary superintendents to begin the task of curriculum development.

Although this group will, without a doubt, develop a national curriculum for school district leaders, less certainty skulks around how it will be received and used. Turf battles and power struggles are not uncommon when changes are suggested to preparation curriculum.

> While there are arguably several courses that should be added to the professional preparation curriculum, conflict arises when faculty try to determine which courses should be displaced. The area of management studies offers an excellent example. While practitioners and professors often debate the extend to which management courses are included in professional preparation, they uniformly recognize that superintendents require a firm grounding in responsibilities such as finance, law, facility planning, and personnel administration. They also recognize, however, that contemporary conditions nurture expectations that superintendents are adequately prepared in areas such as communication, multiculturalism, shared decision making, democratic institutions, policy development and analysis, and child development. (Kowalski, 1999, p. 19)

Thus, it is unclear whether educational leadership professors will see the national curriculum as a resource or as yet another "ideology," posturing "as reasonable or scientific attempting 'to map out the social order and guide political action'" (English, 2004b, p.5 citing Boudon, 1989, p. 25). The response may resemble the reaction educational leadership professors have had to the ISLLC and ELCC standards for the preparation and practice of school leaders, which has not been entirely supportive.

RETHINKING STATE POLICY TO SUPPORT EFFECTIVE
SUPERINTENDENT PREPARATION

As noted in the introduction to this chapter, consensus has grown around the belief that schools must become more successful with an increasingly wider range of learners and that educational leaders play a role in that success. However, with regard to the subject of leadership, consensus stops there. Although the preparation of district leaders has come under increased scrutiny, concern is chiefly focused on numbers.

Apparently, fewer educators are seeking advanced licensure, fewer individuals are applying for administrative job openings, and large numbers of practicing administrators will be retiring in the near future. These trends have led to predictions of a nationwide shortage of school system leaders. Reasons proposed for the shortage include but are not limited to: expanded expectations and responsibilities; stressful conditions; unreasonable demands on personal time; inadequate preparation; dwindling resources; greater difficulty in recruiting qualified staff; and insufficient salaries and benefits (Glass, Björk & Brunner, 2000; Young, 2003).

A sense of urgency has accompanied the shortage predictions, making suggestions that focus on the long-term, such as investing in preparation or making licensure and accreditation more rigorous, appear folly. Indeed, the typical response to shortage predictions is to open up licensure and bypass higher education. Both of these strategies, though they may indeed expand the candidate pool (at least in the short term), will lead to a less well-prepared cadre of school system leaders.

In a recent UCEA monograph, Young and Kochan (2004) proposed an alternative route for state policy leaders. Their recommendations include the following:

> 1) strengthen state licensure policies, 2) ensure rigorous program accreditation and approval, 3) focus state resources on preparing a quality (as opposed to large quantities) cohort of leaders, 4) require institutions of higher education to thoughtfully invest in strengthening leadership preparation programs, 5) encourage programs in the state to collaborate on preparation improvement efforts, and 6) invest in the development of a rigorous and useful leadership preparation program evaluation system. (p. 121)

The first suggestion, which is unquestionably within the purview of state leaders, is to strengthen state licensure policies. Critics have argued that licensure, rather than being a system for ensuring that only qualified individuals are granted access to educational leadership positions, has been a barrier for excellent leaders to enter leadership positions (Fordham Foundation, 2003). However, it is not licensure that these critics should be focusing on. Instead they should be concerned with how licensure policy is shaped and enacted. Currently, the process is neither consistent across states nor rigorous. Most states that have licensure policies use of instruments like the School Leadership Assessment (an instrument produced by ETS-Educational Testing Services) to determine suitability for licensure. These exams, however, provide limited information about an individual's potential as an educational leader. Young and Kochan (2004) suggest using more performance-based licensure examinations and requiring a Masters Degree in educational leadership. Performance assessments, such as the assessment centers provided by NASSP, provide information that can be used both to assess an individuals readiness to take a leadership position as well as to plan for that individuals professional development needs. Moreover, the benefits of a Masters Degree (from an accredited institution) that is focused around developing learning focused leadership is essential for leadership preparation and the profession (Kowalski, 2004). "If licensure is to be a true "gate-keeper" for quality leadership, its rigor must be enhanced" (Young & Kochan, 2004, p. 122).

A second recommendation is to ensure rigorous program accreditation and approval processes. The accreditation process is designed to ensure that all preparation programs provide candidates with a knowledge and experiential base necessary for practice. Accreditation creates confidence in the public realm (Cibulka, 2004) and makes the preparation of educational leaders more visible and thus understandable. In increasing the rigor of accreditation, it is essential that the process demand that programs are aligned with national professional standards (input, content and performance standards) and that they are producing quality leaders (Young & Kochan, 2004). National professional standards are important because such standards tend to reflect the fact that knowledge continues to grow and have built into them a process for renewal (English, 2004b). Those that do not meet both of these criteria should be neither accredited nor approved by the state for the purpose of licensure. States are best positioned to stop the sprawl of inadequate preparation programs through accreditation. In several states to date (e.g., Delaware, North Carolina), state level reviews of educational leadership programs have led to the improvement or closure of inadequate programs.

The third recommendation provided by Young and Kochan (2004) is to focus on quality over quantity in the candidate pool.

> Although there are multiple calls to prepare more and different kinds of people for leadership positions, we believe we could more effectively provide an adequate supply of excellent leaders by focusing and doing a better job with recruitment and selection. One example is the model used at the University of Texas-Austin. The selection process for the UT principalship program involves tapping by leaders in the field, an orientation to the program followed by an assessment center (assessment centers involve inbox

exercises, interviews, public speaking), and, perhaps most important, class-room visits where each candidate's teaching is observed. The UT faculty and their district leadership partners are looking for individuals who work well with all populations of children and who are excellent instructors. (Young & Kochan, 2004, p. 123)

Some alternative programs, such as New Leaders for New Schools, also invest heavily in selection. What we know about effective school leaders (Leithwood & Riehl, 2003) as well as national professional standards (e.g., ISLLC) provide ample guidance regarding the characteristics or disposi-tions that we should be looking for in leadership candidates. Moreover, candidates past performance and experiences in educational settings are generally powerful indicators of a candidate's future potential.

Putting resources into selection makes it more likely that the individu-als in whom programs invest preparation resources will have the disposi-tions and capacity to lead. This is especially important today, given that the majority of states have made dramatic shifts in its budget and budget trajectory (e.g., 31 states have cut their budgets and 29 have tapped new resources); it is essential that we use our resources wisely. States should require accredited institutions to use rigor in the recruitment and selec-tion of candidates for leadership preparation.

Young and Kochan's (2004) fourth recommendation, like the third, urges states to indirectly change behavior in higher education by tying investments in program improvement to accreditation. Over 1,200 col-leges and universities in the United States house a college, school or department of education; some states have close to 60 state-approved programs, yet in very few of these institutions can one find a school, col-lege or department of education that is adequately supported (Zimpher, 1996). This resource problem is played out in terms of the quality of facil-ities, technology, and instructional resources as well as faculty access to professional development.

Several national organizations, including NCAELP and UCEA, have offered guidance for the development of effective programs. Some of this work, specifically that which focuses on program content and program features, is discussed in earlier sections of this chapter. Thus, the path toward more effective preparation is clear. What programs need is the support necessary to take that path toward the goal of improved prepara-tion.

The final recommendation, which also focuses on program improve-ment, is for states to invest in the development of a program evaluation system (Young & Kochan, 2004).

It is essential that states, either alone or in cooperation with one another or with UCEA, develop a process for evaluating preparation programs that provide valid and reliable measures of the success of preparation efforts and that can be used to improve programs. (p. 125)

Faculty members currently have little reliable data upon which to base programmatic change efforts. Although many programs collect data on candidates, most forms of evaluation do not reveal how well candidates will perform once they are in the field. "Until we have a process for determining whether or not educational leadership preparation has any of the impacts that we hope for them, it is not likely that we will have adequate information to engage in effective program development" (Young et al., 2002, p. 147).

To Young and Kochan's (2004) list, I would add one other recommendation: support seamless leadership development. Professional learning should not be considered complete when an individual completes a preparation program. Rather, leaders should have ongoing opportunities to understand their strengths and weaknesses and to build knowledge and skills that will enhance their abilities to serve their students, teachers and communities. States, through both policy and their ability to support collaborative endeavors between key stakeholders, could lay the groundwork for an infrastructure of professional learning. Staged expectations for continued learning within a credible system of professional certification and a quality system of professional learning opportunities could solidly support lifelong learning among school system leaders.

As a result of these combined initiatives, focused on improving licensure, accreditation, recruitment, preparation, and development, states could substantially improve the preparation and practice of school system leaders. There are, of course, other initiatives that would further enhance the practice of school system leaders (e.g., induction programs, advanced certification); however, the suggestions reviewed above should be considered initial priorities.

CONCLUSION: THINKING AGAIN ABOUT COLLABORATION

In this chapter I have attempted to examine critical issues concerning the preparation of school system leaders. Although, I hardly profess to have all the answers for advancing leadership preparation and practice for school superintendents, I do assert what I believe should be some of the major planks in a reform agenda. While the resolution of many of the problems facing preparation has been laid at the feet of the states, states acting alone will make very little headway. Indeed, if we are to achieve the goal of ensuring educational excellence and equity for all children, we must first recognize that our work, at its core, is interdependent. In a number of recent articles and chapters, I along with my colleagues asserted the importance of collaboration to the success of any effort to improve leadership preparation and practice (Young & Kochan, 2004; Young, Petersen & Short, 2002; Young, in press). Here I assert it once again: Collaboration is essential.

The set of recommendations presented above, if implemented, would involve or impact (at a minimum) various units/agencies within state departments of education, institutions of higher education and practicing administrators. Thus, a commitment among educational leadership stakeholders to finding common ground around these issues and to working together to realize collaboratively developed goals is key. Although the above recommendations confer primary responsibilities to the state, no single stakeholder group can do this important work alone and effectively. These efforts must be collaborative.

In writing this chapter, I came across a monograph published by the NASSP (1992). In it the authors highlighted five stakeholder categories with an interest in high quality preparation:

1. The higher education institutions that provide preparation and services to school administrators
2. State agencies and governmental units that license administrators and establish policies and regulations relative to administrative performance
3. Local and intermediate districts that employ school administrators
4. Professional organizations at state and national levels that represent the interests and offer professional development opportunities to school administrators
5. Other agencies such as centers, academies, unions, etc. that provide advice, training, and other services to school leaders (1992, p. 16).

Although each of these stakeholder groups has an interest in quality preparation and a responsibility to support quality preparation, rarely have the activities deriving from these groups been coordinated. "Rather than functioning symbiotically, the agencies have tended to pursue their own policies and programs" (NASSP, 1992, p. 177). Perhaps the primary responsibility of the state, then, is to convene and lead the reform of preparation of school system leaders. Quality preparation depends on coordinated and collaborative efforts. We must redevelop policies and practices to ensure that our school districts have effective leaders.

REFERENCES

American Association of School Administrators. (1994). *Roles and relationships: School boards and superintendents*. Arlington, VA: Author.

Björk, L. (1993). Effective schools-effective superintendents: The emerging instructional leadership role. *Journal of School Leadership, 3*(3), 246-259.

Björk, L., & Gurley, D. K. (2003, November). *Superintendent as educational statesman, politician and democratic leader: Implications for professional preparation in the 21st century*. Paper presented at the annual meeting of the University Council for Educational Administration, Portland, OR.

Björk, L., Grogan, M., & Johnson, B. (2003, July). The reality and myth of the superintendent shortage: Implications for research and educational policy. *Journal of School Leadership, 13*(4), 451-462.

Björk, L., Kowalski T. J., & Young, M. D. (in press). National education reform reports: Implications for professional preparation and development. In T. Kowalski & L. Björk (Eds.), *School district superintendents: Role expectations,professional preparation, development and licensing*. Thousand Oaks, CA: Corwin Press.

Bratlein, M., & Walters, D. (1999). The superintendency: Preparing for multi-dimensional roles in complex and changing environments. In F. Kochan, B. Jackson, & D. Duke (Eds.), *A thousand voices from the firing line* (pp. 87-102). Columbia, MO: University Council for Educational Administration.

Callahan, R. E. (1966). *The superintendent of schools: An historical analysis*. (ERIC Document Reproduction Service No. ED010 410).

Capper, C. (Ed.). (1993). Educational administration in a pluralistic society: A multiparadigm approach. In *Educational administration in a pluralistic society* (pp. 7-35). Albany: State University of New York Press.

Cibulka, J. G. (2004). The case for academic program standards in educational administration: Toward a mature profession. *UCEA Review, 46*(2), 1-5.

Crowson, R. L. (1988). Editors introduction. *Peabody Journal of Education, 65*(4), 1-8.

Cuban, L. (Ed.). (1988) Superintending: Images and roles. In *The managerial imperative and the practice of leadership in schools* (pp. 111-147). Albany: State University of New York Press.

Culbertson, J. A., & Hencley, S. P. (1962). *Preparing administrators: New perspectives*. Columbus, OH: The University Council for Educational Administration.

Ebmeier, H., Twombly, S., & Teeter, D. J. (1991). The comparability and adequacy of financial support for schools of education. *Journal of Teacher Education, 42*, 226-235.

English, F. W. (2004a). Learning "Manifestospeak": A metadiscursive analysis of the fordham and broad foundations' manifesto for better leaders for America's schools. In T. Lasley (Ed.), *Better leaders for America's schools: Perspectives on the manifesto* (pp. 52-91). Columbia, MO: UCEA.

English, F. W. (2004b). Undoing the "done deal": Reductionism, ahistoricity, and pseudo-science in the knowledge base and standards for educational administration. *UCEA Review, 46*(2), 5-7.

Farkas, S., Johnson, J., & Duffet, A. (2003). *Rolling up their sleeves: Superintendents and principals talk about what's needed to fix public schools.* Washington, DC: Public Agenda.

Fordham Foundation. (2003). *Better leaders for America's schools: A manifesto.* Retrieved February 11, 2004, from http://www.edexcellence.net/doc/manifesto.pdf

Glass, T. (1992). *The 1992 study of the American school superintendency.* Arlington, VA: American Association of School Administrators.

Glass, T. (1993). Through the looking glass. In D. Carter, T. Glass, & S. Hord (Eds.), *Selecting, preparing and developing the school district superintendent* (pp. 20-36). Washington DC: Falmer Press.

Glass, T. (2004, April). *The superintendent as manager.* Paper presented at the annual meeting of the American Educational Research Association, San Diego, CA.

Glass, T., Björk, L., & Brunner C. (2000). *The study of the American school superintendency 2000.* Arlington, VA: AASA.

Goodman, R. H., & Zimmerman, W. G. (2004). *Thinking differently: Recommendations for 21st century school board/superintendent leadership, governance, and teamwork for high student achievement.* Marlborogh, MA: New England School Development Council.

Grogan, M. (2003). Laying the groundwork for a reconception of the superintendency from feminist postmodern perspectives. In M. D. Young & L. Skrla (Eds.), *Reconsidering feminist research in educational leadership* (pp. 9-34). Albany: State University of New York Press.

Grogan, M., & Andrews, R. (2002). Defining preparation and professional development for the future. *Educational Administration Quarterly, 38*(2), 233-257.

Guthrie, J. W., Sanders, T. (2001, January 7). Who will lead the public schools? *The New York Times,* pp. 4A, 46.

Hallinger, P., & Heck, R. (1996). Reassessing the principal's role in school effectiveness: A review of empirical research, 1980-1995. *Educational Administration Quarterly, 32*(1), 5-44.

Hess, F. M. (2004). A license to lead? In T. Lasley (Ed.), *Better leaders for America's schools: Perspectives on the manifesto* (pp. 36-51). Columbia, MO: UCEA.

Hodgkinson, H., & Montenegro, X. (1999). *The U.S. school superintendent: The invisible CEO.* Washington, DC: Institute for Educational Leadership.

Howard, R., Hitz, R., & Baker (1997). *Comparative study of expenditures per student credit hour of education programs to programs of other disciplines and professions.* Bozeman: Montana State University.

Hoyle, J. (1982). *Guidelines for the preparation of school administrators* (2nd ed.). Arlington, VA: American Association of School Administrators.

Hoyle, J. (1993). *Professional standards for the superintendency.* Arlington, VA: AASA.

Hoyle, J. (2002. *Superintendents for Texas school districts: Solving the crisis in executive leadership.* Fort Worth, TX: Sid W. Richardson Foundation.

Hoyle, J., English, F. & Steffy, B. (1998). *Skills for successful 21st century leaders: Standards for peak performers.* Arlington, VA: American Association of School Administrators.

Hoyle, J., Björk, L., Collier, V., & Glass, T. (2005). *The superintendent as CEO: Standards-based performance*. Thousand Oaks, CA: Corwin Press.

Kowalski, T. J., & Keedy, J. L. (2004, April). *Superintendent as communicator in the information age: Implications for training in the Superintendency*. Paper presented at the annual meeting of the American Educational Research Association, San Diego, CA.

Kowalski, T. J. (1999). *The school superintendent: Theory, practice, and cases*. Columbus, OH: Merrill.

Lomotey, K. (1989). *African-American principals: School leadership and success*. New York: Greenwood Press.

Marshall, S. (1996). *The officer as a leader*. Harrisburg, PA: Stackpole Books.

McCarthy, M. M., & Kuh, G. D. (1997). *Continuity and change: The educational leadership professoriate*. Colmbia, MO: The University Council for Educational Administration.

Miklos, E., & Ratsoy, E. (1992). *Educational leadership: Challenge and change*. Edmonton, Alberta, Canada: Department of Educational Administration.

Milstein, M. (1993). *Changing the way we prepare educational leaders: The Danforth experience*. Newbury Park, CA: Corwin Press.

Milstein & Associates. (1993). *Changing the way we prepare educational leaders: The Danforth experience*. Newbury Park, CA: Corwin Press.

Murphy, J. (1992). *The landscape of leadership preparation: Reframing the education of school administrators*. Newbury Park, CA: Corwin Press.

Murphy, J. (1993). Changing role of the superintendent in Kentucky's reforms. *The School Administrator, 50*(10), 26-30.

Murphy, J., & Hallinger, P. (1986). The superintendent as instructional leader: Findings from effective school districts. *The Journal of Educational Administration, 24*(2), 213-236.

Murphy, J., & Vriesenga, M. (2004). *Research on preparation programs in educational administration: An analysis*. Columbia, MO: UCEA.

Myers, M. (1992). Effective school and the superintendency: Perception and practice. *Contemporary Education, 63*(2), 96-101.

National Center for Education Statistics. (1997). *America's teachers: Profile of a profession*. Washington: U.S. Department of Education.

National Commission for the Advancement of Educational Leadership Preparation. (2002). *Anchoring statement for the National Commission for the Advancement of Educational Leadership preparation*. Columbia, MO: UCEA.

Nestor-Baker, N., & Hoy, W. (2001, February). Tacit knowledge of school superintendents: Its nature, meaning, and content. *Educational Administration Quarterly, 37*(1), 86-129.

Osterman, K. (1990). Reflective practice: A new agenda for education. *Education and Urban Society, 22*(2), 133-152.

Pajak, E., & Green, A. (2003). Loosely coupled organizations, misrecognition, and social reproduction. *International Journal of Leadership in Education, 6*(4), 393-414.

Parker, L., & Shapiro, J. P. (1992). Where is the discussion of diversity in educational administration programs? Graduate students' voices addressing an omission in their preparation. *Journal of School Leadership, 2*(1), 7-33.

Paulu, N. (1989). Key player in school reform: The superintendent. *The School Administrator, 46*(3), 8-12.

Pellicer, L., Anderson, L., Keefe, J., Kelley, E., & McCleary, L. (1988). *High school leaders and their schools.* Reston, Virginia: National Association of Secondary School Principals.

Petersen, G. J. (2002). Singing the same tune: Principals' and school board members' perceptions of the superintendent's role as instructional leader. *Journal of Educational Administration, 40*(2), 158-171.

Petersen, G. J., & Barnett, B. (2003, November). *The superintendent as instructional leader: Evolution, future conceptualizations and implications for practice and preparation.* Paper presented at the annual meeting of the University Council for Educational Administration, Portland, OR.

Pounder, D., & Merrill, R. (2001). Job desirability of the high school principalship: A job choice theory perspective. *Educational Administration Quarterly, 37*(1), 25-57.

Skrla, L., Scheurich, J. J., & Johnson, J. F. (2000, September). *Equity-driven achievement-focused school districts. Report on systemic school success in four Texas school districts serving diverse student populations.* Austing: The Charles A. Dana Center at The University of Texas.

Stein, M., & Spillane, J. (2003, April). *Research on teaching and research on educational administration: Building a bridge.* Paper presented at the annual meeting of the American Educational Research Association, Chicago, IL.

Young, M. D. (2004, February). *Reorienting the profession of educational leaders.* Testimony delivered during the Missouri State Board of Education Study Session on School Building Leadership, Jefferson City, MO.

Young, M. D., & Kochan, F. K. (2004). Supporting leadership for America's schools. In T. Lasley (Ed.), *Better leaders for America's schools: Perspectives on the manifesto* (pp. 115-129). Columbia, MO: UCEA.

Young, M. D., Petersen, G. J., & Short, P. M. (2002). The complexity of substantive reform: A call for interdependence among key stakeholders. *Educational Administration Quarterly, 38*(2), 137-175.

Zimpher, N. L. (1996). Right-sizing teacher education: The policy initiative. In L. Kaplan & R. A. Edelfelt (Eds.), *Teachers for the new millennium* (pp. 45-67). Thousand Oaks, CA: Corwin Press.

CHAPTER 9

FUTURE RESEARCH DIRECTIONS AND POLICY IMPLICATIONS FOR SUPERINTENDENT-SCHOOL BOARD RELATIONS

Lance D. Fusarelli

In the preceding eight chapters, readers have been exposed to a variety of theoretical perspectives and methodological approaches to the study of superintendent-school board relations. As Young observes in Chapter 8, much of the research on school leadership focuses on school principals. Most administrator preparation programs are designed to prepare principals rather than superintendents, in large measure because the number of principals nationwide far exceeds that of superintendents. Since fewer scholars specialize in the superintendency, it stands to reason that comparatively less research has been conducted on superintendents (and also on school boards) than in other areas of educational leadership. This is unfortunate, since as Petersen and Williams observe in Chapter 2, "the relationship between the superintendent and the board of education has a significant impact on the quality of a district's educational program" (see also Blumberg, 1985; Fusarelli & Petersen, 2002).

The Politics of Leadership: Superintendents and School Boards in Changing Times, 181–195
Copyright © 2005 by Information Age Publishing
All rights of reproduction in any form reserved.

In many respects, the diversity of perspectives (some testing and applying decades-old theory, others exploring new concepts and ideas) addressed in this book exemplifies the status of research on superintendents and school boards. In this chapter, I call attention to some of the shortcomings of our approaches in studying this critical nexus of school governance and highlight some promising areas of research—venues that could yield valuable insights into school governance and deepen our understanding of the dynamics of the relationship between superintendents and school boards. Let us first turn to shortcomings in our research paradigms.

BEEN THERE, DONE THAT: SHORTCOMINGS OF RESEARCH ON SUPERINTENDENTS AND SCHOOL BOARDS

The first and most obvious challenge to charting new territory in studying superintendents and school boards is that the research road has been well traveled, extensively so, particularly from the late 1960s through the 1980s. Fusarelli and Petersen (2002) are "disturbed by the lack of recent theoretical research on school boards and superintendents" and observe, "the 'golden age' of theory building in this area seems to have occurred in the late 1960s and early-mid 1970s. Many of our theoretical constructs are decades old" (p. 290). In fact, two chapters in this volume (Björk's and Alsbury's) test theories developed in the early 1970s. While the authors do an admirable job exploring the utility of McCarty and Ramsey's community power theory (1971) and Lutz and Iannaccone's dissatisfaction theory of democracy (1978) on superintendent-school boards relations, the authors retest theories developed three decades earlier.

In previous research, Björk and Lindle (2001) replicated McCarty and Ramsey's study and found a disconnect between the characteristics of school boards (dominated, factional, pluralistic, or inert) and how superintendents work with school boards. Björk and Lindle found that while 19% of superintendents identified their boards as factional, less than 2% adopt the role of political strategist (i.e., they work to get a board majority to support initiatives). Nearly half of superintendents (48%) identify their role as decision maker, while less than 13% have inert boards (i.e, boards who let the superintendent make all the decisions). Confirming McCarty and Ramsey's earlier findings, Björk and Lindle conclude that superintendents tend to assume roles incongruent with community power structures and suggest that many superintendents are politically naïve when dealing with school boards (it may violate norms of professional culture). However, a more likely explanation is that while superintendents view themselves as professional educators and not politicians, nearly all adopt political strategies in dealing with board members, staff, and the community at large. Occupationally, superintendents may not be politicians, but all recognize the political environment in which they work and maneuver accordingly. As Björk himself has observed, the push for systemic reform forces superintendents to engage a wide array of community groups and generate broad-based community support for school improvement initiatives (see also Stanford, 1999). Superintendents are required to develop relationships with a wide array of policy makers in diverse policy subsystems to build enough civic capacity to initiate and sustain multilevel systemic reform initiatives (Stone, Henig, Jones, & Pierannunzi, 2001). Building and sustaining alliances with multiple civic actors, therefore, is not playing politics but rather is an essential leadership skill. Although McCarty and Ramsey's research (and multiple replications thereafter) have made a valuable contribution to our understanding of community power structures and leadership, the importance of engaging with multiple policy makers throughout the community to initiate and sustain reform is now well established as an essential leadership behavior of successful superintendents.

In Chapter 7, Alsbury tested Iannaccone and Lutz's dissatisfaction theory of democracy, which attempts to relate community dissatisfaction and school board turnover to superintendent turnover. Alsbury refines dissatisfaction theory by distinguishing political and apolitical school board turnover. This addresses one of the major limitations of earlier tests of the theory, since board turnover is not always (perhaps not even most often) due to community dissatisfaction with board members. The formulation and application of dissatisfaction theory to schools is 35 years old, with some studies, including Alsbury's, supporting the basic tenets of the theory and others less so. Alsbury recommends that superintendents pay close attention to community dissatisfaction and engage in continual two-way communication with board members and the community. By keeping their hand on the pulse of the community, superintendents will be more effective at responding to public concern and ensuring the success of leadership initiatives.

One problem with studies of dissatisfaction theory is that low voter turnout in local school board elections, coupled with the rise of single issue candidates and an increase in the politics of personalism, may mean that board (and therefore superintendent) turnover is less a reflection of a schism or lack of congruence between the community's values and those of the board and superintendent, and may be more a reflection of individualistic or personalistic politics. At their core, studies of community power structures, school board-superintendent relations, and board and superintendent turnover reflect a concerted effort by scholars to develop a better understanding of political conflict in school systems and of the discontinuity of leadership produced by such conflict. The requisite organizational capacity necessary to implement and sustain systemic reform is not possible in districts with unstable governance and high administrator turnover. While Alsbury's revisions to dissatisfaction theory are valuable, in the current environment it may be time to create a more dynamic theory of superintendent turnover that more accurately captures the tenuous nature of leadership. The dynamic political nature of many communities, in which a relative handful of angry citizens can cause a superintendent's ouster (as opposed to broad community dissatisfaction), suggests the need to develop better theories of superintendent turnover. Given the critical importance of sustainable leadership, the development of such theories is much needed.

A second problem, related to the first, is that, as Björk observes in Chapter 1, the problems faced by superintendents and school boards have not varied much over the past several decades, including inadequate financial support, uneven curriculum development and alignment, complying with state and federal mandates, and effectively handling disciplinary issues and drug abuse (see also Glass, Björk, & Brunner, 2000). The enduring nature of these problems suggests that much of what scholars think of "new" in superintendent-school boards relations may simply be a recasting or rehashing of old ideas and problems. Furthermore, repeated studies of superintendent-school board relations indicate that few superintendents (about 15%) leave their positions because of conflict with their boards (Glass, Björk, & Brunner, 2000). In fact, the vast majority of superintendents have good relations with their school boards. What, then, is "new" about the challenges and problems faced by superintendents and school boards?

Some scholars have wondered whether "the study of board-superintendent relations is an intellectual dead end, having been studied and analyzed to the point where there is nothing new to discover and learn. For example, the most recent *Handbook of Research on Educational Administration* contains scant mention of superintendent or school boards" (Fusarelli & Petersen, 2002, p. 288) in few of its 548 pages (Murphy & Louis, 1999). Perhaps scholars have mapped out all the conceptual domains and dimensions of superintendent-school board relationships. Furthermore, as Fusarelli and Petersen (2002) observe, "patterns of board-superintendent interactions follow fairly well established patterns of behavior along a continuum from amicable support to outright hostility" (p. 288). Wirt and Kirst (1997) agree and conclude that, "Different styles are all versions of the classic 'fight-flight' or 'exit-voice-apathy' characterization of how individuals act when confronted by threatening situations" (p. 166). Numerous studies of school boards have classified boards as either hierarchical or bargaining or as political or professional (Greene, 1992; Tucker

& Zeigler, 1980). Research on superintendent-school board relations suggests that over the past 30 years, nearly all superintendents play one of two dominant roles in working with school boards—that of professional advisor (48%) or decision-maker (49.5%) (Glass, Björk, & Brunner, 2000). If the dimensions, domains, and terrain of superintendent-school board relations have been well mapped, then what value is added by additional studies confirming what we already know?

In an effort to chart new conceptual terrain, some scholars are adapting and applying insights from critical theory, feminism, interpretivism, and postmodernism to the study of superintendents and school boards. For example, in Chapter 3, Watson and Grogan assert that power relations between superintendents and school boards are under-researched in part because the field remains dominated by traditionalistic paradigms of power. According to the authors, school board members, community leaders, and superintendents may understand power very differently. If so, it is important that policy actors better understand the dynamics of these power relationships if they are to achieve their goals. Increasingly diverse communities may have multiple centers of power to which superintendents and school boards must attend if they are to engage in systemic reform and school improvement. Grogan and Sherman (2003) note that superintendents, even those who are successful, lack enough personal power to single-handedly achieve their goals; they must work with and through others to operate effectively.

Watson and Grogan assert that researchers will gain a better understanding of power in schools by using feminist poststructuralist theory (particularly concepts of structure, process, and agency) to analyze superintendent-school board-community relations. The authors argue that, "Without a multi-dimensional knowledge of power and how it operates, district leaders remain limited in their activities." However, such an approach has two major shortcomings. First, the application of alternative or nontraditional approaches to studying school leadership is no longer a novel approach; in fact, a number of scholars have applied these methods to problems of school leadership over the past 15 years. Differences in power and how such differences affect decision making have been well established and researched in the literature (See English, 1994; Fusarelli, 1999; Kreisberg, 1992; Maxcy, 1994; Scheurich & Imber, 1991; Schumaker, 1991; Strike, 1993). The second shortcoming in the method advocated by Watson and Grogan is that feminist poststructural theory is not readily accessible to practitioners or easily applied to issues of school leadership. It is unclear, exactly, how, and in what specific ways superintendents and school boards can use feminist poststructural theory to change their current practice and improve educational opportunities for all children. What this approach value-adds that other, previous research has missed, is unclear to many scholars and practitioners. The big questions that remain unanswered are, "How specifically can feminist poststructural theory improve the working relationship between superintendents and school boards?" "How can a superintendent use the theory to work more effectively with the school board to improve learning outcomes for all children?" If the purpose of elaborate theory is to improve practice, the linkage between theory and practice must be more clearly elucidated and these questions must be answered.

REVISITING THE PAST AND REASSESSING THE PRESENT: PROMISING AND EMERGENT RESEARCH INITIATIVES

Lest we be too negative or pessimistic in our assessment of research and policy on superintendents and school boards, several contributors to this volume question the utility of what we think we know about school leadership and assert that fundamental changes in the external environment of schooling have significant (and understudied) implications for school governance. In Chapter 1, Björk argues that recent changes in the external environment of schooling have affected relations between superintendents and school boards. These changes include demographic changes, heightened interest group activity, greater federal and state (including judicial) usurpation of local control, economic instability, divergent, competing values, and the constant pressure for systemic education reform. Fusarelli and Petersen (2002) identified three trends that are impacting and changing the relationship between superintendents and school boards: demographic change, school reform, and changes in superintendents themselves. Our society is becoming increasingly poor (with a widening gap between the very rich and the very poor), our children are becoming increasingly more diverse, our nation's elderly (mostly white) are placing ever-greater demands on limited resources, and the percentage of households with children is decreasing (Reyes, Wagstaff, & Fusarelli, 1999; The Twentieth Century Fund, 1992).

The combination of these demographic changes is placing enormous pressure on superintendents and school boards to do more with less resources. Intense pressure for outcomes-based systemic school reform—including standards, accountability, and testing, testing everywhere—has relocated much power and authority from superintendents and school boards to state legislatures and governors, state education departments, state and federal courts, and the federal government (Fusarelli, 1999; 2002). Wirt and Kirst (1997) observe that school boards have been steadily losing power as mayors, state legislators, and the federal government have usurped many of the roles and responsibilities of local school boards. As Kowalski notes in the Foreword, "increasing federal and state authority at the expense of local school board authority would diminish the stature of superintendents [as well as school boards] because their role would entail [or be reduced to] managing predetermined and pervasive policy." How does this trend affect the school board's relationship with the superintendent? This question is largely unexplored in the literature. Björk suggests that these changes have fundamentally altered patterns of district governance and superintendent-school board relations, increasing the probability for conflict as well as offering an opportunity to redefine the nature of the superintendent-school board relationship.

Some scholars argue that school boards (and therefore superintendent-board relations) have become increasingly politicized over the past 30 years, making effective district leadership more difficult (Björk, Bell, & Gurley, 2002). In AASA's most recent study, more than 90% of superintendents in large urban districts said interest groups exert political pressure on school boards (Glass, Björk, & Brunner, 2000). Most superintendents, including those in medium and smaller districts, acknowledge that interest groups are active in their communities (Glass, Björk, & Brunner, 2000). One significant change in interest group activity that has implications for superintendent-school board relations is the shift from centralized efforts to grass roots, individual lobbying (Goldstein, 1999; Opfer, 2001). In her study of political conflict over evolution in Cobb County, Georgia, Opfer (Chapter 4) observes that "a by-product of this grassroots, individual participation is a politics of personalism" in which extreme voices come to dominate public debate and affect superintendent and school board decision making (See also Fiorina, 1999). While this politics of personalism ("What's in it for me and my child?") is not new, it often conflicts with superintendents' and school boards' efforts to act in the best interests of *all* children. To mitigate this politics of personalism, Opfer suggests that superintendents (and school boards) take measures to open up processes that limit participation and channel participation in useful ways.

For their part, school boards must be cognizant of the individualistic, personalistic nature of interest group activism and recognize that individuals who engage in such activities seldom represent the moderate center of opinion on school issues. If superintendents and school boards fail to recognize this trend, school policy risks becoming embroiled in "unnecessary conflict, animosity, delay, gridlock, and policy nonsense." Drawing from Björk's research, as the influence of interest groups expands, scholars should focus more attention to studying the political dynamics of intensely factional school boards and should map out the political strategies superintendents use in dealing with such boards. Since the majority of superintendents report good relations with their school boards, research on how superintendents deal with and manage dysfunctional school boards would yield valuable leadership insights.

All-too-frequent turnover of superintendents and school board members makes initiating and sustaining comprehensive systemic education reforms problematic (if not impossibly unrealistic). One area in which additional research is needed is in examining the effects of superintendent-school board turnover on school systems. Studies comparing districts with low turnover of superintendents and low turnover of board members with districts with high turnover of superintendents and high turnover of board members need to be conducted to determine whether and how turnover impacts school improvement and reform, particularly sustainability efforts. If a simple 2×2 matrix were constructed, a number of interesting and useful studies of superintendent-school board turnover (and the impact on the relationships therein) and on school improvement could be conducted that would add considerably to our understanding of the effects of these complex forces on school reform and improvement. As Bonnie Fusarelli notes in her chapter, frequent superintendent-board turnover inhibits strategic planning and the implementation of systemic reform initiatives. Furthermore, it makes it difficult to develop sufficient institutional capacity to sustain effective learning organizations.

Much research on superintendents and school boards fails to take into account differences due to district size—studies of organizational or political dynamics involving superintendents and school boards assume districts face similar problems, have similar levels of complexity, and equal capacity (both pressure and support). While the job of superintendent is generally the same across the country, Björk (Chapter 1) and Young (Chapter 8) suggest that superintendent-board relations may vary with respect to district size. Large urban districts may have greater diversity of conflicting interests and more special interest and community groups with which to contend, appease, and accommodate. This is not to discount the often virulent school-community politics with which superintendents in smaller districts must contend, as evidenced in the chapter by Bonnie Fusarelli. While the intensity (and often nastiness) of politics may be similar across district size, the number of organized interest groups and diverse community interests that daily confront urban superintendents can be overwhelming to all but the most hardy individuals. In such large districts, superintendents function more as chief executive officers (CEOs). In smaller districts, superintendents tend to be more directly involved in day-to-day management responsibilities. As Kowalski (1999), himself a former superintendent, notes, the size and complexity of a school district are "key factors in determining what superintendents actually do on a daily basis" (p. 12). Accordingly, a need exists for more nuanced research on superintendent-school board relations that takes district size into account.

The intense accountability pressure to improve student achievement noted by several contributors to this volume is another significant trend impacting relations between superintendents and school boards. Increased emphasis on public school accountability, as evidenced by the push for expanded school choice (especially charter schools) and the detailed public reporting of school performance data mandated by the No Child Left Behind Act (a type of "accountability via transparency"), rests upon the assumption that public reporting of detailed school performance data will generate enormous pressure for school improvement. Interestingly, this assumption, widely shared among conservative policymakers, is largely untested in the research. In their study of Missouri's annual Public Education Evaluation Report (PEER), Placier, Hager, and Hull (Chapter 5) examine the impact of public reporting of school system performance data on the relationship between superintendents, school boards, and the community. The authors found that data dissemination (even bad news) does not always generate public pressure on school leaders for improvement. Lines of communication between schools and the public remain limited in some school districts and media coverage is seldom comprehensive or investigative. Furthermore, school leaders and board members occupy positions of formal authority in school systems and can use that authority to cast doubt on the credibility, usefulness, validity, and reliability of test data and school comparisons.

Contrary to conventional wisdom, in some districts, school leaders perceive (and count on) public apathy. Sometimes, superintendents are able to ignore, discount, and effectively counter any negative messages conveyed by the seeming transparency of school performance data. The authors conclude that the notion that "the public reporting of school performance [data] will foment school accountability by transferring the impetus for change from school leadership to the lay public" is overly simplistic and often erroneous. The authors conclude that "the intentions of external reformers can be radically transformed within the dynamics of those [superintendent-school board] relationships, based on local norms and conventions." Since a major behavioral assumption of the No Child Left Behind Act (and many similar state accountability policies) is that an informed citizenry will pressure educational leaders to improve schools, much more research needs to be conducted to test the validity of this hypothesis. If efforts to publicly report school performance data fail to trigger a public response that in turn forces school leaders to initiate reforms, then a major component of our school accountability policies is brought into question and will need to be reworked and revised. Policy makers may find that "you can't get there from here" and may need to fundamentally rethink efforts at school reform and improvement.

Research by several contributors to this volume highlights several other promising areas for research on superintendents and school boards. With respect to the relationship between superintendents and school boards, one promising area of inquiry is exploring the relationship between superintendents and school board presidents. As Petersen and Williams observe, little research has been conducted in this area, despite the fact that school board presidents are often the most influential members of school boards. As such, the dynamic between board presidents and superintendents may be an influential factor in successful district leadership and improved educational outcomes for all students. According to Petersen and Williams, the board president-superintendent-school board dynamic (which is largely unmapped) is pivotal in school reform and restructuring efforts.

Another promising avenue of exploration is the application of social influence and social capital theory as lenses through which to interpret and understand relations between superintendents and school board presidents (Petersen & Short, 2001). Petersen and Short found that a superintendent's credibility (trustworthiness and expertness), social attractiveness, assertiveness, and emotiveness are key components of successful superintendents' leadership styles that enable them to receive board support on multiple policy initiatives. A follow-up study by Petersen and Williams (Chapter 2) extended the analysis and drew upon social capital theory (human, social, cultural, and economic) to explain how superintendents can effectively lead school systems (and develop good relations with school boards) amidst often intense pressure to boost student achievement and eliminate the achievement gap while doing more with less money.

Finally, as states loosen their requirements for superintendent certification and licensure (Cooper, Fusarelli, Jackson, & Poster, 2002), a number of non-traditionally trained leaders have moved into the superintendency. Although only about one percent of superintendents nationwide are non-educators, about fifteen percent of superintendents leading large urban districts come from outside the traditional education establishment (Council of the Great City Schools, 2003). The movement of non-educators into top leadership positions in schools has generated much controversy and rhetoric (on both sides) but little solid, empirical research to date. Neo-conservative critics and an increasing number of state policy makers have begun to question the utility and effectiveness of university-based preparation programs for superintendents (Tucker, 2003). Under the mantle of superintendent as CEO, some policy makers believe military training in leadership, business expertise, or politics is sufficient to effectively lead school systems. Young (Chapter 8) asserts that superintendents must have successful experience in education as both a school leader (administrator) and as an educator (teacher), although the true measure of leadership lies in the ability to place the right people in the right positions in schools. Young argues that the research evidence suggests non-traditionally-trained superintendents (the superintendent as CEO role conceptualization is particularly applicable here) are not as effective in leading districts as those who come up through the ranks and have licenses and degrees from university-based administrator preparation programs (See also English, 2004).

A paucity of research exists on the effectiveness of non-traditional superintendents in leading school improvement and creating high performing learning systems. Paul Houston, executive director of the American Association of School Administrators (AASA), concluded that the performance of non-educators in leading school improvement is mixed (Council of State Governments, 2004). Observing the differences in culture between education, the corporate environment, and the military, Houston notes that many non-traditional superintendents are frustrated by the political aspects of the job. Research by Bonnie Fusarelli (Chapter 6) explores the issue of how traditional superintendents-school board relations are altered when non-educators (those from outside the traditional education establishment pipeline) become superintendents. Fusarelli found that although conflict can be expected when outsiders unfamiliar with the culture of education assume leadership positions in schools, the precedent history and pattern of superintendent-school board relations are important factors that can affect any superintendent's leadership initiatives, be they an insider or an outsider.

As the number of superintendents coming from outside the educational ranks increases, more research is needed on the leadership styles of superintendents. A tendency exists to assume that retired military leaders and some corporate executives would be more autocratic than educators who rose through the ranks of school systems. However, little research exists to either support or disconfirm that hypothesis. Limited anecdotal evidence suggests that such notions are overly simplistic and sometimes erroneous (Stanford, 1999). While it is assumed that non-educators would lead school systems differently than those from the traditional educational establishment, researchers have yet to establish that outsiders are less conventional or more innovative than their traditionally-trained peers (Public Agenda, 2003). Bonnie Fusarelli suggests that "it is not the fact that individuals are educational outsiders that makes the difference, bur rather that they have the interpersonal qualities, political acumen, and leadership skills required to lead a school district and work with a school board."

Fusarelli and Petersen (2002) observe that the rise of non-traditional school leaders to the superintendency has significant implications for superintendent-school board relations. Questions such as, "What happens when an individual unfamiliar with the education culture and workings of school boards is chosen to lead a school district? (or) What happens when the board interferes in personnel decisions made by the superintendent?" have been inadequately explored in the empirical literature on superintendent-school board relations (p. 287). Veteran school administrators are used to board interference and experienced with collaborative governance. However, non-traditional superintendents, particularly those from the military and corporate environment, may not be used to having their judgment questioned or may not have worked in an environment where the formal lines of decision making authority are not always clearly defined. Fusarelli and Petersen (2002) ask, "If understanding role differences is a major factor contributing to successful superintendent-school board relationships, then how easily will nontraditional superintendents unfamiliar with school processes and culture 'fit' or meld into the culture of school boards?" (p. 287). If school boards value professional expertise, would they be more likely to intervene or meddle in issues that nontraditional superintendents may be less expert in, such as curriculum and instruction? Such questions are largely unexplored in the research on superintendent-school board relations.

Finally, much more research is needed on the "culture clash" that often occurs between superintendents and school boards that have long histories of "uniqueness." Every school board in every community has a particular history, a way of doing things, that greatly affects (either positively or negatively) the leadership initiatives of superintendents. This local context plays a major role in shaping superintendent-school board relations (Burlingame, 1988). Bonnie Fusarelli's case study (Chapter 6) underscored just how important a role the community's history and the history of school board-superintendent relations play in constraining a superintendent's leadership initiatives, in affecting their leadership success, producing turnover, and undermining the sustainability of reform. As Kowalski observes in the Foreword, the dividing line or demarcation between board member as policymaker and superintendent as policy implementer is "frequently very thin, and at times, even invisible." As Bonnie Fusarelli observes, some districts have such contentious, micromanaging school boards that superintendent longevity is impossible. Superintendents, be they veteran educators, corporate leaders, or retired military officers, all face the challenge to lead and deal with the politics of leadership in an increasingly hostile environment.

CONCLUSION

Throughout this volume, readers have been exposed to a wide body of research on superintendents, school boards, and the political dynamics between these important policy makers. Some of the research tests decades-old theory, while others reflect new and innovative approaches to studying emergent issues confronting superintendents and school boards, with significant implications for school leadership and school improvement. As Fusarelli and Petersen (2002) observe, "The world of educational administration is changing; so too must our theories, concepts, and understanding of that world" (p. 290). Joining Petersen, I conclude with a call for a re-examination of our theories and constructs, particularly in light of the changes and issues facing superintendents and school boards discussed in this volume. A better, more comprehensive understanding of the politics of school leadership will lead to more reflective practice, more effective leadership, and improved educational outcomes for all children.

REFERENCES

Björk, L. G., Bell, R. J., & Gurley, D. K. (2002). Politics and the socialization of superintendents. In G. Perreault & F. Lunenburg (Eds.), *The changing world of school administration* (pp. 294-311). Lanham, MD: Scarecrow Press.

Björk, L., & Lindle, J. C. (2001). Superintendents and interest groups. *Educational Policy, 15*(1), 76-91.

Blumberg, A. (1985). *The school superintendent: Living with conflict.* New York: Teachers College Press.

Burlingame, M. (1988). The politics of education and educational policy: The local level. In N. J. Boyan (Ed.), *Handbook of research on educational administration* (pp. 439-454). New York: Longman.

Cistone, P. J. (Ed.). (1975). *Understanding school boards.* Lexington, MA: D. C. Heath.

Cooper, B. S., Fusarelli, L. D., Jackson, B. L., & Poster, J. (2002). Is "superintendent preparation" an oxymoron? Analyzing changes in programs, certification, and control. *Leadership and Policy in Schools, 1*(3), 242-255.

Council of State Governments. (2004, January 16). *AASA Director Paul Houston talks about the "Politics" and the "politics" of school leadership.* Retrieved June 29, 2004, from http://www.csg.org/CSG/Policy/education/Dr.+Houston+interview.htm

Council of the Great City Schools. (2003, October). Urban school superintendents: Characteristics, tenure, and salary. *Urban Indicator, 7*(1), 1-7.

English, F. W. (2004). Learning "manifestospeak": A metadiscursive analysis of the Fordham and Broad Foundations' manifesto for better leaders for America's schools. In T. Lasley (Ed.), *Better leaders for America's schools: Perspectives on the manifesto* (pp. 52-91). Columbia, MO: University Council for Educational Administration.

English, F. W. (1994). *Theory in educational administration*. New York: HarperCollins.

Fiorina, M. (1999). Extreme voices: A dark side of civic engagement. In T. Skocpol & M. Fiorina (Eds.), *Civic engagement in American democracy* (pp. 395-425). Washington, DC: Brookings Institution Press.

Fusarelli, L. D. (1999). Education is more than numbers: Communitarian leadership of schools for the new millennium. In L. T. Fenwick (Ed.), *School leadership: Expanding horizons of the mind and spirit* (pp. 97-107). Lancaster, PA: Technomic.

Fusarelli, L. D. (2002). The political economy of gubernatorial elections: Implications for education policy. *Educational Policy, 16*(1), 139-160.

Fusarelli, L. D., & Petersen, G. J. (2002). Changing times, changing relationships: An exploration of current trends influencing the relationship between superintendents and boards of education. In G. Perreault & F. C. Lunenburg (Eds.), *The changing world of school administration* (pp. 282-293). Lanham, MD: Scarecrow Press.

Glass, T., Björk, L., & Brunner, C. C. (2000). *The study of the American superintendency 2000: A look at the superintendent in the new millennium*. Arlington, VA: American Association of School Administrators.

Goldstein, K. (1999). *Interest groups, lobbying, and participation in America*. New York: Cambridge University Press.

Greene, K. R. (1992). Models of school board policy-making. *Educational Administration Quarterly, 28*(2), 220-236.

Grogan, M., & Sherman, W. H. (2003). How superintendents in Virginia deal with issues surrounding the black-white test-score gap. In D. Duke, M. Grogan, P. Tucker, & W. Heinecke (Eds.), *Educational leadership in an age of accountability* (pp. 155-180). Albany: State University of New York Press.

Kowalski, T. J. (1999). *The school superintendent: Theory, practice, and cases*. Columbus, OH: Merrill.

Kreisberg, S. (1992). *Transforming power: Domination, empowerment, and education*. Albany: State University of New York Press.

Lutz, F. W., & Iannaccone, L. (Eds.). (1978). *Public participation in local school districts: The dissatisfaction theory of democracy*. Lexington, MA: D. C. Heath.

Maxcy, S. J. (Ed.). (1994). *Postmodern school leadership: Meeting the crisis in educational administration*. Westport, CT: Praeger.

McCarty, D. J., & Ramsey, C. E. (1971). *The school managers: Power and conflict in American public education*. Westport, CT: Greenwood.

Murphy, J., & Louis, K. S. (Eds.). (1999). *Handbook of research on educational administration* (2nd ed.). San Francisco: Jossey-Bass.

Opfer, V. D. (2001). Beyond self-interest: Education interest groups in the U. S. Congress. *Educational Policy, 15*(1), 135-152.

Petersen, G. J., & Short, P. M. (2001). The school board president's perception of the district superintendent: Applying the lens of social influence and social style. *Educational Administration Quarterly, 37*(4), 533-570.

Public Agenda. (2003). *Rolling up their sleeves*. New York: Author.

Reyes, P., Wagstaff, L. H., & Fusarelli, L. D. (1999). Delta forces: The changing fabric of American society and education. In J. Murphy & K. Seashore Louis

(Eds.), *Handbook of research on educational administration* (2nd ed., pp. 183-201). San Francisco: Jossey-Bass.

Scheurich, J. J., & Imber, M. (1991). Educational reforms can reproduce societal inequities: A case study. *Educational Administration Quarterly, 27*(3), 297-320.

Schumaker, P. (1991). *Critical pluralism, democratic performance, and community power.* Lawrence: University Press of Kansas.

Stanford, J. (1999). *Victory in our schools.* New York: Bantam Books.

Stone, C. N., Henig, J. R., Jones, B. D., & Pierannunzi, C. (2001). *Building civic capacity: The politics of reforming urban schools.* Lawrence: University Press of Kansas.

Strike, K. A. (1993). Professionalism, democracy, and discursive communities: Normative reflections on restructuring. *American Educational Research Journal, 30*(2), 255-275.

The Twentieth Century Fund. (1992). *Facing the challenge: The report of The Twentieth Century Fund task force on school governance.* New York: Author.

Tucker, H. J., & Zeigler, L. H. (1980). *Professionals and the public: Attitudes, communication, and response in school districts.* New York: Longman.

Tucker, M. (2003, Fall). Out with the old. *Education Next, 3*(4), 20-24.

Wirt, F. M., & Kirst, M. W. (1997). *The political dynamics of American education.* Berkeley, CA: McCutchan.

ABOUT THE AUTHORS

Thomas L. Alsbury is an assistant professor in educational leadership and policy studies at Iowa State University. Dr. Alsbury's research interests include the superintendency, organizational governance, school boards and school leadership. Dr. Alsbury, a past, longtime public school administrator has worked collaboratively with state agencies and through grants to create unique collaborations leading to the development of principal and superintendent mentoring and career professional development programs in Iowa. Dr. Alsbury's national research on superintendents and school boards and their relationships has recently appeared in *Educational Administration Quarterly* and the *International Journal of Leadership in Education*. [alsbury@iastate.edu]

Lars Björk, is the director of the Institute for Education Research (IER) and associate professor in the Department of Administration and Supervision at the University of Kentucky. In addition, he serves as the co-director of the University Council for Educational Administration's Center for the Study of the Superintendency. Dr. Björk has served as a senior associate editor of *Educational Administration Quarterly* and presently a member of the editorial boards of the *South African Journal of Education, Journal of Thought*, and the *Journal of School Public Relations*. He has co-edited *Higher Education Research and Public Policy* (1988), *Minorities in Higher Education* (1994), and *The New Superintendency: Advances in Research and Theories of School Management and Educational Policy* (2001, with C. C. Brunner), and the *Contemporary Superintendents: Preparation, Practice and Development and Licensing* (2005, with Theodore Kowalski). In addition, he has co-authored *The Study of the American Superintendency 2000: A look at the Superintendent of*

Education in the New Millennium (2000, with T. Glass and C.C. Brunner), *The Superintendent as CEO: Standards-based Performance* (2005, with J. Hoyle, L. Collier, & T. Glass). Dr. Björk holds PhD and EdS degrees in educational administration from the University of New Mexico. [lbjor1@pop.uky.edu]

Bonnie C. Fusarelli is assistant professor in the Department of Educational Research and Leadership at North Carolina State University. Dr. Fusarelli recently co-edited the *Politics of Education Yearbook: Curriculum Politics in Multicultural America* (2004) and co-authored "Educational Governance and the New Public Management" in *Public Administration and Management*. Her research is focused on educational leadership and policy, superintendents, social justice, equity, and diversity issues in schools. She is currently completing a national study of award winning superintendents. [bonnie_fusarelli@ncsu.edu]

Lance D. Fusarelli is associate professor and program coordinator of the Educational Leadership Program in the Department of Educational Research and Leadership at North Carolina State University. Dr. Fusarelli is the author of two books, an edited volume, and more than 30 journal articles and book chapters—many on school leadership. He is the author of *The Political Dynamics of School Choice* (2003) and co-authored *Better Policies, Better Schools: Theories and Applications* (2003). He co-edited *The Promises and Perils Facing Today's School Superintendent* (2002), which examines school leadership issues confronting superintendents nationwide. His recent work focuses on state political and policy responses to the No Child Left Behind Act. [lance_fusarelli@ncsu.edu]

Margaret Grogan is currently professor and chair, Department of Educational Leadership and Policy Analysis, University of Missouri-Columbia. She is the immediate past president of the University Council for Educational Administration. She edits a series on women in leadership for SUNY Press. Prior to Missouri, she was at the University of Virginia teaching in the principal and superintendent preparation programs there. Her current research focuses on the superintendency, the moral and ethical dimensions of leadership, women in leadership, and leadership for social justice. Recent publications include two articles, "Keeping a Critical, Postmodern Eye on Educational Leadership in the United States: In appreciation of Bill Foster" in *Educational Administration Quarterly* (2004), and "Women Leading Systems" with Cryss Brunner in *The School Administrator* (February, 2005). With Gary Crow, she also published a chapter, "The Development of Leadership Thought and Practice in the United States," in *The Handbook of Educational Leadership* (2004). [groganm@missouri. edu]

Douglas R. Hager is a research associate for the Office of Social and Economic Data Analysis at the University of Missouri-Columbia. His research interests include school accountability reform, teacher learning, school leadership, educational technology, and policy analysis. Recent publications include "The Paradox of Professional Community: Tales from Two Cities: (with J. P. Scribner and T. R. Warne) in *Educational Administration Quarterly* (2002) and "An Exploratory Study of Career and Technical Education Teacher Empowerment: Implications for School Leaders" (with J. P. Scribner, A. D. Truell, and S. Srichai) in *Journal of Career and Technical Education* (2001). [hagerd@missouri.edu]

Angela M. Hull is a school policy specialist on the governmental relations team with the Missouri State Teachers Association. In December 2005, she plans to graduate with a doctorate in policy studies from the Department of Educational Leadership and Policy Analysis at the University of Missouri-Columbia. Her areas of interest include school finance and state level policy development. She is a member of the American Education Finance Association. [amhd7f@mizzou.edu]

Theodore J. Kowalski is the Kuntz Family Chair in Educational Administration at the University of Dayton. He has held a number of positions in the public schools of Illinois and Indiana ranging from teacher to superintendent. Prior to his current position, he taught at Purdue University, Saint Louis University, and Ball State University, having served as dean of the Teachers College at Ball State for 13 years. He is editor of the *Journal of School Public Relations* and serves on the editorial boards of three other professional journals. Since 1986, he has delivered approximately 100 invited lectures at universities across the United States and in foreign countries. He is the author of 18 books, the most recent of which include *Contemporary School Administration* (2nd ed., 2003), *Public Relations in Schools* (3rd ed., 2004), *Case Studies in Educational Administration* (4th ed., 2005), and *The School Superintendent: Theory, Practice, and Cases* (2nd ed.) (2005). [Theodore.Kowalski@notes.udayton.edu]

V. Darleen Opfer is director of the Ohio Collaborative: Research and Policy for Schools, Children and Families. She is also an associate professor in the School of Educational Policy and Leadership at Ohio State University. Prior to coming to OSU, she was an assistant professor of educational policy studies at Georgia State University. She has worked in the Florida and Virginia Legislatures and as a policy specialist for the Association for Supervision and Curriculum Development in Washington, DC. She also taught severely emotionally disturbed children in both Florida and Virginia. Her research interests have included interest group influence, the political aspects of policymaking, and the impact of high stakes account-ability policies on schools, teachers, and students. She has completed both large- and small-scale policy evaluations for state and international agencies and currently serves as the research and policy consultant for the integrated schools in Northern Ireland. [opfer.6@osu.edu]

George J. Petersen is an associate professor of educational leadership and administration at the California Polytechnic State University, San Luis Obispo. He is also an adjunct associate professor in the educational lead-ership and organizations program at the University of California, Santa Barbara. Prior to coming to Cal Poly and UCSB, he was the associate director of the University Council for Educational Administration (UCEA) as well as an associate professor of educational leadership and policy analysis at the University of Missouri-Columbia. His research inter-ests have focused on the executive leadership of the district superinten-dent. This work has examined superintendent beliefs, roles, and work in the area of instructional leadership, policy decision-making, and social influence in addition to the organizational mission and academic success of the district. His work has been published in journals such as *Educational Administration Quarterly, Journal of School Leadership, Journal of Law and Education, Journal of School Administration and Educational Policy Analysis Archives.* He holds a BA (philosophy) from the Pontifical University of St. Thomas Aquinas, Rome, Italy, and a BA (cultural anthropology) from the University of California, Santa Barbara. He also holds an MA and PhD in educational policy, organizations and leadership from the University of California, Santa Barbara. [gjpeters@calpoly.edu]

Peggy Placier is an associate professor in education policy studies pro-gram of the Department of Educational Leadership and Policy Analysis at the University of Missouri-Columbia. Her areas of teaching include social foundations of teacher education, sociology of education, history of edu-cation policy, and policy analysis. In her courses she emphasizes a critical analysis of schooling in the social contexts of political structures, cultural communities, and ethical perspectives. Dr. Placier conducts qualitative research on the topics of teacher education practice and policy, state and district policy formation, and the language or rhetoric of policymaking, using sociolinguistic and ethnographic approaches. Her articles have been published in journals such as *Educational Evaluation and Policy Analy-sis, Education Policy, Curriculum Inquiry, Qualitative Studies in Education, and Educational Administration Quarterly,* and she has also published a number of book chapters. She holds a BA (English, secondary education) from Ohio University, and an MA in anthropology and PhD in educational foundations from the University of Arizona. [PlacierP@missouri.edu]

Sheldon T. Watson is a doctoral candidate in the Department of Educational Leadership & Policy Analysis at the University of Missouri-Columbia. Upon graduation he will assume a position as an assistant professor of educational leadership at Connecticut State University. Sheldon's research interests integrate strands of leadership and policy studies, and the social foundations of education. He has taught eighth grade social studies, and is a former archaeologist; having conducted fieldwork in both Italy and the American Southwest. Current research foci include collaborative leadership activity and school improvement, the ethics of policy implementation, and the historical development of the use of patriotic policies in public schools. Sheldon has a strong methodological interest in qualitative research methods, particularly the application of discourse and conversation analytic techniques to the study of educational leadership. He is a contributing author to a chapter on the use of such methods in *Educational Leadership and Reform* (2005), a volume in Research and Theory in Educational Administration; a series edited by W. Hoy and C. Miskel. [stwa43@mizzou.edu]

Barbara Morrow Williams earned a Juris Doctorate from the Lewis & Clark Northwestern School of Law in Portland, Oregon, and she is a PhD candidate in educational leadership and policy analysis at the University of Missouri at Columbia, Missouri. Her dissertation case study and her research agenda include examining the socialization experiences of women public school superintendents and mid-life professional women in formal organizations, and the intersection of school district parent-involvement policies with parent-led, community-based efforts to improve the delivery of public education in metropolitan areas. She was recently selected as a UCEA David L. Clark Seminar fellow at the 2005 AERA convention. Prior to coming to Missouri, she was active in community not-for-profit organizations that help women and girls meet the challenges facing them and their neighborhoods. A native of California, she earned her bachelor's degree from Mills College in Oakland, and a master's degree from the University of California at Berkeley. She is married to an educator with three adult, college-educated children. [bamw46@hotmail.com]

Michelle D. Young is the executive director of the University Council for Educational Administration and a faculty member in educational leadership and policy analysis at the University of Missouri, Columbia. Dr. Young received her PhD at the University of Texas at Austin in educational policy and planning and then served as an assistant professor in the department of Policy, Planning and Leadership Studies at the University of Iowa. Dr. Young serves on the editorial board of the *Educational Administration Quarterly*, *Educational Administration Abstracts*, *Journal of Cases in*

Educational Leadership and *Education and Urban Society*. She also serves on the National Advisory Board for ERIC, the Wallace Foundation's Education Advisory Committee, the National Policy Board for Educational Administration, and the National Commission for the Advancement of Educational Leadership Preparation. Her scholarship focuses on how school leaders and school policies can ensure equitable and quality experiences for all students and adults who learn and work in schools. Dr. Young is the recipient of the William J. Davis award for the most outstanding article published in a volume of the *Educational Administration Quarterly*. Her work has also been published in the *Review of Educational Research*, the *Educational Researcher*, the *American Educational Research Journal*, the *Journal of School Leadership*, the *International Journal of Qualitative Studies in Education*, and *Leadership and Policy in Schools*, among other publications. [youngmd@missouri.edu]

INDEX

Printed in the United States
32531LVS00003B/10-36

9 781593 111694

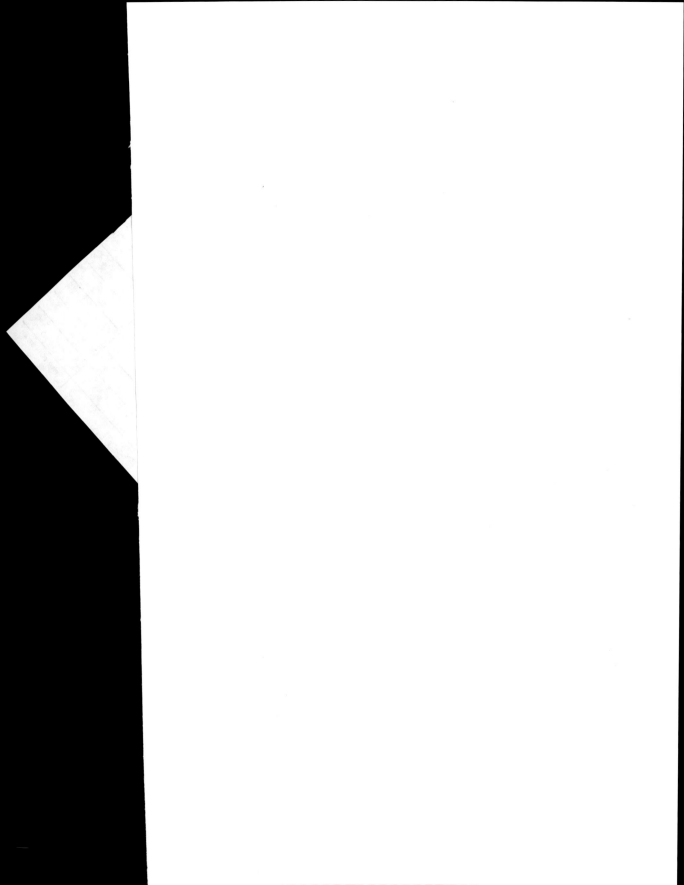

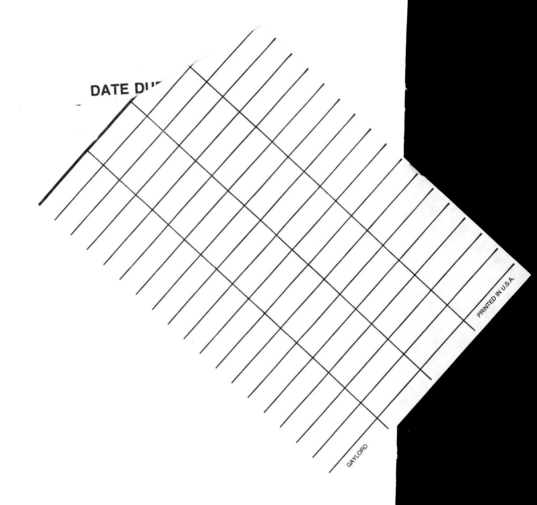

DATE DUE